Louise Monaghan (top right) with her sister Mandy (top left), daughter May (bottom left) and RTÉ TV and radio presenter Ryan Tubridy (bottom right) after Louise appeared on *The Late Late Show* on RTÉ One just after her escape from Syria.

This edition, 2013

First published in Great Britain in 2012 by
MAINSTREAM PUBLISHING COMPANY
(EDINBURGH) LTD
7 Albany Street
Edinburgh EH1 3UG

ISBN 9781780575919

This book is a work of non-fiction based on the life, experiences and recollections of the author. In some instances, names of people have been changed to protect the privacy of others. The author has stated to the publishers that, except in such respects, not affecting the substantial accuracy of the work, the contents of this book are true.

A catalogue record for this book is available
from the British Library

Printed and bound by
CPI Group (UK) Ltd, Croydon, CR0 4YY

1 3 5 7 9 10 8 6 4 2

Stolen
Escape from Syria

LOUISE MONAGHAN
AND YVONNE KINSELLA

MAINSTREAM
PUBLISHING

EDINBURGH AND LONDON

Acknowledgements

Nobody walks alone on any difficult journey. Your loved ones, although they might not be with you, feel the same pain, fear, terror and complete hopelessness that you experience. It was the acknowledgement of this fact that kept my spirit soaring and gave me hope on my own journey. I knew in my heart that no matter how far away from home I was, I was never really alone.

During my ordeal in Syria my biggest dread was nightfall, and in my darkest hours, while I cried myself to sleep, I knew that those who loved me cried with me. My sister, Mandy, endured the agony of my confinement in Syria, the treacherous journey to Damascus and every horrific setback that befell myself and my daughter, May. Our parting of ways in Turkey will be forever etched in my memory. Although it went unsaid, I truly believed that I would never see her again, and that alone, setting aside the magnitude of the situation, was absolutely heartbreaking. I love her unconditionally. She is the most inspirational woman I have ever known.

My father, Frank, or Frankie as he is known everywhere, paced floors, cried tears, pleaded and prayed for our safe return. A popular man in our area, he generated great interest in our story and his raising awareness of our plight aided our return more than he will ever realise. You are a good man, Dad, a great man, and we love you.

Josh, my little man, my nephew, is a truly courageous child. He lives with illness every day, and despite the daily medication he never complains. As a child he was happy and carefree and a constant source of joy to my late mammy and all his family. As a teenager, he is self-assured, sensitive, wise and a friend.

Sean, Mandy's fiancé, committed himself to minding Dad and Josh, allowing us peace of mind in that respect.

I had many hours when, frustratingly, I had to just wait, and during these times my mind would wander back to carefree moments in Cyprus.

Janine and I spent hours just talking, debating and sorting out all of the world's problems. Her daughters and May were truly like sisters. Janine and I shared the same passion, a love of the 'simple life'. We walked through rain-soaked forests in the winter and basked in the sun on quiet beaches in the summer. I loved our morning coffees together, and we laughed, always. I love her, and she will forever be in my heart and thoughts.

I met my other dear and fantastic friend Nicola on my first day at work at Olympic Holidays. During my best and worst days she was by my side. Forever constant, she is the definition of a true friend. Her mum, Irene, a fantastic and strong Scottish lady, was always the voice of reason, and I wish to thank them both for caring enough to make a difference.

Deirdre, my 'Irish friend', dropped everything when she got a call. A fantastic person, so full of life, she brightened up even the worst days.

Everyone needs a hero in life and mine, apart from my dear departed mammy and May, is my Aunty Kathy. A champion for those in need from all walks of life, she has selflessly dedicated herself to helping people, without asking for gratitude or reward. Always a tower of strength, she worked tirelessly with my sister to get me and May home, and during real times of despair she was the voice of hope.

Elaine, Kathy's daughter, my cousin and dear friend, I always felt love for me radiate from her every time we were together and it was always so comforting. I love her too and could not imagine not having her in my life.

My cousin Tash came to Cyprus with my sister and endured the nightmare with us, and I thank her for being there.

Yvonne Kinsella came into our lives unexpectedly. It's astonishing to discover you have so much in common with a person you didn't know six months ago. Yvonne never relented in aiding us with our struggle and we will be forever friends.

May and I were astounded by the support we received from all other family members, friends and neighbours throughout our ordeal and on our return. There really is no place like home.

I cannot finish my acknowledgements without mentioning how eternally grateful I am to the many angels I met in Syria. They saved my life. There are so many people whose names I have had to change to protect them, but they know who they are. You were all a huge support to me when I needed it most. Some of you had never even met me or May until we were stranded in a strange country in the midst of war, but without you all we would not be here today. That is a fact, and I say this in particular to Sayed and Rahil.

I learned that despite race, religion and cultural differences, people are all the same. There is good and bad everywhere. But sometimes you only notice these things when you are at your lowest ebb and alone. My situation certainly opened my eyes. And I will never forget this.

In summing up, I also want to thank Mainstream Publishing for giving me the opportunity to get my story out there to help others in similar situations. I also wish to thank the officials in the Departments of Foreign Affairs in Ireland, Cyprus, Syria, Turkey and Egypt, especially the Irish ambassador based in Cairo at the time, Her Excellency Isolde Moylan. At times I was so frustrated by the delays in getting myself and May out of Syria that I lost all hope in your help, but you got us there eventually and you will never know how grateful we are for that. Far too many to mention personally are all the other politicians, both local and international, who helped us. Joe from the Dublin Passport Office worked tirelessly to ensure we had the correct travel documents. Finally, I would like to thank Mary Banotti, who, on my return, was my confidante and mentor.

And last but by no means least I want to thank my beautiful and courageous daughter, May, who at just six years of age took on a mammoth task, terrifying at many times, and was her mammy's rock as we made our escape from Syria. May, you truly are the best child any mother could have and every minute of my journey to get you safely home to Ireland was worth it. I would do it all again in a heartbeat to know that you are safe. You mean the world to me.

If I have forgotten to mention anyone, please believe me it is not intentional. Anyone who came into my life before and during our horrible ordeal will always be in my thoughts and prayers, no matter what. I am blessed with my family and my friends and will always be indebted to you all.

Love always, Louise

Contents

Preface

In September 2011 my world was torn apart when my ex-husband, Mostafa Assad, the father of my six-year-old daughter, May, brutally abducted his own child during one of his routine visits.

Against all odds, he managed to smuggle her out of Cyprus, where we were living, in and then out of Turkcy and finally into his homeland of Syria. He managed all of this despite the fact that he had no valid passport for our child and she was on a 'stop list' preventing either of us from taking her outside of the country without written permission from the other.

I had cancelled May's passport a year before this horrible day when I realised that he had taken it from my home, despite me being her legal guardian. It was a tip-off from a teacher in her playschool back then that alerted me to a possible plan by Mostafa to abduct our child. Never in my wildest dreams did I think he would actually succeed in doing it. And the authorities in Cyprus simply dismissed all of my concerns as those of an overprotective mother.

Having gone through the immediate fear and natural hysteria brought on by the kidnap of my baby, and then realising that to make matters worse she was now in a Middle Eastern country in the grip of war, I made the hard decision to bow down to the demands of my very controlling ex-husband and I started to play a game. A game that saw me pretend that I actually wanted to make a go of our marriage again, despite our divorce, but a game that I knew I had to play if I was to ever see my beautiful daughter again.

With a longing heart, eager to be reunited with my child as quickly as possible, I walked into Syria alone, amidst gunshots and bomb blasts, and I too became captive in a house of tyranny.

Locked up with little food and no contact with the outside world, hidden from Mostafa's family and neighbours, I prayed that Turkish human traffickers paid by my family would somehow find us and save us.

But they never came.

Left with no choice but to escape, and miraculously given a freak chance to do so, we ran, myself and May. And, after many hours on the road, having faced many heavily armed checkpoints along the way and having endured the intimidation of armed men, we somehow, miraculously, made it to a 'safe house'.

But, despite the initial relief, we soon realised that we weren't actually safe just yet. Hours turned into days and days into weeks, but when all hope was lost, and believing there was a warrant out for my arrest and that I could be stoned to death or jailed for life for kidnap under sharia law, we somehow managed to flee.

And with many terrifying twists and turns along the way we eventually made it back to Ireland and the safe arms of our loving family.

This book tells the harrowing details of that fateful day when Mostafa Assad tore my world apart and that of my child, and it reveals the horrific journey we had to make to eventually reach safe ground.

Today, we are alive and well, but our lives will never be the same again. We must now live under assumed names and have been forced to move away from the family who fought so hard to save us, simply because one man has set out to

destroy our lives and could strike again at any time. If he
does not do it himself, I know he has others only too willing
to wait in the wings until he decides that the time is right to
try again. I know that even if he is in a prison cell, he could
very well still make plans, and next time we might not be so
lucky.

I decided to write this book in a bid to help others who
might one day find themselves in a similar situation.

I have learned an awful lot about parental abductions on
my journey, a journey I wish I had never needed to take, and
if I can even save one person, man or woman, from a similar
ordeal, then this will have been worth every painful minute.
More than 200,000 family abductions took place in the USA
alone in 2009, according to the 2010 Report on Compliance
with the Hague Convention on the Civil Aspect of
International Child Abduction prepared by the US
Department of State's Office of Children's Issues. With such
a huge number of abductions occurring, there has never been
a better time to advise people on how to prevent kidnappings
from happening. The reason for May's abduction lay in the
cultural differences between myself and her father, so I think
it is important to advise people on some of the pitfalls of a
mixed marriage in the hope that they can avoid finding
themselves in the same situation as I did. I am not for one
minute telling people not to get into a mixed marriage, as
those that fail are probably few and far between, but what I
do want to do is to advise people to talk about their plans for
the future, their ideas for bringing up children, what they see
as the best options for raising a family and then to amicably
work things out that suit both parents.

My little girl was abducted because she was due to start her
education the very next day in a European school and not an
Islamic school. It was as simple as that. And my ex-husband's
unwillingness to even talk through his views with me led to a
situation that will not only affect me for the rest of my life but
will haunt our child for ever, too.

If I could turn back the clock I would, but all I can do now is to try to mend the damage done to my beautiful child and to help others who find themselves in similar situations.

Hopefully, I can.

Louise Monaghan

CHAPTER ONE

◆

The Worst Day of My Life

Wednesday, 7 September 2011 is a day that I will never forget for as long as I live. A day that will scar my life for ever, a day that absolutely shattered the idyllic lifestyle I had been living for nearly six years in the popular holiday resort of Limassol in Cyprus.

This day started out just like any other: the sun was shining and there wasn't a cloud in the sky. But my little girl, May, was extra excited that morning because she knew that she was due to start what we all called 'big school' the following day. We had everything ready to go, and her little white polo shirt, her navy skirt and her new shoes sat proudly on the single bed in her princess-themed bedroom. Her little baby-pink schoolbag with a picture of a puppy on the front, which she picked out herself, was filled with her new school books and copybooks just waiting to be used. Her first day at school was a day I had been dreading for a long time, like all mammies do, as it's the most obvious sign that your little baby is growing up and from here on in she is shaping her future and becoming her own little person.

But I knew that May was all excited about her new endeavour and so I was excited for her. She had been to preschool the previous year and she absolutely loved it. I had enrolled her in the 'big school' at Mesa Yitonia. I never had a problem getting her up in the mornings because she actually loved getting dressed up to meet her friends in 'school', as she called her preschool, so I knew the transfer to the big school wouldn't be a problem at all. She had lots of friends who would be starting in the same class on that same day. Everything was just fitting nicely into place.

I know that all mothers think their child is extra special, but, honestly speaking, May has always been great, never complaining and always wanting to make her mammy happy.

On Tuesday night, May's father, Mostafa, whom I had divorced in November 2010, rang to say he would take May to the beach the following morning, as after we separated he had been given access to our daughter on a court order for a few hours every Monday, Wednesday and Saturday.

I was never happy with him taking May at any time because our relationship had become very strained over the years and he had very little time – and, in my mind, love – for our child. I genuinely believed that he only wanted to see her because he knew it upset me to let him be with her. However, I had noticed in recent months how he seemed to be making more of an effort with her, and he was definitely more patient.

I believe that he insisted on seeing May not just because of his controlling nature but also because he was Muslim, and not being allowed to see his child would diminish his parental rights and insult his religion.

But I had no choice in the matter, as the courts in Cyprus just weren't prepared to listen to my concerns when we discussed guardianship rights. On several occasions I was threatened with imprisonment if I failed to comply with the orders of the court, so I was left with no alternative but to go ahead with the arrangements and trust that Mostafa wouldn't hurt our little girl or try to take her away from me.

At one stage, May and Mostafa had to go for one-to-one counselling because May just didn't want to be around her father. She was very distrustful of him. But all of my worries just fell on deaf ears. No one listened. Despite my concerns that he may actually have mental issues, given his tendency to lash out verbally and physically, Mostafa's access to our child was actually extended.

During the court hearing in July 2010 he was also given access to her every second Christmas and Easter, but he was not allowed to keep her overnight, which was a relief to me. They said that his housing wasn't suitable for overnight stays, as he lived with a number of other Syrian men in rented accommodation.

Mostafa lived about five miles away from us in a town called Zakaki, an old village on the outskirts of Limassol, just under two miles from Lady's Mile beach, which May and I always visited. Zakaki has become newly developed in recent years and it is now home to My Mall, the biggest shopping centre in Cyprus. This is a place where people from all over the country come to shop for clothes or to meet friends for a coffee and a chat. It has a huge food mall and is also a very popular place for tourists.

On Wednesday morning, when Mostafa arrived to pick May up, I was on the floor doing some daily exercises, as I was suffering from an illness that affected my hips and back and left me in an awful lot of pain and very stiff. When he arrived, I got up and went into the kitchen to pack a little lunchbox for May.

He was quieter than usual that morning, and he actually followed me all around the rooms as I sorted May's clothes for the beach. I could feel him watching my every move. Normally he would just stand there, waiting, knowing that he wasn't welcome, but on this day he seemed to have an air of cockiness about him that should have alerted me to something being wrong but that I somehow dismissed.

I remember putting May's beloved Nintendo DS into the bag and packing her little bikini and some suncream as I ran around the place, trying not to delay him. Mostafa never had money, he lived from day to day all the time, and so as he was leaving I asked him if he needed some cash. He suddenly looked very agitated and he just ignored the question. But I wasn't thinking of him; I wanted to make sure that he had enough money to buy May an ice cream, as it was a very hot day and they would be out in the heat for a few hours. So I decided to take no notice of him, and as they left the apartment I went back in for my purse and I handed May a twenty-euro note over the veranda.

As she went to walk away, smiling nervously as she always did when she was forced to go with him, I noticed that I hadn't brushed her hair, so I called her back to fix it. But Mostafa was having none of it. He grabbed May by the hand, dragging her towards the car, saying that he had a hairbrush in the car and he would do it himself.

We didn't really get on, myself and Mostafa, but I do remember thinking that he had been extra cool with me that morning, but then again he had days when he could be like that so once again, to my peril, I just brushed it off.

I remember as they left, I was looking down at May from the veranda and thinking how pretty she looked that day. She was a beautiful child, inside and out, but she just looked radiant in her little T-shirt and a gorgeous cream-coloured dress with pink and purple flowers that I had picked up for her in a Debenhams store the week before and a little pair of girly flip-flops. She had a lovely hairband in her hair, and she stood at the gate and said, 'Mam, I love you so much.'

I said, 'I love you too, my angel,' and she walked away.

As she got into the car I suddenly got a very weird feeling, a sick feeling in the pit of my stomach. Something just wasn't right in my mind. I rang him almost immediately and I said, 'Mostafa, is everything OK?'

He snapped at me and said, 'Yes. Why?'

I said, 'You were acting a little bit strange this morning.'

He snapped back, 'Oh, Louise, you are starting again. I have access to see my daughter, and she *is* my daughter after all.' He got very defensive, saying it was his time with May and insisting that he just wanted time with his child, so he sort of reassured me a little. I spoke via the loudspeaker on his phone to May, who said they were going to the beach. She sounded fine, so I felt relieved and I just carried on with what I was doing.

I busied myself getting ready for work, and I headed out the door at roughly 11 a.m. I was working at the time in a company called Olympic Holidays, a British tour operator based in Cyprus. I was a sales consultant in their call centre, and I did hours to suit myself really. Now that the summer rush was over things were much quieter, leaving me more time with May, which suited me perfectly. I had worked for Olympic for five years and I absolutely loved my job. I was one of their best sales people, even though I only worked part-time to enable me to look after my daughter. We were like one big happy family at Olympic, which is very rare in workplaces today. I was on a good basic salary every month and earned great commission, so May and myself had a lovely life in Cyprus. We normally spent our weekends in various upmarket hotels on the island, enjoying their swimming pools and being pampered. I got some really good discounts in all of the hotels because of my job, and we really made the most of it when we could. Life was great. We were very close and I was so happy with our life as a little family.

I missed my dad and my sister, who were living back in Dublin, but that week I was looking forward to my dad and his friend coming over to visit us, as they were due to arrive in Larnaca on the following Sunday. May was excited to be seeing her granddad, as they were very close, and she was his only granddaughter so he spoiled her rotten whenever he did get to visit.

We had lost Mammy in 2001 in a devastating car accident, and we all rallied around my dad after that, as he was lost without the woman who loved him and made every day easy for him. They were very united. Their only children are myself and my younger sister, Mandy, who lives in Dublin with Dad, and we are a very close-knit family. Every visit he made was important to me and I loved it when he'd ring to say he was coming over. I knew that we were due to have a busy week, with May starting school and my dad arriving, but we were both so excited over it and had everything ready for his visit.

But as I sat in the office at about noon that day a very uneasy feeling came over me again. I cannot explain why I felt that way, as Mostafa wasn't due to drop May back until 1 p.m. – those were the terms and conditions of his visitation rights – but for some unknown reason my stomach went into a knot, and I immediately picked up the phone and dialled his number.

When it signalled that his phone was switched off I knew instantly that something wasn't right. A mother's instinct, maybe, but I just knew.

I immediately switched my computer off and I said to my friend and colleague Nicola, 'I'm leaving, Nic. I can't get Mostafa on the phone. I just know there is something wrong.'

I didn't even wait for her reaction; I just grabbed my handbag and raced out of the office as fast as I could and jumped into the car. At this stage my heart was racing and my mouth was dry and I knew there was something not right with May. I could sense it.

I drove to the local beach that we often frequented, which was where Mostafa had said he was taking her. It had swings and a slide and May loved it, but on this day it was basically isolated. It was windy and the sand was blowing around, looking like little tornados, and as I looked around and saw they weren't on the beach, I knew there and then that he had taken her away from me.

I felt a sick feeling in my stomach, and I pulled my phone from my handbag and immediately rang my sister, Mandy, back in Dublin. In a blind panic I said, 'Mandy, he's taken her, she's gone.'

Mandy asked me what did I mean by 'he's taken her', and I said to her that I knew in my heart May was gone. I actually said to her, 'Mandy, I know he has gone to Syria.' I had no real reason to think that, he had not mentioned any plans to do so to me, but my gut instinct told me that he had abducted our little girl and he was gone, they were gone, and I knew deep down that I might never see my baby again.

Poor Mandy was frantic, and I'm sure she must have felt even more helpless than I did right then, as she was 2,300 miles away. I knew that she would be getting on to the Garda back home to alert them, but I knew that the only people who could do anything for me at this stage were the Cypriot police, the CID or myself. I told Mandy that I would keep looking for May and Mostafa and I would ring her back as soon as I had more news.

I felt weak and nauseous, and I hadn't been feeling the best as it was, even before this happened, as I had a serious illness that affected my bones. Somehow, though, I put all the pain I had been experiencing in my back and my hips to the furthest corner of my mind, and without even realising it I started to act on autopilot.

I had already ruled out the beach, so I jumped back into the car and drove straight to the apartment where Mostafa lived, praying that I was horribly wrong and that I would see the car there, hoping that something minor had happened to delay him and everything was OK, but the car was gone. He had taken my other car, as he always did when took May out, so when I realised it was nowhere to be seen, my heart sank. I rang some of my friends in an awful state. I don't even know what I said exactly, as the words were just spewing out of my mouth in a state of panic. But they were brilliant. They all left their workplaces or their homes and said they would meet me at my apartment.

As I approached home, I tried to tell myself yet again that Mostafa might be there, just waiting for me to get back. My heart was racing. I was praying and praying that I was wrong and that he hadn't taken her at all, but once again I was wrong. There was no car and no sign of him or May. There was absolutely no doubt now that they were both gone. I had no hope left.

I was devastated. I couldn't think straight. I was crying and panicking and praying and I felt helpless. I kept ringing Mostafa's mobile. Nothing. When my friends heard what was going on, that he was late back and had his mobile turned off, one of them offered to take me to the local police station. As we pulled up outside, I jumped from the car, ran inside and screamed, 'My child has been kidnapped. Please help me.'

Despite my panic over the fact that my child was missing, I felt the Cypriot police did not respond appropriately. Unfortunately, I had frequented St John's Police Station many times before, reporting Mostafa over assaults, and I knew only too well what reception I would be facing, but because of the seriousness of this situation, I genuinely thought that it would be different this time.

They told me to sit down and calm down, that they would not accept this type of behaviour in the station. I continued to tell them that I knew my ex-husband had taken my daughter and I knew in my heart that he was taking her to Syria. Eventually, they directed me into the CID office, where they investigate serious crime. I hurriedly made my way upstairs to the office, followed by my friend, and we were met by an officer, who sat us down and was joined by another officer. I tried to stay calm, knowing that it was the only way they would listen to me, and I explained to him why I thought Mostafa had taken May to Syria.

I explained how the court order worked: that he was due to bring her back to me by 1 p.m. I told them that I had tried his mobile phone time and time again and I could not reach him, and I explained that his phone was never turned off. I told them that in all the years I had known him, his phone had never been turned off. There were many times when he would ignore my calls and just not answer, but he never turned the phone off.

I tried to tell them that as a mother I knew that my daughter was in trouble. I knew she had been abducted. I probably sounded like I was insane, but I knew in my heart that May was gone.

All the time I was speaking to them I was frantically dialling Mostafa's number, but every time I got the same message: that the person I was calling had their phone turned off, repeated over and over again in Greek. I knew that I probably looked like a madwoman, as it had been less than an hour since May was due back, but, thankfully, miraculously, they suddenly started to take me seriously and they began to take a statement. I told them everything. I explained how Mostafa had been acting strangely that morning, how I had a gut feeling as soon as he walked out the front door that something was going to happen.

Thankfully they sent out an all-points bulletin (APB), giving other officers a description of the silver BMW he had been driving and the registration number. They immediately radioed Dispatch and relayed the details to all the police cars on the roads around Limassol, urging them to try and find the car.

They asked me for a recent photograph of May. I didn't have one in my handbag at the time, so I sent my friend back to my home to get some pictures. At that moment I remembered all the photo-fits of missing children in this station, and it suddenly dawned on me that May would now be up on that wall with all the others who, until this day, I had felt sorry for. I thought they would probably never be found. Suddenly my child was one of those people. And I was one of those very parents.

As I recounted everything in detail to the police officer I felt as if I was in a movie. It all felt surreal, like a dream, a bad nightmare, the worst nightmare, and I just could not believe that the fears and dread I had experienced for years, the fears I had expressed so many times to the Cypriot authorities as Mostafa fought me for visitation rights, were suddenly all becoming a reality.

As I sat there, I started to think on my feet. I knew that he was taking May out of the country, and I knew that he would try to take her through the occupied territories of Northern Cyprus, which are effectively under the control of Turkey. I gave the police my telephone number, and my friend Deirdre and I said that we would head towards the border in Deirdre's car in the hope that we could catch him before he made his way across into Turkey.

I couldn't figure out how he would manage to get May across a border, any border, into another country, as she had no current passport. I had cancelled her passport in September 2010, because I knew even back then that Mostafa might try to abduct her, and even if it never happened I wasn't prepared to take the chance that it could. I knew that with Mostafa anything was possible: if there was a will there was a way, and I had no time to lose.

As we started the car, ready to pull away, I tried Mostafa's phone again. I was shocked when it actually rang, but sickened when I realised that it was an international dialling tone, confirming my worst fears: that he was already outside of Cyprus.

All of a sudden he answered the phone. I felt my stomach churn. I tried to remain as calm as I could, but my heart was racing. I said, 'Oh my God, Mostafa, I've been ringing you all day. Where are you?'

He calmly replied, 'I am in Syria.' I don't know what came over me, but I tried to stay as unnerved as possible, even at that moment, and I asked him why he was in Syria. He replied, 'I am in Syria because I am taking May to Syria.' I asked him if he was already there and he said he would be there in an hour. I asked him if I could speak to May, and he immediately put her on the phone. I didn't want to upset May, so I stayed calm and asked her if she was all right. She said she was fine, but I could barely understand her because she sounded so upset. She said she was in a big shopping mall. I asked her if she had been on an aeroplane, and my heart dropped when she replied, 'Yes, Mama, I have.'

May and I spoke English to each other all the time, but she was also fluent in Greek and even spoke a little Arabic. I told May that I loved her, and I promised that I would see her soon. I knew that she would be missing me, because we were together day and night and she was never out of my sight for more than a few hours, when she was in preschool or with her father on his rare visits. I knew she had very little trust in her father and that she would be fearing the worst.

Deirdre and I knew that it was pointless now to drive any further, as Mostafa was well and truly gone from Cyprus, but I rang CID straight away to tell them that I had spoken to him and that he was on his way into Syria. I begged them to get Interpol involved immediately, in the hope that they would have more control internationally. But CID told me to relax, that they would sort everything. They even tried to convince me that they would have May back with me safely within a few hours. But they were gravely underestimating my ex-husband. I knew that, but they wouldn't listen to me.

In a state of frustration and not knowing what to do or where to go next, I went back to my friend's house. By this stage, all of my friends had heard what had happened and they were all there, waiting for news. I contacted a friend who knew a lot of people in Turkey, and he said he would try to find out exactly where Mostafa could be if he was, as he said, an hour away from Syria.

Having tried to be strong for so long, as I tried to convince the police to take me seriously, I suddenly cracked. It was as if all of my emotions just exploded at the one time, and I was overcome with grief and heartache. I got very weepy and I felt my body collapse from beneath me and I began to have a panic attack. It wasn't something I had usually, but I knew that it was caused by sheer stress. I must have just fainted almost immediately, as the next thing I knew I was waking up in an ambulance and vomiting repeatedly. I thought I could hear Deirdre saying that they had caught Mostafa at the Turkish border, but it was all in my head, as I was totally confused.

I then collapsed a second time, because I remember waking up again, this time in hospital, and going into another fit of panic because I knew that I had to get to my mobile phone as quickly as possible, as Mostafa had said that he would ring me when he reached Syria. I knew that he would wonder what was happening if I didn't answer the phone, and I knew that I would have to get out of the hospital urgently if I was to find my little girl, so I signed myself out with no treatment, feeling absolutely awful, very weak and very weepy.

My friend told me that Mostafa had phoned while I was in the hospital, and he told my friend to tell me that he was at his home in Syria and I was to ring him when I woke up. When I looked at the number on the phone it had a dialling code of 0096. I then knew for a fact that he was, as he said, in Syria.

I was very emotional, but I tried to be as calm as possible. I didn't want Mostafa to think I was annoyed with him, because I didn't know what he would do with May if he thought I was a risk and that I was going to get the police involved by reporting him as having kidnapped our child. I instinctively knew that I had to remain cool when speaking to him, to try not to give him any reason to think that I was worried about May. I had to make him believe that I understood him and that I just wanted to see our child.

Mostafa told me that she was very happy and that she was playing with her brother and sister, two children he had from a previous marriage in Syria. He told me that everything was going to be OK. He said, 'Listen, Louise, just leave your job, sell up everything and come over to Syria. I will get the BMW back to you and you can sell that too. Take all your money and come to us here and we will start a new life together. We will sort something out.'

I tried to play a game with him, even though I wanted to be sick from the panic. I said, 'Listen, Mostafa, this is a lot for me to do. You know I am waiting on the results of my hospital tests and I don't know yet if I have cancer.'

I had been very sick for a long time, and a recent trip to the hospital had confirmed that I had a condition called osteoarthritis and I was in a bad way. I needed to have both of my hips replaced urgently. They also informed me that I had a spinal condition called spondylitis, and they had found two large cysts on my hips that they believed might be cancerous. I had been sick with worry since the day they broke the news to me. I was still trying to come to terms with the fact that I needed a hip replacement, as I was so active each day in the gym and in the swimming pool, but cancer was a word I had prayed I would never hear.

I had been very concerned about the cancer tests from the day I went into hospital, but now the situation seemed even worse than ever. Now, not only had Mostafa taken my child, but there was also a possibility that I might have cancer. If I did, then I knew that I needed to get to May and get her back as soon as possible. I needed to get her home to my family in Dublin so that Mostafa couldn't take custody of her.

But, despite my obvious concerns, Mostafa didn't seem concerned at all as I relayed my fears to him on the phone. He simply said, 'Well, I am sorry, but you left me with no choice. She was to start school tomorrow and you knew that I didn't want her to go to school there.'

Suddenly the real reason for him abducting May became crystal clear. May had been attending the local Greek preschool, and she was about to start national school, and it wasn't a Muslim school. Mostafa hadn't been happy about May attending the non-Muslim pre-school, but because it would only be for a short time he put up with it. But the primary school would be her place of education for six years, and he could not accept that. The school was literally across the car park from where I worked and it was so handy for both myself and May. I had sent her there because in most mixed marriages in Cyprus, the parents don't force religion on their children. In this school, instead of having to go to Orthodox religious class every day, the children could opt out and would do mathematics or some other subject instead. It is the same with their diet: the school gave the children lunch, but if they had a Muslim parent they wouldn't give them ham or pork. They are very open-minded in Cyprus.

I was happy with the school's attitude, because I would never insult the fact that May is half Syrian. I liked to think that I was bringing her up with respect for both sides of her parentage, so that when she got older she had a taste of both cultures and could choose her own path in life.

She had been doing so well at preschool; the teachers there had told me that she was a very intelligent child and had a very high IQ. They loved May and she loved them. The school knew of the problems I'd had with Mostafa, as Social Services had informed them of the situation. I had experienced physical abuse at his hands over the years, but May had been given her own social worker after Mostafa hit me one day in one of his rages and struck May as well by mistake as she was sitting on my knee. It was a day I will never forget, as I had tried hard to conceal from my little girl all the abuse I'd had to endure over the years, both physical and mental. That day changed everything for her. I had never wanted her to witness any of his irate behaviour, because I didn't know how she would react to it. I didn't want her to fear him as I did, but my efforts to protect her were destroyed that day. She wasn't badly hurt – not physically, anyway – but I will never know how it affected her little mind. I'm sure that is something we will probably discuss as she gets older, something that she will lock away until she feels ready to open up.

Social Services had to be informed of the assault, and after it was all investigated they instructed the school never to allow May to leave the school with her father. The only person with permission to take her off the premises was myself.

May starting her new school, I could now see, was the main reason why he had taken her that day. It perhaps wasn't his main reason for abducting her, but it was definitely why he had to do it that day. He was so devious and controlling that he abducted his own flesh and blood, took her from her mammy and the comfort of her home to a war-torn country simply because he, a non-practising Muslim himself, wanted our little child to grow up as he saw fit: in his world, with his beliefs.

The hypocrisy of this man was sick, as he never practised his faith, he never prayed on a prayer mat, he seldom went to the mosque or did anything to show he was a practising Muslim other than his not eating specific kinds of meat and demanding that I dress a certain way, yet suddenly he was pretending to be devout and wanted his daughter to grow up with a faith he had not adhered to himself. This was definitely one of the main reasons for turning our world upside down, and he didn't care who he hurt in the process.

The other reason was money. He had ordered me to sell everything I owned: that was the demand I had to meet if I ever wanted to see my little girl again. He'd instructed me to clear my bank account and bring him whatever money I had, so that we could live happily in a slum in Syria. And in his warped mind this order was meant to entice me to come to him. He knew the only reason I would ever obey any of his orders or demands would be to see my daughter again, and he was clever enough to know that the only way for me to see her was to do as he wished.

He sickened me to the pit of my stomach, but I had to try to put the deep hatred and abhorrence I was feeling for him at that moment to the back of my head. I knew that I needed to do whatever he asked of me if I was to see May again alive and well. I had no choice. And he knew that.

As the calls continued throughout the evening and on into the night, I somehow managed to keep Mostafa calm. I didn't want him to worry that I might have reported him to the authorities and so I tried my best to keep him onside. I warned him that it could take some time for me to sell everything before I could join him. I told him how I wanted to get there as soon as possible to be with May, but that I couldn't just sell everything overnight, it would take time. I did this because I knew that if I got inside Syria I would also be held captive, and myself and May would be sentenced to a Muslim way of life. I knew that we would be locked in his home and made to live a life where neither May nor I would ever have any rights. And I knew that if he had been violent to me in a European country like Cyprus, he would stop at nothing to display his authority in his home country, where he, as a male, had all the rights and myself and May, as females, had none.

To give me time to work out the best options and to see if there was any way the Irish or Cypriot authorities could do anything to help us, I played a game.

I reassured him that I would take all of my life savings out of the bank as soon as I could and that I would make my way over to Syria. I knew that I had no choice in what I said and how I handled him: I had to think of May's safety at all times. I didn't want him to think I had any plan other than to get all the money I could together and to join him so that we could live together as a family again. The fact that we were legally divorced didn't come into the equation. To him, this was all a game and he held the trump card. He knew that I would do absolutely anything for my daughter. Admittedly, he probably still had feelings for me, but I knew that his main objective was to gain access to my money and to feel like he had beaten me by taking May. He knew only too well that my life revolved around my child and that nothing or no one could keep her from me. She was his ticket, as he saw it, to a cash windfall.

He might have had normal parental feelings for May, but I knew that primarily he was doing this to hurt me and to send me a clear message that, despite the fact that I had been given full guardianship of our daughter in court, he ruled our family. He was the person in full control now, and by taking May to Syria he was showing that he had won.

He knew that I would sell my soul for my child, but he also underestimated me. He hadn't realised how strong I had become since our divorce and that I would not only sell my soul for my child but, despite the circumstances, I would also risk my life to get her back.

He never thought I would plan to make my way into a Muslim stronghold, a blonde European mother, and a Catholic to boot. He totally underestimated a mother's love for her baby, and that was his biggest mistake in his otherwise faultless abduction plan.

All of the time I was playing him, trying to keep him onside to protect May and keep him calm, I was praying that the fact that May had an Irish passport meant that the Irish government could somehow move in and through diplomatic means they could demand the release of one of their citizens. But I was very wrong.

As Mandy made phone call after phone call back in Dublin, trying to get government ministers, the Department of Foreign Affairs and the media on board to help us, she was getting nowhere. I was on the phone to her every few minutes. I missed her more than ever before, as without my little girl I felt I was totally alone now in a foreign country, when all I wanted was to have my family around me to support me. I needed them to console me as I cried. I needed them to listen to me, face to face, not on a phone, where the conversation was manic at times. I wanted nothing more than to feel my dad's love: a father's love that my own child unfortunately had never felt. I was desperate.

Between the phone calls back and forth to politicians and doing interviews with Irish newspapers and radio stations, Mandy booked a flight to Larnaca. I knew that she had to first fly from Dublin to London, then wait for another flight to get to Cyprus, as direct flights from Ireland to Cyprus had stopped some time ago. Knowing Mandy, I bet that although she would be shattered from the long journey, she would still be charged up when she finally arrived, high on adrenalin caused by stress, and I knew that she would immediately be ready to start planning in depth how to get May back to us safely. I was so relieved that she would be with me soon and I started to count down the hours to her arrival. We spoke every hour at least.

Mandy was trying to keep Dad relaxed at the same time. She had to be honest with him but tried to keep all of the worrying details back from him. We were terrified that if Dad knew just how bad it was he would collapse from stress, so we had to keep him as calm as possible. My dad is a very quiet and inoffensive man whose life was turned upside down when he lost my mam, and we cared for him as if he was another child. We knew we had to protect him from the whole truth, as he idolised May and he had always feared the worst would happen with Mostafa. Dad had seen through him nearly from day one.

Mandy's partner, Sean, was our saving grace for keeping Dad relaxed. Himself and Josh, Mandy's son from another relationship, who was just 16, agreed to take care of Dad while Mandy was away, as they lived in the same house. Mandy and Sean were saving for their wedding day in 2012, so they and Sean lived with Dad and looked after him. Mandy was a little bit more relaxed about leaving because she knew Dad was with the boys. Both Josh and Sean must have been terrified waving goodbye to Mandy at the airport, not knowing what was to lie ahead, but they knew she was determined to go to support me. A sister's love is incomparable to any other love in times of trouble, and I needed Mandy then more than ever before and she knew that.

While I waited for Mandy to arrive, I prayed and prayed that Mostafa would not hurt May. I was so grateful that at certain times when I rang he would let me talk to her, but I was worried sick, because although she claimed that she was OK, I could hear the fear in her little voice.

She would never let him know she was scared, though, I knew that. She had seen me play the game for years, trying to keep him calm when he was stressed out, and I could actually tell from the phone calls we had that she was doing exactly the same thing. She had obviously watched me before as I battled to keep him onside and she was clearly being nice to him to make him believe she was happy to be with him, to protect herself.

That first night without my child was the worst night of my life. I had never felt more alone. I stayed that night in a friend's house, and it was 4 a.m. before I actually went to bed. I was still ringing Mostafa every hour, checking if May was OK and trying to reassure him that it would all be fine as soon as I got to Syria. He had started to panic a bit halfway through the night, and at one stage he actually said to me that he didn't know why he had done what he had done, but he knew that it was too late to turn back.

I kept playing the game. I kept telling Mostafa that it was all right and that I understood that he did what he did simply because he loved May. I had a lump in my throat saying those words and I can never explain the hatred I felt for him at that point, but I needed to keep on his side. My biggest fear was that he would totally panic and lose it and run. And if he ran he would take May with him, switch off his phone and I would never hear from him or see my daughter again. It was a real possibility, and I knew that I was the only one who could control the situation, not the authorities, not the police: it was up to me to keep him calm and keep my daughter alive and safe.

I reckon I only slept for about an hour that night. It was horrible. The next day I received a call from my solicitor. This man had handled all the proceedings for me when I was battling for custody and pleading with Social Services and the courts not to give Mostafa any visitation rights on his own. This man knew only too well what I'd had to endure with my ex-husband for the years prior to this, and I had phoned him as soon as I realised Mostafa had snatched my child. But it took him a whole 24 hours to return my call. I knew that it wasn't the time for arguing and so I didn't vent my frustration at his seeming lack of concern. I just listened to him telling me that it would all be fine and that he was sure I would have May back with me in two to three days. Hearing these words, I was relieved because they were coming from someone in the know, as far as I was concerned, so my level of hope rose dramatically.

He asked me to drop into his office for a chat if I got a chance but I knew exactly where I wanted to go that day. I had made it my priority to go to the offices of Social Services, to let them know what had happened, because I blamed them for not listening to me in the first place. I had warned them all that this could happen when they were looking at custody and visitation rights, but no one had listened. Now it was too late.

I really felt that they had let me down miserably. I went to the office and I spoke with our social worker and I told her that Mostafa had taken May. I said, 'I told you he was a flight risk. I told you all that he would take her and that's exactly what he has done.' I think they were all in shock.

I had asked them time and time again to assess him mentally, because I felt that he was unstable. In fact, I had requested on four different occasions that he be mentally assessed, and no one had listened.

The social worker immediately got annoyed at me and went on the defensive, shouting and roaring, trying to insist that this wasn't their fault. Then, suddenly, she started to calm down and she said that this was actually 'a good thing', as he would now immediately lose parental rights to May.

I remember thinking that it made absolutely no difference now, as I wasn't sure that I could ever get my child back from Mostafa. It was totally irrelevant now, because he was in Syria and, parental rights or no parental rights, the law there was on his side. He had all the rights in that territory and I had none. So unless I got him back to Cyprus with May, and I knew that wasn't going to happen, I was the one with no rights.

The social worker didn't want to get involved with the abduction because, she said, my case was now closed, but she gave me a few hints on what I should do and where I should go. I was hoping that any advice she could give me would be helpful, but it was all too little too late. May was gone, and as far as I knew it was now out of the control of the Cypriot government. When I left her office I was feeling very low. It seemed no one could help me in Cyprus and so I went straight to my solicitor's office to see if he could offer any more assistance and give me more hope. All he could do was say that I would get her back. He couldn't tell me how, just that it would happen. I left his office very depressed, knowing deep inside that all I could do at this stage was wait.

CHAPTER TWO

———◆———

The Plan

When Mandy arrived in Limassol on Thursday night I was so relieved. I literally fell into her arms, sobbing uncontrollably and shaking with grief. My friend had picked up Mandy and our first cousin Natasha at the airport and then brought them to me, as I was in the CID office.

I remember thinking how composed I was at this meeting, prior to Mandy's arrival, as I gave a statement to the police in English. I had a Cypriot translator who ensured that every word I said was taken down accurately in Greek and not misunderstood. Her attendance at this meeting made sure there would be no way that anyone could say later on that something I told them during the interview was lost in translation.

But when Mandy walked through the door, all of my emotions exploded. I sobbed like the rain, and at one stage I looked at the translator and she was crying. I think she suddenly realised the seriousness of the issue and that the abduction was not a fear, it was a reality.

I can honestly say that at times it felt as if May was dead. Not having her beside me, not being able to touch her, to hug her, left me feeling like I had lost my little girl for ever. Having my sister beside me didn't make up for that loss, but I knew that she would help me to cope with everything so much easier.

On a few occasions when I stopped for a minute or two, I would think to myself, 'How can he be so gullible as to accept that I am just getting on with my life without May?' I couldn't understand how he could believe that I was so calm when I knew she was in a war-torn country where everything was so volatile that she could be killed at any moment. I just didn't comprehend how his mind worked.

I continued to push the authorities in Cyprus to try to get May out of Syria as soon as possible, but it became clear, very fast, that I was getting nowhere.

Mandy told me how the media in Ireland had been brilliant and how every newspaper in the country was covering the story. We'd had to contact the newspapers in order to put pressure on the authorities to help us. Because I had purposely cancelled May's passport 18 months previously, fearing that this very situation could happen, Mandy had requested a new passport for her. But she had been told categorically that it was impossible for the Irish Department of Foreign Affairs to reissue a new passport without both parents' signature on the form.

I could not believe what I was hearing. How the hell could they justify what they were saying? I was May's mother and I had full guardianship of her. I had cancelled her passport myself with the Irish embassy in Nicosia after completing all the necessary documents in my local police station, and she was also on a stop list that prevented her leaving the country without written consent from both her parents, because of my concerns for her safety. Despite this, Mostafa had abducted our child, and was wanted for her kidnap in Cyprus and had somehow managed to get her through two borders on a cancelled passport, yet he would have to sign a form to get her a new passport so that I could rescue her from her abductor: *him*.

At that stage, I thought I would lose all hope. My own

country, the country where May had been born, could not help us. Why? I kept asking myself this over and over again. I had seen films and read books in which you see the authorities in whatever jurisdiction an abduction took place doing everything they can for the mother of the child and eventually getting the child back, but I was being told, straight out, that there was nothing they could do for me or May.

That was when we really decided to pull in the help of the media to highlight the case, to put pressure on the authorities. I was disgusted that we had to go down that road, but we felt that we had no choice. In fairness to the Irish media, most of them were absolutely fantastic and did everything they could for us, putting pressure on the Department of Foreign Affairs, demanding to know why this little Irish child could not be looked after and why her passport could not be issued. They were amazing.

It was Friday now: we had gone for three days in Cyprus with absolutely no contact from the Cypriot police. We didn't know what, if anything, they were doing to try to locate my child. It was very frustrating. We had seen no one from the Irish Embassy in Nicosia either. We had thought that having an Irish government representative in the same country that we were living in would help us as well, but we were wrong there also, because during those nightmare days we saw no one and heard nothing. It was so upsetting, because I felt that we had been abandoned.

We were very careful to keep all media coverage away from Cyprus, because we feared that if Mostafa heard there was publicity in newspapers or on radio about the abduction of an Irish child in Cyprus he would just flee. Then everything would change and we would have lost little May for ever. So we asked the Irish media who printed newspapers for sale in Cyprus and Turkey, like the *Irish Sun* and the Irish *Mirror*, not to allow the story to leak into these editions and, thank God, they didn't. They were fantastic.

The pressure the journalists were putting on the Irish

authorities finally resulted in a phone call from the Irish government on Friday. It had taken that long for a response. But despite a promise from an official that he would ring back later that day, it never happened.

We were getting used to these empty promises by this stage. The Irish weren't the only ones deserting us. Up until Saturday we had no visits from the Cypriot police, even though we had contacted them to tell them that we were being followed by associates of Mostafa who had seen us go into and leave the CID office on Friday. We had told them that we were absolutely terrified, that we knew that these guys were following us to report everything back to Mostafa and that they were capable of doing anything to us. We were frightened that they could force their way into the house and maybe beat us up, kill us even, we didn't know what they were capable of, but I knew only too well that honour amongst these men was everything and that they were protecting their friend and fellow countryman. I knew that every little move we made was being reported back daily, if not hourly, to Syria, but the Cypriot police never came to see if we were OK or offered us any form of security. We were on our own and that was being made very clear to us.

On Friday afternoon while I was sitting in the house I got a phone call from Mostafa's first cousin. I didn't know why he was ringing me, but he said he had my car and he asked me where he should leave it. Mostafa had obviously decided that I should get the car back, the car that he had used to kidnap my child, in which he had taken her to the Cypriot–Turkish border, and I was to sell it to get some more money to bring to Syria with me. I was absolutely devastated.

When Mostafa's cousin arrived, I went out to meet him at the door. I watched him take all of May's little bits and pieces from the car, her kiddies' rucksack with her little bikini, her packed lunch untouched and her suncream still unopened. He literally walked in and, without a second thought, threw the bag into the hall. I knew that he was trying to make his way into the house to see who was there, because he was looking all around the apartment as he entered into the hall, so I asked him if he would go out to the car to get me something I thought might be still there. I used this as an opportunity to run inside and tell Mandy and Natasha to hide in the back room. I knew he would come into the main living area to have a good look around, but I was sure that he wouldn't go into the bedroom. And, just as I had anticipated, he came into the apartment and looked all around to see if anything looked out of place or if anyone was around.

Thankfully, all was quiet, and as brazen as you like he took out his mobile phone and he dialled Mostafa. He obviously didn't realise that I could speak some Arabic and understood it quite well, because in Arabic he told Mostafa that everything was OK and there was no one in the apartment. I knew that my ex-husband had obviously directed him to check out the house and that he would be reassured by confirmation that there were no police around and nothing suspicious happening.

I rang Mostafa later that night and he was in an awful state: he was really emotional, crying and very agitated. He said that he knew that we had been to the CID office on Wednesday. It turned out that a friend of his had been arrested that day and happened to be in the station and overheard everything. Mostafa was panicking, thinking that there was a warrant out for his arrest. I tried to appease him, telling him that everything was fine and that I had called in to CID in a panic on Wednesday, as I thought back then that he had kidnapped May because I couldn't get him on the phone. But I told him that I had contacted them straight away once he had been in touch with me and I had informed them that everything was OK now. I told him no charges had been filed. He seemed to believe me and he appeared to relax a little.

Myself, Mandy and Tash went to sleep on Friday night feeling totally dejected. I felt as though someone had pulled a plug on me and my energy levels were zapped. I was having a lot of discomfort from my hips and my back, and even sitting down for long periods was affecting me. I was due to have a double hip replacement the following week, but all I could think about at this stage was getting May back. I knew that the operation was definitely not going to happen now, even though I had built myself up so much for having it done, and I was looking forward to a new way of life for myself and May with my new mobility.

I was also hoping that cancer tests I'd recently had would come back negative, but to be honest I couldn't even think about the consequences if they weren't. There were much more important things to sort now.

All of my efforts were now directed in one way, and nothing could get me to deviate from that. I tried to get some sleep that night, but once again my mind was racing and my thoughts were all about May. Needless to say, when I woke the next day I was very low. I felt hopeless.

We sat down, all three of us, and we agreed that we were on our own in this. No one was going to help us, and the only option we had was to go it alone.

And so we started to make our own plans. An aunt of ours who had been constantly on the phone offering support throughout this ordeal loved to visit Turkey. She went there a few times every year and had a lot of friends who had a lot of contacts. She told us that she knew a Turkish man who might be able to help us. She had been talking to him on the phone earlier and he had told her to give his number to us and he would see what he could do. There were a lot of Syrians living in Turkey as well as in Cyprus, as they tend to go to stay in countries not too far from Syria once they leave or escape. Our aunt was thinking that some of the Turkish men he knew might know of a way to get into Syria without being arrested and that they might be able to snatch May from Mostafa's house and get her back into Turkey.

Parts of Turkey bordered Syria, and it looked like this could be a good way of getting May back if the legal route wasn't working. I knew that these guys, if this man knew them, would be illegal people smugglers and would probably have to be paid in advance, but I was prepared to give every last cent I had to get my child back in my arms. I didn't care how illegal it was to pay these smugglers. I had foolishly put my trust in the authorities and they had let me down badly. I knew that if I waited for them to move, if they ever did, it could be too late.

Immediately, I picked up the phone and I dialled the Turkish number our aunt had given us. The guy answered, and when I told him exactly what had happened and where Mostafa had taken May, his response was, 'Why didn't you call me earlier? I will get some men over there and we will snatch her back for you.' Needless to say, I was over the moon. This was the first really positive response I'd had in days, and I really felt this would work. He said he would sort the men out and get back to me with a price. At that stage I would give him all the information I had on Mostafa, exactly where the house was and so on, and they would tell me where to send the money to.

Having had so many disappointments in the last few days, Mandy and I decided that we would come up with Plan B just in case Plan A failed. We knew it would be very messy, but we decided to pack some clothes and head to Turkey ourselves, so that if all else failed at least I would be nearer to Syria if I could persuade Mostafa to come to the border to meet me.

I knew he wanted me to stay in Cyprus until I had sold everything, including my cars, a BMW and a Honda Logo, and had taken any money I had from the bank. The apartment I lived in was rented, so he knew that I didn't have any money in property, but he just wanted everything he could get his hands on. I decided that I could convince him that I needed to leave Mandy in Limassol to sell everything, including any furniture I had, because it wouldn't sell overnight and I needed someone whom I could trust to make sure they got the best price for everything I had. I trusted my friends in Limassol with all my heart, but I needed to use Mandy as my lifesaver when it came to Mostafa, because if I managed to get into Syria, he would need to allow me to have contact with Mandy all the time on the phone because she was his passport to cash.

Myself and Mandy started to pack a few bits and pieces. Tash was to travel back to Dublin, and her job was to reassure everyone back home that we were both OK. She was in bits leaving us, but we couldn't risk anything happening to her; we didn't want to jeopardise her safety as well. But, as sisters, Mandy and I would stick together – at least until we got to the border of Syria and Turkey, where we both knew we would have the very hard task of saying goodbye to each other. Hopefully it would be for just a short time, but realistically we both knew that it could be for ever. We would deal with that if and when the time came, although we both knew it was on our minds every step of the way.

We honestly didn't know where we were going exactly, or how we were going to get there, but we did know that the journey we were about to take would not be a pleasant one for either of us. We could read each other's minds, but neither of us mentioned the unmentionable. We just got stuck into organising our passports and money and picking out some clothes that would not make us look too much like European tourists.

I rang my friend again, and he had a contact who was a Turkish-Syrian Cypriot. He arranged for this man to take us that afternoon to the Cypriot–Turkish border, as he knew the route very well. This would mean we could take a flight from somewhere within the northern territories, which were effectively under Turkey's control, to somewhere near the Turkish–Syrian border. There was no direct flight into Turkey from Larnaca or anywhere in Cyprus because of the tense atmosphere between Cyprus and Turkey over ownership of land. The north of Cyprus was really operated by Turks and therefore our only way into Turkey was through this route. This man, we were told, would take us all the way to an area not too far from Nicosia, where we would then take one, maybe two flights to get us to a town near the Turkish border with

Syria. The prospects of doing all this alone with my sister were terrible, but we had to put our fears behind us.

That Saturday afternoon, the Turkish-Syrian man, who I had never met before, arrived at the apartment to pick us up. I had to trust this man even though he was a complete stranger. Despite my concerns, I convinced myself that my friend would never put us in danger and this man must be someone he trusted implicitly. One way or another, the plan was made, and I wasn't about to chicken out now. We knew we were extremely lucky to be getting a driver at all, never mind a local driver who knew the best and safest routes to take, to get us to where we needed to be.

Once in the car we drove for about one hundred kilometres through Cyprus towards Nicosia, the capital. After a while it became clear that we were entering an area that was not habitable. Suddenly we were in an area with fewer houses and shops; it was mostly just fields and derelict sites. I was aware that this area was quite dangerous. It was basically a no-man's-land. We had left civilisation, as I knew it, behind a few miles away from this place.

We drove up to the Cypriot border in a semi-built area of Nicosia and then into the UN-controlled section of the border. Oddly enough, this is still a very dangerous area, as anyone in Cyprus will tell you. The terrain is still covered in landmines and is extremely dangerous for people who do not know about them.

As we approached the border, which was straddled on either side by two white houses that were probably used by the border control, we saw a man sitting down smoking a cigarette. He was sitting in a makeshift border-control box and we started to get our passports ready for inspection. But he never even looked up at us; we simply drove through.

At this stage we had driven through the Cyprus border area and into UN territory. I knew I was in a UN base, but we didn't see one soldier along the stretch of road. All we saw was just a big field with barbed wire along the route. But as far as Mandy and myself were concerned we were one step nearer to my little girl and the relief was already hitting us.

We proceeded on for about 500 metres up the road when suddenly, out of nowhere, there was a queue of cars. It just hit us from out of the blue, as it had been desolate all the way along until then. As we got nearer to the outposts, the driver turned around to us and asked for our passports, which we gave him. He got out of the car and walked up to an area where there were four or five different passport-control boxes. We were straining our heads to see what he was doing, but at the same time we didn't want to bring any attention to ourselves, and within five minutes or so he was walking back to the car. We suddenly realised that nothing was certain and, in fact, there was a possibility that we might not actually get a visa to enter Turkey. These things do happen; we just had to pray there wouldn't be a problem. There was no way of knowing how it had gone as the driver approached the car, as his face gave nothing away. With our stomachs sick, we watched him casually pull on his seat belt and start the car up again. With that, he simply turned around to us, handed back our passports, which had been stamped, along with the visas, and said nothing.

We proceeded to drive into what was technically another country with no one checking Mandy and myself to see if we were the passport holders. There were no checks at all on us. It proved there and then how easy it had been for Mostafa to take my baby away from me through not one but two foreign countries with no passport (or, if he had her passport, it was a cancelled one). I remember Mandy and I simply looking at one another with disgust. We could say nothing as we sat in the back of this man's car, because we were with a stranger who we couldn't trust 100 per cent, but it was sickening to think how easily we had done it.

We carried on driving for about half an hour through rough ground, making our way to Ercan airport in the occupied north of Cyprus. The driver pulled in when we reached the airport and told us to go on in to see which flights we could get to somewhere close to Syria in Turkey while he parked the car.

Myself and Mandy walked around all the flight desks, explaining that we needed to book a flight for two people to the closest point to the Syrian border. At each and every desk they looked at these two blonde Irish women as if we were mad. One agent told us that we would have to stay overnight in Ercan and take a flight the next morning. Thankfully our driver came in and he asked the rep which was the best route to the Syrian border, and he was told that we could take a flight within an hour with Turkish Airlines first to Istanbul and then on to another flight to a place called Adana. This city was roughly 160 miles away from the Syrian border. We were shocked at how the airline staff had so easily dismissed us simply because we were Western women but also delighted that we had someone with us who could actually work on our behalf. We checked in our luggage and boarded our 9 p.m. flight to Istanbul. It was a two-hour flight, and though we were drained, myself and Mandy spent the whole time chatting about how I would try to get May out of Syria if the Turkish people smugglers let us down. We were still very hopeful that Plan A would work, but, like most things in life, there was always a slight worry that something could go wrong and so I had to prepare myself for that.

We tried to doze off for a few minutes, but the tiredness had worn off and we were high on stress, just counting the minutes, not the hours, until we got to Istanbul before we jumped on our next flight.

All the time I was worrying about Mostafa, as I had turned my phone off in case he rang me and heard us driving along in a car or heard an intercom at the airport. I was paranoid that he would hear something he shouldn't, making him panic and flee with May.

Luckily, we had been thinking on our feet before we left. I had given my friend a key to the house and told her that if Mostafa rang the house phone she was to tell him that I had got sick again and collapsed and ended up back in hospital. I thought that this would put him off the scent for a while, as I knew that his mind would go into overdrive if he wasn't able to get me on the phone. If nothing else, this story would buy me a little time, as long as he didn't think of ringing the hospital to check that I was there. That was something I never even considered until much later.

We finally got to Adana at 12.30 a.m. – drained! What we didn't know until later was that Adana is a mostly Kurdish-controlled area, mainly occupied by Turks and Arabs. It is a very volatile part of Turkey where trouble could break out at any time and where women get very little respect, especially Western women travelling alone; therefore, two blonde Irish women in European clothes would stick out like a sore thumb.

We walked outside the very small airport and onto the street, and even though it was the dead of night we could see that we were in what could only be described as a very poor-looking area. It just looked very desolate, and any women we saw were well covered up in the hijab or burka. The men were dressed in sandals and typical Turkish robes or long clothing, and some wore fezzes. We stood to have a cigarette outside and decided that we had no choice but to stay in a hotel that night and begin planning our next move after a sleep.

All this time I was worrying frantically over May. I knew it had been a whole day since she had spoken to me and I hoped that she didn't think I had abandoned her. I was also worrying about Mostafa, praying that he wasn't letting his mind run away with him because he was unable to contact me. My head was filled with all sorts of scenarios, none of them good.

As we stood smoking, myself and Mandy, a taxi pulled up in front of us and the driver jumped out and opened the door. I think he was very surprised to see us there, two women in a strict Muslim area who looked completely out of their comfort zone. We asked him to take us to the best hotel he knew. He nodded, and after a few minutes' drive we arrived at the Airport Hotel.

We were absolutely starving as we hadn't eaten all day, so we asked the man in the lobby where we could get some food, seeing as it was the early hours of the morning. He looked at us as if we each had two heads and in broken English he said, 'You cannot go outside of the hotel. You are two Western women, blonde women, it is too dangerous.'

We were fit to collapse with hunger and tiredness combined. I think he saw the dejection on our faces, and though he said nothing he came back about 45 minutes later with some beers and chips he had cooked himself. We paid him about 20 euros and we were absolutely delighted with our little feast. It felt as if someone had just handed us a thousand euros.

We sat in our rooms and we demolished those chips. We were delighted to have been eating anything. We were obviously very naive to think we could just go out onto the street at 1.30 a.m. in a city of 1.6 million people, the fifth largest city in Turkey as I found out much later, and be safe. We were very grateful that we had chosen this particular hotel, because any other hotel manager would have probably started to ask questions as to why we were there, where we were travelling to and so on, so we got lucky that night.

However, the hotel was extremely basic. There were no luxuries, and you basically had to just be grateful that you had a bed and a toilet and shower in the room – and we were. Luxuries were the last thing on our minds that night.

The next morning while I was getting ready, Mandy went down to the hotel reception and spoke to another man on duty. She asked him how we could get to the Syrian border. They were astonished that she wanted to go into Syria, but she didn't tell them our reasons for going, she just said we needed to get as near to the Syrian border as possible.

The hotel porter on duty said he could get a driver to bring us right down to a place called Hatay Province. This is an area that used to be owned by the Syrian government, and Syrians call it Liwa' aliskenderun. It was the cause of much dispute over the last few decades in particular, but tensions had eased in more recent times. A law requiring people from Turkey or

Syria to hold visas if they were travelling back or forth across the border was stopped in early 2009, and these people were finally told that they could pass without problems to visit family either side of the border over the Christmas holidays or Eid. Eid is a religious holiday celebrated each year by Muslims, and it is a hugely important family time for them. The opening of the border during this time frame was seen as a huge stepping stone towards improving Syrian–Turkish relations.

We were advised by the hotel porter that this area was still extremely dangerous, especially for women travelling alone. We knew that there would be very few places that would not be dangerous on our travels, and I had decided that once in Hatay Province I would look for a hijab to wear as I travelled across the border. It might not be a lifesaver, but I knew wearing the garment might make my crossing slightly safer.

We were told that it was roughly 192 kilometres from Adana to Hatay and it would take up to two and a half hours to get there by car, but that the driver who would take us there was very trustworthy and we would not be in danger with him. This distance meant nothing to us at this stage, and once again we had no choice but to put our trust in yet another stranger.

As I saw it, Mostafa Assad was an embarrassment to his culture, and he gave a bad impression of Middle Eastern society and people. Over the last 24 hours, I had encountered Middle Eastern men who had helped us with no questions asked as we attempted to travel to an Islamic culture while dressed in Western clothes and with no explanation as to why we needed to get there. They all wanted to know, I am sure of that, but so far we had got help at every place we stopped and as yet nothing bad had happened to us. I thanked God for being with us every step of the way and once again put my trust in him that this new driver would be just as trustworthy as the people we had met along the way to date.

Myself and Mandy got our bags from the room, paid the hotel porter and waited for the driver to arrive. He took our bags and put them into the boot of an old car. He didn't say much to us, but we handed him over 100 euros before we drove off and just hoped that he wouldn't leave us stranded along the way. I asked him to take us to the best hotel in Hatay and he told us, in Arabic, that he knew of a very good four-star hotel and that it was very nice. Myself and Mandy tried to remain positive as we looked at each other, because a four-star hotel in Turkey is definitely not what we call a four-star hotel in other European countries. The last hotel was allegedly four-star as well, but it resembled nothing more than a bed and breakfast, and a bad one at that. However, beggars can't be choosers, and we had been delighted the previous night, not just for the bed but for feeling somewhat safe.

The journey took us through a very mountainous area with barren land all around us. It was obvious on leaving Adana how huge the city was and how commercialised it was compared with other parts of Turkey. It was also obvious, however, that the Muslim influence was very much a big part of this particular area of Turkey, as women were either fully covered up in burkas or were wearing headscarves and were covered from the neck down.

We stopped at a little shop, a very basic place, to get drinks and to use the toilets, and I will never forget Mandy's face when she saw we had to wee into what was literally a hole in the floor. It was primitive, to say the least.

We noticed a lot of trucks along the route, and as we approached Hama itself the traffic became quite heavy, with lots of commercial vehicles seemingly heading for the Syrian border town.

When we eventually arrived at the Buyuk Hotel, after roughly two hours in the car, the driver took our bags from the boot, walked us into the lobby and organised a room for us. We thanked him and proceeded to check in.

We were very hot, as we had travelled non-stop in a car where the air conditioning didn't appear to be working, and opening the window just made it even hotter. There was nowhere we could have stopped along the way for a coffee, not like at home;

there had been a few little makeshift shops along the route, but we didn't see anywhere selling coffee. Luckily we had packed some bottles of water and we sipped them as we drove along. We hadn't eaten breakfast at all that morning, we simply drank some very strong Turkish coffee as we stood outside the hotel door and hoped that we would be able to go for a walk in this town to buy some food for the room and look to buy a hijab. Looking around us, though, it was clear that of all places we had visited to date, Hatay Province was a very strict Islamic area.

When we eventually made our way up to the bedroom, we were shocked to see that it was even more basic than the last one. There was, once again, cheap carpet laid on the floor but it hadn't even been cut properly and it extended up the walls. In the bathroom, there were no shampoos or any little luxuries you would expect in a four-star hotel, just cheap bars of soap. But the bed linen and towels appeared to be clean, and the room was neat. A bonus was that we had a TV and it had BBC World News. We were delighted to be able to hear English voices. We knew at this stage that beggars couldn't be choosers so we simply made the best of what we had. We got a mobile phone signal too, which was a blessing, as we knew that we had to seriously up our game now and start putting our plans into place.

We woke to the sound of prayers from the mosque, and those prayers continued throughout the day intermittently. For someone not used to this lifestyle it was quite frightening and, to be honest, I was terrified.

There are more than 540 miles of border between Turkey and Syria, and Hatay Province occupies 50 or so miles of this land, maybe more if you take in the sea areas. Nearly all refugees trying to flee Syria use the Hatay area to make their escape. Many thousands have taken the route over the years and many have lost their lives trying, but on 20 June 2011 the border had been closed because the Syrian government was trying to control the mass exodus. There were no 'good news' stories in

Syria, that was for sure, and President Bashar al-Assad knew this, so he ordered a total ban on foreign journalists entering the country. As the fighting and street protests escalated in cities and towns the length and breadth of the country, border controls were tightened.

I knew that this was happening because I had been following the news on TV throughout Turkey as we travelled along. I was watching CNN and Fox News, and I knew that it wasn't looking good. But this escalation in violence in Syria made it even more necessary for me to go in and save my child if the Turkish people smugglers failed to help us. It was still Plan B, but we both knew that it could very well become a possibility if all else failed.

I knew that if it came to it that Mandy would be terrified for my safety and that of May, but I had to keep reminding Mandy that she had a child herself and I knew that in a similar situation she would do exactly what I was doing. Reluctantly, she agreed, but she was also terrified of what could be lying ahead for both May and myself. That was if I actually managed to get into Syria at all, given the high security at the checkpoints.

Since May had been kidnapped, I often lay in bed at night hoping to God that she was safe and that she couldn't hear gunshots or see people being shot dead in the streets. Bad as he was, I hoped that Mostafa would shelter her as much as possible from witnessing any of the violence erupting. I knew other children living in Syria would be used to this sort of volatile situation, not that this was any consolation to them, but my little girl was used to a nice quiet life, going to the beach every day, playing with her friends and eating healthy dinners and ice cream for a treat. Now I dreaded to think what she was witnessing. But despite everything on the TV and everything I was hearing from home, I was determined to get in there and save her.

I was now fewer than 40 miles away from the dividing line between civilisation and war. But to me it was the dividing line between life and death, because without my little girl I might as well have been dead. She was my life and I needed to save hers. That was the bottom line.

We settled down in the room and took out the laptop. Thank God we were thinking on our feet and had taken it with us from Cyprus. We weren't sure if we could get an Internet connection along the way, but thankfully when we turned the laptop on the Internet worked.

We started to look at stories in the news on Syria, finding out exactly what the latest updates were. We also emailed family at home, letting them know that we were safe and telling everyone to take care of our dad. He was still our big concern, as we knew he would be worried sick with both of his daughters alone in a foreign country and his only granddaughter kidnapped by a father she feared and taken to a country savaged by war. We had been talking to Sean and Josh over the last few days while we were travelling and we had spoken to Dad, too, trying to keep him calm, saying we were fine and urging him not to worry.

At one stage we turned on the TV in the bedroom and watched the coverage of the tenth anniversary of the 9/11 bombings in the States. I have to say that was a horrible thing to have to watch. Especially as we had been there, in New York, when it happened. I remember saying to Mandy how odd it was to be sitting there watching the news unfold, because if I had been in Dublin we would have been doing the very same thing, probably watching that very same station. If I had been in Cyprus, I would have been watching it with my dad and his friend. But it was all so different now.

Back home, our aunt was still trying every avenue to get the Irish government to help, but she was getting nowhere fast. While we were in the hotel we got a call from the Department of Foreign Affairs advising us that they were doing everything they could, but that it wasn't easy. They were still having problems getting May a passport because, even though her father kidnapped her, the Irish government, which ruled the department, was still insisting that he would have to sign papers to get a new passport issued. We were distraught, as we knew this would definitely never happen.

Just drained by it all, I contacted our new 'friend' in Turkey who was supposed to be organising the people smugglers to get May out. I told him that I was now only a few miles from the Syrian border and that I would wait here until the men snatched May. Then they could bring her straight to me in Hatay or I could get nearer to the border at Reyhanli/Bab al-Hawa quite easily once I knew they had her. I asked this man how things were progressing with the group of men he was organising for the escape plan. All of a sudden, the goalposts started to shift in what was supposed to be an easy job for him to organise, and he started making excuses, saying that the escape plan was proving harder than he had expected. There were bigger risks than he had thought for the men. He said that because of the extremely volatile area where Mostafa lived, he was having problems getting men to agree to go in and risk their lives. He said that he needed more time to sort things out and that he was still trying to get three or four guys onside to organise an escape plan. We realised that this man was not telling us everything, and we started to wonder if he was just acting the 'big guy', pretending he had contacts and that he could organise an escape. We got very worried.

After that conversation, myself and Mandy just sat on the bed looking at each other, not knowing what to do next, not knowing what to say. I remember looking at Mandy's face and seeing the sheer exhaustion etched on it with every line. She looked absolutely shattered, but that night more than ever I was so grateful to her for being with me. I realised that she had put her own life in danger to come this far, and I knew that although she absolutely loved me she was also worried sick about her own safety and would be thinking that if anything happened to her, Josh would be alone and Dad would be distraught.

For now, we needed to bide our time and give our Turkish contact a little longer to organise a rescue plan for us. We hadn't been given a price from him either and judging by the last conversation any price he'd had in his head was about to go up as the risk of danger rose. So I rang my friend back in Cyprus and asked her to ring Mostafa again and tell him that I was still in hospital, sedated, but that I should be able to ring him if I was OK the next morning. She was a great friend and she did what I asked.

We got back onto the Cypriot police as well but realised that there was no help coming from their end. They did not even offer a slight ray of hope for us. Up until then I know we had both been hoping and praying that the Turkish guys would get to the border and go across, snatch May and bring her back out to me in Hatay. But, judging by the last phone call, this hope seemed to be fading fast. I think at that stage we knew that time was ticking away and that I would have no choice but to go into Syria and face whatever there was to face.

Here we were, two sisters in a deplorable hotel room, if you could even call it that, on the border of a strange, war-torn country, and we had no plan that we knew would get myself and May home to Ireland safely and put Mandy's mind at rest. Although I knew that I had to face Plan B now and walk into a living hell, because that is how I envisaged Syria, I also knew that poor Mandy would somehow have to make her way all the way back along the same route we had just taken to get a flight back to Ireland, alone.

Mandy and myself just sat there on the bed in silence for a good ten minutes, neither of us knowing what to say but both of us knowing what had to happen next.

I explained to Mandy that I felt as if I had no choice but to risk my life and try crossing the border. She was in an awful state, crying and hugging me, but I felt as though I was losing May, and my hopes of her being rescued by these Turkish guys were fading fast.

We knew that if I went in, we had the mobile phones to chat on, but we had to play that very safely as well if I did get into Syria. Apart from Mostafa hearing us speak, I was also worried

about whether the Syrian government was tapping the phones
of Westerners entering the country. I knew that anything was
possible, so if I went in Mandy and I had to plan our steps with
military precision to protect everyone involved. I decided that
if I did go across I would let the Turkish contact know in
advance, and Mandy could keep him updated after she had
phoned me. Mandy would communicate everything to me, as
we would have our own coded way of talking to each other and
getting messages across. We had decided to do this because
although Mostafa knew that I needed to be in touch with
Mandy by phone because she was supposed to be selling up all
that I owned in Cyprus so that she could send the money on to
me to give to him, I knew that he would be listening and
hanging on to my every word as we spoke. So we had come up
with a code whereby if Mandy asked me if I felt OK and if my
back or hips were bothering me and I said I was sore, that
meant the opposite, as in I am OK, he is not being aggressive
towards me and you are not to worry.

I knew that we could plan an escape all we liked, for just May
and myself to run, but the likelihood of that happening was
extremely low in such a volatile country, and a strictly Islamic
country where the women and children did everything with
their men and rarely got out alone.

That night, neither of us slept. The thought of what was
about to happen haunted the night for us both. We were always
extremely close as sisters, best friends really. We had only fallen
out once in 30-odd years, albeit for a long time, and it had all
been about Mostafa and how my sister and family felt he was
ruling my life. But Mandy and I were never closer than that
night.

I knew Mandy feared that even if Mostafa didn't kill me, I
would lose my life anyway in Syria, either through war or from
the oppression Mostafa would force on me. She felt I was in a
no-win situation and as we both tried to doze off I knew that
we were both praying for the same thing: that these Turks
would live up to their promise and that at daylight I would

receive a call to say they were on their way. It was a dream that we both knew in our hearts would probably never come to fruition, but we lived in hope. I had already planned to give May's little toy Justin to the smugglers to take in with them as reassurance that her mammy had sent them to rescue her and she wasn't being snatched by total strangers. I just prayed and prayed that early the next morning the phone would ring and Plan A would be up and running. But, in reality, I wasn't too hopeful.

As we woke the next morning we grabbed the mobile phone to make sure we had not missed any texts from our Turkish contact. When there was nothing, we knew what we had to do.

We got dressed and went down for breakfast, which consisted of strong coffee, bread and jam, and then we headed out to do some shopping for a hijab. We went to an ATM and Mandy suggested that I take two or three thousand euros from my account, but I knew that life was cheap in Syria and so I decided to take out five hundred euros and the equivalent in Turkish lira, so that we had two denominations in case some people we met and needed help from along the way wanted a specific currency as payment. I put the euros in one cup of my bra and the lira in the other cup.

As we walked through the shops in our regular Western-style clothing, our appearance attracted attention. We stuck out a mile, but we carried on, ignoring the whispers and the stares as much as we could. We looked at the prices of the hijabs and they were absolutely ridiculous. They wanted 80 to 100 dollars for an ordinary garment, and I felt that we were being totally ripped off because they saw us as tourists, so we left the shopping. I decided that I would just cover up as much as I could in my own clothes to get across the border, because I knew that once there Mostafa would have clothing that he felt I should wear – appropriate clothing, as he would see it – already waiting for me. I was also concerned about handing out such a large amount of money for clothes, as we were trying to hold on to cash to pay for flight money for Mandy and the likes of the Turkish guys, and all of our money was being eaten up as it was on taxis, planes and accommodation.

We headed back to the hotel and we decided that I would ring Mostafa and tell him where I was. I was doing this very reluctantly, but both Mandy and I knew that it had to be done. When he answered the phone he sounded frantic and he asked where I was. When I told him Hatay, he didn't even question how I had got there, even though I was meant to be in a Cypriot hospital up until last night. He just said, 'You are only half an hour away from me, Louise.' I played on his insecurities, because he hated me being anywhere on my own where there could be men, so I said, 'Please come and get me, Mostafa. I am very scared. There are loads of strange men around, and I am worried sick.'

I asked him to come across the border into Turkey to talk to me. I was shocked when he said he would, and he told me to give him five minutes: he would ring back. I thought that he wanted to try to organise something, but I soon realised something more important and much more dangerous had just evolved.

Within minutes, he rang me back. It appeared that a call had been waiting to come through to his phone while he was speaking to me, and it was a call that was to dash all of my plans. If I hadn't acted as I did, it was a call that could have put not only my life but also May's in jeopardy.

When I answered the phone, Mostafa started to scream and shout. He was like a madman. He said he had received a call from Interpol asking about my whereabouts. He immediately thought that I had reported him for kidnapping May. My stomach flipped over. I was holding the phone slightly away from my own ear so that Mandy could also hear what he was saying. We both froze. I saw Mandy's eyes widen in shock and she put her hand to her mouth in disbelief. We were in trouble now.

I don't know how I thought of it, but I seemed to immediately blurt out, 'Mostafa. Hang on a minute. Don't be panicking. I'll get to the bottom of this. No one knows anything, there must be an explanation.' He was ranting and raving, so I said, 'Give me the number and I will ring them and see what is wrong. It is nothing for you to be worried about. It's obviously nothing to do with you because they don't know anything.' He seemed slightly more relaxed and he told me to ring him straight back.

The number they had called from was Cypriot. In a temper and totally fuming, I dialled the number. I don't think I even took a breath. I told the man on the phone who I was. He replied, 'Louise, we have been trying to contact you and your phone was off.'

I replied, 'My daughter has been kidnapped and you have just rung her abductor. I want to talk to your supervisor.'

He replied, 'No, you can't.' And with that, he put the phone down on me.

At that stage I just wanted to scream. I could not believe how Interpol had just gone and messed everything up for me. I knew that Mostafa would panic, and I was terrified that he wouldn't believe whatever excuse I gave him and that he might just pack his bag and run with May. I was worried sick that he might think it was a set-up and that they might trace his phone. In his mind, that would mean they could be looking for him right there and then, that they could possibly even be on the way to arrest him.

Mandy was frantic. But I had to think quickly. I immediately redialled Mostafa's number and I said, 'Mostafa, thank God it's all OK. Nothing to worry about. Basically, my dad hasn't heard from either Mandy or myself for days now and he was worried sick so he contacted Interpol. It's OK now. I have told them we are fine and that I will be in touch with my dad. Do you really think they would ring your number, tipping you off, if they were trying to find *you*! Would you not be so ridiculous, you are panicking for nothing.'

So that appeased him a bit and calmed him down, but then he said, 'That has just unnerved me a little, so now instead of me coming over the border to you, you will have to now come over into Syria to me.' I was sick, because I thought that if I got him over into Turkey, myself and Mandy could try to persuade him to let us take May home. It would have been a huge gamble, but it might have worked: he might have been so scared that he could be arrested that he might have agreed to save himself any further trouble, because I knew he was feeling some regret – not out of love for our daughter, but out of fear of what could possibly happen to him, having kidnapped a child. One stupid phone call from the international police force had jeopardised everything and possibly ruined any prospect of him agreeing to bring May back across the border to me.

I wanted to scream, but I had to stay calm. I had to continue playing the game. So I agreed to come across to him. I told him I would come over, and I would meet him between 7 and 8 p.m. Immediately his suspicions were aroused again, and he wanted to know why I had chosen this particular time frame. I said that I had to pack and I needed to lie down for a while, as my hips were causing me a lot of pain and I knew that I wouldn't make it all the way if I didn't rest up first. I told him I was very, very scared. After warning me not to do 'anything funny' or he would flee with May, he finally agreed to the plan. As I put the phone down, I looked at Mandy and I knew that she was thinking exactly as I was. Within hours we were to go our separate ways and the reality was, and she knew it only too well, that we might never see each other again.

I was walking into a war zone, to a husband who had beaten me to a pulp over many years while we lived in a civilised society. Now I was making my way into a country where women were subservient to their men, did what they were told, when they were told, and lived their lives dominated and beaten down in many cases. I was now going into *his* country. *His* life. I was going back to a man whom I had divorced less than 12 months before in fear of what he was capable of doing to me. Now I was walking back into his arms and into a life a million miles from my world.

But if I didn't go, what then? If I didn't try to save my daughter I feared that she would grow up to be one of those subservient women, with an arranged marriage, probably to a cousin, at fourteen years of age. She would have to be obedient and bow down to her husband's domination all of her life and she would always think that her mammy had abandoned her, left her to live that life alone, with no support.

I couldn't do that, and Mandy knew that only too well. I had to do what any other loving mother would do. I had to put my life on the line to save my daughter, and that's what I was going to do.

After I packed my few belongings, myself and Mandy went out for a bite to eat. We sat in a pizza place, oblivious to anything that was happening around us, ignorant of people's stares or whispers for the first time. It felt to me like Jesus must have felt at the Last Supper. We were both sick to the pit of our stomachs and we ate without saying a word. It was as if this was to be the last meal I would ever have with the sister I adored and loved. I felt as though I was being sentenced to death.

I was worried sick about how Mandy was going to make her way back on that same route we had taken together and then get back to Ireland, and yet all she was worried about was me. There had been no call from our Turkish 'friend' and now he wasn't even answering his phone. Reality was dawning that I was on my own. Yet, weirdly, we still hoped that it all might happen when I was in Syria, and if this was the case they would take both me and May, which would have been much easier on May as I would be there to explain what was happening and reassure her that we were both safe.

Mandy and I decided as we sat eating pizza that our code for the men coming would be based on something silly. We would use Sean as the subject matter, and if they were coming, Mandy would say, 'Sean is still off the drink,' insinuating he had given up his few pints of Guinness. And if there was no sign of the men, she would say, 'Sean is still having his few pints.' It sounds ridiculous to people who don't know us, but we had to say stupid things so Mostafa could never guess what we really meant. Mandy had all the code words written down. I couldn't take them with me, as it would have been too dangerous in case Mostafa found them, but I tried to memorise them as best I could.

Once we were both aware of what would be said and what it would mean, we made our way back to the hotel. In silence.

I wanted so much to be able to take a camera into Syria with me so that I could one day show everyone at home what the place was like, to give them an insight into the life little May would have had to live if I hadn't gone in to save her. Unfortunately, though, I knew that I would never get into the country, let alone into Mostafa's home, with a camera. Syrians didn't want any foreigner knowing what really went on behind their borders, and much as I wanted to attempt to take one in with me I knew that the consequences could be lethal. So I didn't risk it.

We asked the hotel porter to call the taxi that would take me to the border. They were very suspicious in this particular hotel as to why I needed to get to Syria, especially as I was clearly a single woman dressed in clothes that were totally contradictory to Muslim beliefs. I think they must have believed that I was going into Syria on a secret mission for a reason that I could not discuss, and so they ushered us out of the back door to avoid any attention from passers-by on the street outside.

When we reached the exit, the taxi was waiting for me and I just wanted to cry. I knew that Mandy had to stay here alone for the night, and I prayed that I wouldn't break down when I left her. I put my black handbag onto the back seat of my taxi as well as a fake Louis Vuitton luggage bag that Mandy had bought in Cyprus. I hadn't taken much with me, just some long dresses I had bought in Cyprus, some cardigans and a photo of Josh that we had planned to give to the Turkish guys along with May's toy if they were going in for her, to reassure her that these men were sent from her mammy.

I also made sure that I had plenty of medication with me.

My doctor had told me that all I could take before the hip replacement was rosehip, and so I had this in my bag, but we also put in a cocktail of over-the-counter drugs removed from their packaging, such as adult Motilium, infant Motilium, painkillers and anti-inflammatory tablets. Mostafa would not have known any of these drugs. We knew that May and myself would probably be sick from the food, but I had planned not to tell Mostafa which drugs were for which ailment. I would just let him think that they were all for my hip and for cancer, in case I did actually have the disease. But I knew that if I was eating food that I knew would upset my stomach I would at least have something to help me cope with it and he would never know. I was well equipped, or so I thought, for any illness that I could be hit with.

But nothing could have prepared me for leaving Mandy. I don't think I will ever be able to explain how I felt, watching my sister walk away. We were both crying, and the final hug we gave each other could have broken bones. My body felt weak, yet I felt no pain from the hip problem that had caused me so much agony in the weeks prior to this. If anything, I felt stronger than in a very long time. I was absolutely dreading seeing Mostafa Assad but longing to see and hold and squeeze my little girl. I had been living in anticipation of this for days, and now it was only hours away.

I dreaded what was going to happen if I succeeded in getting across the border, as I still wasn't sure if Mostafa knew anything about the publicity back home about his abduction of May. He was so devious that I feared telling Mandy that I thought he might actually know what had been going on all along and was actually playing a game with me as I played one with him. I had feared for days that Mostafa getting me into Syria could be a ploy to beat me up and teach me a lesson, or that he would trick me into thinking that I was going to see May and play happy families when in fact he might have left her with a family member and would never let me see her until he felt I was being an obedient wife. He knew that my life revolved around my child and that absolutely nothing could hurt me more than losing May. I didn't want to tell Mandy that I feared Mostafa was only letting me see May because he thought I might have cancer and because he knew that my visa would only last for a short period. He knew I would have to leave Syria at some stage, and if I was diagnosed with cancer on my return and I died, my family would have a harder battle to get May back to Ireland because he would already have her in Syria. My mind had been racing over the previous days, but there was only so much I could burden Mandy with.

As I started to make my way to the taxi, Mandy ran back and grabbed me. Swinging me around, she said, 'Louise, if I let you go people are going to think that I let you go and that it was my fault.' But I reassured her, and I told her to tell our family and friends that she had no choice but to let me go. I reminded her that she would do the same if it was Josh, and she nodded. We were both heartbroken. But I had a job to do. I had to go into this country and get my child back and nothing and no one could stop me now.

As I drove off, I looked behind and I remember seeing Mandy sobbing. I remember how she put her hands to her face and then ran them through her hair, as if she was desperate. It is funny how certain things stick in your mind, but this was a vision I was to hold on to for a long time. A vision that made me realise how much my sister loved me and I her.

As we drove along in the taxi, the driver got a phone call on his mobile. He spoke in Arabic to this person and then he turned to me and handed me the phone. A man I did not know told me in English that because of the dangers associated with me going into Syria the driver would not be able to take me all the way to the border but that he would drop me off as close as possible. He feared for the safety of the driver if we were stopped at the border. I understood his concern, because I had been on the Internet with Mandy for days as we looked at the possibilities of escape routes and so on, and I had seen that the Syrian government had issued a blacklist of all known protesters and therefore border checks were a huge risk for anyone who was not a known supporter of President al-Assad. I had no idea who this driver was or what his background was, and it was highly possible that he might have been in trouble before with the authorities in Syria or Turkey and his name was on that list, or it could simply have been that he was afraid of being stopped and checked simply because those at border patrol needed no excuse to beat, arrest or even kill someone. They could do whatever they wanted to whomever they wanted, and having a European woman in his car was a problem in itself.

I agreed that this man could not put his life in danger, and we continued to drive along the dirt roads. I noticed how there was virtually no vegetation and no houses, except for some makeshift shacks along the way scattered here and there. It was a vast, very open area with no shops or businesses, just sand and dirt tracks. As we drove, the dust was spraying up behind the car and we were showered with debris from oncoming vehicles. The cars were old and battered, as was my taxi, and you could tell that the cars were considered clean by the standards they held in this area, but they would have been unacceptable in any Western country. But the taxi was a means of transport, and as far as I was concerned it was a godsend to have a driver who had been recommended by the hotel and who I hoped I could trust.

We exchanged a few words as we drove, but I noticed him glancing at me every now and then through his rear-view mirror and I knew he was wondering what the hell I was doing going into a country savaged by war and uprisings when even those living just a few miles across the border wouldn't dream of it.

As I sat there thinking of all different scenarios that could happen once I met Mostafa, I looked out the window to see a refugee camp filled with Syrians that I had seen a number of times on the news. It was a makeshift camp with about five or six hundred white tents. I had heard on the news that these were Syrians who had attempted to get through to Turkey through no-man's-land but were caught and had been refused entry. It was heartbreaking to look at those people. It looked like there could have been a few thousand people there, all fleeing in fear of their lives, all desperate for a new life under a 'normal' regime. There were little children, hundreds of them, it seemed, running around in their bare feet on the sandy, dirty gravel and men sitting around fires, like makeshift barbecues, eating meat. This was the first image I had of what life must have been like for those living in Syria at that time, when there was a war on. If people were prepared to go to these extremes to escape, knowing that this could be the extent of their lives if they were lucky to get out at all, then things were even worse than I could ever have imagined.

The camp was to my left, and, as we made our way up a mountainous road, to my right I saw two men struggling to get under a barbed-wire fence. I first saw a bag being thrown over the fence, then the men jumping down and trying to lift it, pulling and tugging at the fencing. As they saw our car approaching they threw themselves to the ground, trying to hide. I knew immediately that they were Syrian and trying to get into Turkey.

We only travelled another five or ten minutes, and up ahead I could see the checkpoints and the lorries and cars queuing up to get through. The driver pulled in and told me that this was the end of the road for him, he couldn't take me any further, and he held his hand out for payment. I could see that he couldn't wait to get out of this place and so I handed him the agreed payment of 100 euros for bringing me on a journey that took roughly half an hour. I knew that I was being ripped off, but I had no choice but to pay whatever these people were asking, as they put their own lives at risk getting myself and Mandy to and from certain areas. I knew that 100 euros would change that man's life so much and probably keep himself and his family in food for a month. It was a small price to pay for getting me that step closer to my daughter.

As I took my bag and left the car, I was terrified but filled with the anticipation of seeing May. I wasn't kidding myself, I

was walking into a waking nightmare, I knew that only too
well, but it was a nightmare that I couldn't avoid.

As I proceeded to walk towards the checkpoint, three men
who were sitting on the side of the road jumped up and ran
across to me. I knew that they were Syrian. They asked me in
Arabic for money, pushing their hands into my face and tugging
at my cardigan. I knew what they wanted, but I just ignored
them and pulled away and started to walk faster towards the
border. Thankfully, one of the guards, who I now call one of the
many angels I met along my journey, saw what was happening,
and as I ran towards a buzzer that was on a gate he came
running out. As the gate started to open slowly, he grabbed
hold of me and dragged me in. With that he must have hit
another button, because the gate closed behind me almost
instantly.

I just calmly opened my bag, I don't know how I managed to
be so focused, and I took out my passport and handed it to
him. In English, he asked me where I was going to. I said I was
going into Syria. He replied, 'No, you're not. Do you have any
idea what is happening in Syria?' I told him I knew what it was
like. I knew they were killing people but that I had to go. He
replied, 'I can't let you go in, I'm sorry.'

I took out my purse and I said, 'I have money and I will give
it to you if you let me go through.' I was very upset. He still
refused to budge, and obviously the issue wasn't money but my
safety. I then told him that my ex-husband had taken my baby
and that I needed to get in to save her. With that, he took me
past a line of Syrians trying to get back into Syria. And he took
my passport and we went to an outbuilding where there were
three men inside checking documents. As they were all staring
at me and my Irish passport, one man made a phone call. When
he put the phone down, he handed the passport back to my
angel and it was stamped. My angel said that he had no choice
but to let me in, as it was a legal requirement to do so. I kissed
his hand and said, 'I can't thank you enough.' I said goodbye to
him, and he asked me where I was going to next and how I was

getting there. I told him that I was going to walk to the main border, and he seemed totally shocked.

He said, 'It is a five-kilometre walk from here to the border of Syria. It is the most dangerous walk. It is filled with bandits who live in this area because they cannot get into Turkey.' At this stage it was about 7.15 p.m. It was dark already and I was very conscious of the time, as I had told Mostafa that I would be there between 7 and 8 p.m. The man said, 'You cannot go like this, you won't make it.' With that, he walked away from me and over to a car parked nearby. I heard him speak in Arabic to the driver, and then he walked back to me and said that this man was going to take me as far as the Syrian border. He said, 'Do not give him money or gold. This guy owes me a favour.' I heard him tell the driver, in Arabic, that if he asked me for any money he would never work in that area again, and that he had given me his phone number and if anything went wrong I was going to ring him. I will never be able to say how grateful I was to this man, because he truly saved my life that night and he had no reason whatsoever to help me. The driver simply nodded and I got into the car.

The previous day, President al-Assad had declared a ban on motorbikes in towns and cities, as the owners were using them in protests to escape quickly. I had read this on the Internet the night before, and my first image as we drove along the five kilometres to the border was seeing motorbikes abandoned all over the road. At some points there were groups of men trying to repair some of these damaged bikes on the ground. There must have been roughly about five or six hundred of them lying abandoned as we made our way along the dirt roads, dodging motorbikes or spare parts everywhere.

People kept coming up to the car knocking on the windows as we drove along slowly, but we kept driving, totally ignoring their pleas. There were some makeshift tents lining the streets as well, and I saw one man on the side of the road being treated for wounds as the blood ran down his leg. I couldn't make out what had happened to him, but I guessed he might have been a protester beaten up somewhere else but who had made his way back to this area because it was near the border and possibly a safer area to be in than where he had come from.

As we drove up this road, we suddenly came to an area where there were a number of Syrian police officers. I was absolutely shocked to see a huge building, which turned out to be a duty-free centre. It was something like you would see in an international airport, and it looked so out of place. It had big glass windows and revolving doors. I could see there were men dressed in uniforms working away and on the shelves I could see every cigarette brand imaginable and a full range of alcohol: wine, whisky, vodka, everything. It was all clearly visible from outside: shelves upon shelves of what I thought would have been banned substances in a strictly Muslim country. Alcohol is generally not tolerated in Syria, so this was quite a shocking scene for me. Yet I could see people walking around, buying things.

As I was watching all this in fascination, the driver left the car, and then all of a sudden I was startled to hear a knock on the window. As I looked up, I saw Mostafa at the door. He opened it and said, 'Louise, are you OK?'

My hair stood up on end and my blood ran cold. I exclaimed, 'No, I am not, Mostafa. I have been through a horrendous experience, even getting here, my hips are killing me and I am shattered.'

He said, 'Don't worry, I will look after you from now.' With that, he got into the taxi and he directed the driver to continue driving to the border-control area. Seemingly we still hadn't crossed the border into Syria; these were all just points along the way before being granted entry or exit.

When we got to the border-control building, Mostafa took my passport and we both got out of the car to get my visa checked. Mostafa had arranged the visa application but my passport still had to be stamped. He spoke to those in the office, and when we came out with the visa in hand he started complaining over the fact that it had cost him 50 dollars to get it.

We got back into the taxi and he told the driver to take us on up the road to the actual border itself, which he did. He drove us across this very small border, with a chain-link fence. There were two men there, but they didn't check anything. Mostafa had a car parked just over the border and we left the taxi. I thanked the man who had taken me over, as agreed, for free.

When I got into Mostafa's car – his father's car, a maroon-coloured Kia – I asked him how May was. He said she was fine: just that, nothing else. Then from the back seat he plucked a black hijab with delicate beading around the edges and a long black dress with similar beading, and threw them at me and said, 'Put this on. This is what you will be wearing now.'

He made me put it on as we sat in the car. I just pulled it on over the clothes I was already wearing. He helped me fix the hijab in place, rushing in case someone saw me with no veil covering my head. I was still wearing a pair of flip-flops I had bought in Cyprus, which clearly was not acceptable for Muslim women, but he told me that he would sort that and buy me shoes the following day. I told him that I would need to ring my sister to tell her that I was all right and that I was safe.

I knew that he was wondering how I'd managed to get to Syria from Hatay alone and so I told him that I was very upset because I'd had to leave my sister behind in the town and it was very emotional for us both. I said Mandy was very upset. He said, 'Ring her, ring her. Tell her I will bring her over here and she can stay in a hotel.' I knew there was no way that she would come, but I played along. I rang her and I told her I was fine and that I was with Mostafa now. He knew that I had a phone with me and he didn't try to take it from me, which was a huge relief. I told Mandy that everything was fine and, playing along as planned, I said to her that she was to continue selling everything I had and then send all the money over to us.

She said, 'Of course I will. And tell Mostafa I am fully behind you both in this. He has to mind you now. Tell Mostafa I will organise everything for you now and send him the money and ask him how I am best sending it. Keep your phone on and I will update you both.' She was, of course, saying all of this knowing that he could hear everything she was saying as he was beside me in the front seat, driving.

I told her that we would sort all that out and get back to her. I remember asking Mostafa if he wanted to talk to Mandy, but, of course, he was too embarrassed to say a word, and he indicated with his hands and by shaking his head that he didn't want to speak to her.

He believed that Mandy was going to sell everything for me: the cars, the furniture from the apartment and bits and pieces. Mostafa knew that I had savings in the bank from a previous house I had sold in Cyprus before moving from Paphos to Limassol, and in his head Mandy was going to close my bank account as well and transfer everything over to Syria. I told him that I had given Mandy power of attorney through a solicitor to enable her sell everything and transfer the funds, and he believed it all. He knew that he had to keep her and me onside to make his plan work. So he had to be nice to me or the plan would be useless.

As we drove to Mostafa's house, which took half an hour or so, through filthy streets with no footpath markings, no lines in the middle of the road to show you where you were driving and no way of knowing if you were on a road or a pathway, he kept checking my hijab. At a few stages along the way he stopped to rearrange my clothing, as I wasn't used to wearing it, and at one of these stops an open-topped truck pulled up alongside us and asked why we had stopped and whether we needed help. I had seen scenes like these on the news when they were covering the war in Syria, and my stomach tensed up almost immediately. I knew that shootings happened in scenes just like this, because I had witnessed it clearly on TV, but thankfully Mostafa gave some excuse, saying everything was fine, and they drove on. The relief was immense.

We carried on driving, and we eventually arrived in Mostafa's home city, Idlib. Immediately I was hit with the strong smell of sewage. There was filth and dirt and people's household rubbish and clothing strewn everywhere. It was obvious that they did not have rubbish collection in this area, because it was the filthiest place I had ever seen in my life.

There were men driving along in the dark on donkeys, whipping the poor animals as they struggled along these dirt roads. The cars the people were driving were falling apart as they made their way along the streets and would never have passed any sort of roadworthiness test in any other country. It was a deplorable scene, worse than any of the areas I had been through on my route here. I told Mostafa that I had seen what Idlib was like on the news and that I was worried, to which he replied that it was all simply hype by the media. He had only been back in this country a week and he had been brainwashed already, and now trying to brainwash me. The West, as usual, was being blamed for painting a bad picture of his homeland, a land he had hated with a vengeance until he decided to kidnap our child just days before. I sat and listened to his ranting as reality hit me from every angle, even though it was pitch black outside. Dark or not, I couldn't be fooled by what was clearly in front of me.

All of a sudden he pulled in along the roadside, opposite what looked like a fruit and vegetable shop. He told me to wait in the car and not to get out, that he needed to buy something and he would be back in minutes. As he left, I closed the window: he had left it open because it was such a balmy night, but closing the window helped to cover up the foul smell, which, though he was obviously used to it, was unbearable to me. I pulled the scarf over my face to try to block the stench even further, but it was of little help. As I watched him walk across the road, the level of hatred I felt for this man was mighty. I was grateful that he hadn't tried to give me a hug or a kiss when we met, as my real feelings would have been very apparent to him. All I wanted at this stage was to get to May.

I was being as strong as possible, given the circumstances, and I knew I had to keep up the pretence. Within minutes of him leaving the car I heard this deafening noise. It was indescribable. I looked in the rear-view mirror and I saw what looked like a thousand protesters, mostly men, waving flags and carrying an open coffin, a makeshift coffin made from a wooden box. They were all chanting and screaming carrying this body, and to my horror I noticed that they were coming towards the car. I immediately stretched across and locked the doors, fearing they would drag me out and beat me to death. I was a European in a car alone with no one to protect me, and I thought that was it, I was dead. I could see women in the side streets grabbing their children and running and I didn't know what to do. Should I run? Should I hide on the floor? I was desperate.

I totally froze. Suddenly I saw Mostafa, and he looked like he was about to run across the road to me, but then he realised that if he did, they would probably trample him. (I only realised later that if you run into a protest it is seen as disrespectful and you would be beaten to death there and then, so that explained why Mostafa had stepped back into the doorway out of their way.)

As they all marched past the car, it started to rock violently. I thought for a brief moment that they would turn the car over, with me in it, but within a few minutes, as I sat there praying that it would be over fast, they just disappeared around the corner and into another street. As they passed they were chanting in Arabic, 'Death to the president, death to the president.' Mostafa walked across and got into the car, and I turned to him and said, 'No trouble, eh?' He had told me on the phone that everything was fine where he was living. A total lie. He didn't reply to my comment and we continued to drive through the city.

As we approached a checkpoint, he said that it was manned by the army and that it would be fine. We weren't stopped, and we carried on until we passed something that resembled a big motorway. There were rocks and stones strewn everywhere and a dead donkey on the side of the road with the president's name written in paint on its rear. I asked Mostafa what that was all about and he said that anti-government protesters were writing President al-Assad's name on the bottoms and backs of dogs and donkeys and then using these poor animals for target practice.

There were pictures of President al-Assad absolutely everywhere. He was smiling down in various poses from nearly every street, and in some streets there were multiple posters. It was as if he didn't want anyone forgetting who was in charge. You couldn't go from one street to the next without seeing him stare down at you. It was the oddest scene. I had never seen anything like it, even during election time back home, when every politician likes to place himself in our eyeline, everywhere. But this was very different. It was definitely a form of propaganda.

As we went across this main road we came to another checkpoint, manned this time by men who were not in uniform, as they had been at the previous checkpoint, but were instead wearing jeans and shirts and tracksuits. Some were wearing bandanas on their heads. Mostafa told me that these were men guarding his own village and that this checkpoint was OK. I was wearing the hijab, so when they looked into the car I kept my eyes focused down onto the floor so as not to arouse suspicion, and they just waved us on.

We drove along and arrived at Mostafa's village. One of my first images was seeing green lights on the top of three buildings, and I realised immediately that these were all mosques. Most little towns and villages have one mosque, so to see three made me feel very intimidated. It meant that this was a very religious Muslim area and that it would most definitely be practised by everyone. There was a big possibility it could house some very extreme fundamentalists. The village had big walls, covered in graffiti. It resembled a compound.

I only learned afterwards that this particular village was a very dangerous area to live in or even be in. Tensions were running high between locals and the Syrian army, which shot people on the streets most days for protesting. You had to be very careful once you left your home because snipers were everywhere: on roofs, on derelict buildings, everywhere. You took your life in your hands every day. But even if I had known exactly how bad it was going to be, I still would have had no option but to come.

I looked around, and even in the darkness I could see the stark reality of what was around me. The so-called 'houses' had corrugated-iron or tin roofs, and most houses had no doors or glass in the windows, they were just covered in sheets. I remember thinking how it was odd that at nearly 9 p.m. there were children running around the streets, young children, maybe some as young as two or three years old, with no shoes on, and at one stage Mostafa had to swerve to avoid these children because they simply wouldn't move, even seeing an oncoming car heading for them.

I remember trying to make out all the landmarks along the way so I could tell Mandy as much as possible to relay to the Turkish smugglers. I wanted them to get a feel of the area so they could try to pinpoint exactly where we were.

When we pulled up at Mostafa's house I was slightly relieved, as it looked somewhat habitable. He had been sending money home during the good years in Cyprus when he was making money from working in construction. He ushered me straight into the house, and it was obvious that he didn't want anyone to see me. Next door was a two-storey house that towered over his little house, and he clearly didn't want whoever lived in this particular house to see what was happening.

I knew that this street was full of his family, as he had told me years before how one couple built a house there years ago and then all of their family moved in around them as they grew up. So the whole road was filled with the Assad family.

As soon as I got into the house, Mostafa told me to sit there and wait until he came back with May. I remember being elated that I was about to be reunited with my little girl.

I looked around and realised that I was in the standard living room. Most Arabic houses have two sitting rooms: one for the women and the other for male gatherings only. The furniture was a red colour with gold going through it. There were three chairs in this room and gold-framed pictures on the walls depicting sections from the Koran. I then walked into the room where the men clearly congregated for their religious gatherings. It was covered wall to wall with cushions, some on the floor, others that were propped straight up.

This was a typical Arabic home, but it was alien to me, as I had never lived like this before. I had been married to a Muslim, but he was not, I thought, a fanatic. He never demanded his own room to meet with his friends with no women allowed. He had an aggressive nature, and he could be possessive, perhaps because in his culture men enjoyed more rights than women, but I never witnessed a strict Islamic side to his nature. But it was becoming clearer to me that he had been living a lie for years in Cyprus, leading me to believe that his religion didn't really matter to him. I believe now that all that time he was planning to snatch May and take her back to Syria so she could become a devout Muslim. The man I had met all those years ago in a bar was very different to the monster I now knew.

I was so excited, though, as I waited for my little girl to burst through the doors to see her mammy again. I was so anxious about meeting her, praying that she hadn't been hurt by her father or anyone else, praying that he had cared for and protected her all this time.

But as the door opened and she walked through, it took me a minute to recognise her. My little baby was dressed so differently. I was absolutely shocked and horrified. She looked so different. Someone had tightly plaited her lovely long brown hair, and she was wearing a horrible cheap pair of black trousers and red Arabic clogs with a gold pattern running through them. Her top was black and white with horrible cheap lace around the neck and the ends of her sleeves. It was typical Arab village clothing. When she came clomping through the door onto the tiled floor in those horrible clogs she ran over to me, and I remember thinking that although her father had only had her for a week, he had already managed to change her into his way of life.

She clearly didn't know what to say to me as he stood staring at us both. She nervously looked at him before saying, 'Mama. Look. I told you I would mind my Nintendo for you. I kept it safe.' I felt like bursting into tears. She treasured her Nintendo DS and it was obviously a lifesaver to her in this hellhole. She sat on my lap and he left the room. As soon as he was gone, we started to kiss and hug and she was squeezing my leg. Once she knew that he was definitely gone, she looked around and she whispered in a really low voice, 'Mama, I'm really worried.'

I said, 'What are you worried about, love?'

And my heart melted when she replied, 'I was meant to start school.'

I said, 'Don't worry, love. I rang the school and I told them that you were on holiday and they were fine about it.'

Then she said, 'And what about Maria?' Maria was our cat and May idolised her. I reassured her that my friend Janine was feeding Maria and looking after her. I could see her relax once she knew that school and poor Maria were all fine. And I remember thinking how clever she was, because as Mostafa walked back into the room she went back to being obedient to her father. I knew there and then that she was also playing the game. She had seen me so many times trying to push the right buttons to keep him calm and on my side, and I was watching a complete carbon copy of myself as I watched my little girl trying to gain her father's approval and love.

As he came closer, she acted as if she had said nothing to me that would have caused him concern. She immediately said, 'Oh, Baba, did you see my new shoes?' She always called him Baba, the Arabic word for father, and now more than ever it was important that she used that word. This sort of behaviour would keep him happy. Hearing May speak his language would appease him no end.

It was getting late, and I told him that I was in a lot of pain and very tired from the long day. I asked him if he would mind if I slept with May that night, as I had missed her so much. He agreed. He knew that I was sick, and he didn't seem to mind. There were two bedrooms in the house, one with a big wardrobe and a king-size bed and a children's room with three mattresses on the floor and three throws and three pillows. This was the room where May was sleeping with the brother and sister whom she had only briefly met when she was a baby, two children I had only once met for a very short time and had hardly heard of.

That night I met Shazza, the girl, who was ten, and Adele, the boy, who was now eight years old. I was introduced to them very quickly. Neither of them would have remembered that we had met before, when they were both only babies, Shazza four and Adele just two years old. No sooner had we been introduced than they were ushered to another room, leaving myself and May alone.

It was a very unusual feeling, being in this house where my ex-husband lived with two children from a previous marriage, and it must have seemed just as uncomfortable for those children, because now they had a woman in the house who they didn't know: a woman who was very different to any female they had met before in their short lives, and a Westerner who lived a very different life to them. But I had to wait to make my judgement of them, and them of me. I just wanted time with my baby.

I cuddled up with May that night and she was chatting away excitedly, relaxed in knowing that we were back together again. She said that her aunts, 'Baba's sisters', were asking her where she got the marks on her body. Fearing what she was about to tell me, I said, 'What marks, sweetheart?'

She said, 'The marks I got when Baba slapped me to get me onto the plane.'

A knot formed in my stomach, and I hugged her so tightly I thought I would squash her. He had beaten his own child to kidnap her. I wanted to run out and stab him. I was livid. I told her he would never lay a finger on her again and that I would make sure she was never put in danger again, and, gently, I probed her about what had happened that day. We were careful to whisper in case he was listening at the door. Poor little May was well aware of what he was capable of and, as she told me, she constantly checked the door to make sure he heard nothing.

She told me how he had told her that morning that he was taking her to a big new shopping centre and he was going to buy her a new Barbie. She believed him. She thought that this big building was a mall, when, in fact, it was an airport. He bought her a Barbie in the duty-free shop, but when she went outside she suddenly saw the plane and realised what was happening. She said she started to cry and told him that she didn't want to go on a plane. She said that she had told him that her mammy said she was never to get on a plane without her mammy, but he told her that her mammy knew and she was fine because he was taking her on holidays. She said she still wasn't happy and was crying because she wanted to go home to me, but he beat her repeatedly to get her onto the flight as she sobbed and sobbed.

I didn't know what to say except to tell her over and over again how much I loved her and that nothing like that would ever happen to her again.

Looking back on it now, I realise that the only reason he allowed me to talk to May on the phone that first day was to reassure her, because taking her would be a lot easier for him if May thought that I was OK with it. He was even cleverer than I had given him credit for.

That night, we cuddled up and little May fell asleep in my arms. I kept stroking her hair and kissing her forehead. I remember as I lay there trying to sleep in this strange bed how I was terrified to hear gunshots outside the window. I didn't know whether they came from right outside or a short distance away, but I was petrified. I could also hear bangs in the distance from either bombs exploding or tank fire. It was a different world. A different, frightening life.

Somehow, I managed to doze off, and was awoken by the first call to prayer from the local mosque. It was so daunting to hear the chants, and I just wrapped my arms around May and held her as tightly as I could without waking her.

After a short while, I looked around the room and listened out for noise and soon realised that Mostafa wasn't in the house. I immediately went to the front door to look outside and see where I was and what was around me. But as I turned the handle of the door, I found it was locked.

I knew there and then that this was the start of my life now. I was now also a prisoner in this man's house. In this man's country. My lovely life, our life, as I knew it, was over. Indefinitely.

CHAPTER THREE

Meeting Mostafa

Mostafa was not my first husband. I had got married in March 2000 to a lovely man, a man who to this day I would do absolutely anything for, but the relationship was doomed from the start, because although I loved him, it wasn't a love of a wife for her husband.

I loved him as a friend, my best friend, but I married him simply because I felt that I had to. I had been with him since I was 15, we were definitely what you would call childhood sweethearts, and my mother was convinced that we were meant to be together. It was my mother who sort of convinced me that he was the one! And so we married.

My first husband knew absolutely everything about me, unlike Mostafa. He knew my weaknesses and my strengths, and that was why I married him, if I am completely honest. I had been sexually abused for a number of years as a child, and my husband accepted me as I was and fully supported me.

My abuser was someone the family knew very well, and I confided in my mother about it in my early teens. It was a difficult thing to do because we all knew him so well, but I felt that I couldn't go on living in pain any more. Every time I saw him I hated him. Despite me eventually letting it all out, he was never charged and it was never reported to the police, but I didn't complain. Back then, times were very different and things were brushed under the carpet, and I knew that although nothing was done to bring this man to justice, my mother would be watching out for me, protecting me, and I would just have to get on with my life. But, of course, things are never that simple. I didn't get over it; I simply got on with it.

In December 2001, my mammy was killed in a horrific car accident. We thought our world would crumble that month. Losing our mother turned our lives upside down. Like most families, we took our mam for granted. She was such a fit and healthy woman that we never imagined our lives without her. We never expected to lose her at the age of 53 and without having a chance to say our goodbyes, letting her know how much we loved her.

Weird though it may sound, I knew that something was wrong within minutes of the car crash. We had such a close bond, the two of us, and I know that I felt her pass away that day. At around the time of the accident an awful feeling came over me, and within 20 minutes I got a call to say that mammy had been in a crash. I remember turning to my husband and saying, 'She is dead.' He tried to convince me that she would be fine and he just wanted to get me to the hospital, but I knew already that she had passed. I don't know what it was, but I had no hope.

Her death and our loss, such a huge loss, was what triggered a lot of what happened to me later in my life. I basically never got over losing her.

I was married to a lovely man, but I spiralled into a deep depression when Mammy left us. He understood how close we were, myself and my mam, and how, for me, it just seemed like the whole world was caving in on me in the weeks and months after she died. Yet I became so consumed by depression that I could see no escape from its black hole, and soon my marriage fell apart and my husband and I went our separate ways. It was a hard decision for us both to make back then, but thankfully we stayed friends and he understood that I was simply not in control of my emotions at the time. To this day he is one of my best friends. His opinion always matters to me, and I am so glad that he was in my life for so long.

We all missed my mother more than I could ever explain. She was the sticking plaster in our home. She ruled the roost and she held everything together.

She had a very close family herself: six sisters (although one had passed away) and one brother. When Mam died, her family basically became our adopted 'mammies'. They did everything to make sure that we were OK, and, more importantly, they made sure my dad was looked after, because they all knew just how close my parents were. Dad relied on my mother for everything and she treated him like a third child. He idolised her. As time went by, we could see how lonely Dad was looking. He was clearly heartbroken, having lost his backbone, the woman who had been with him to keep him company and partner him through life since she was 25 and he was 36.

We were all shattered by the loss, and although we knew that people meant well, it was very hard walking out the door every day, as people would come up and ask us how we were, how Dad was and how we were all coping. My mother was a very loving woman and she had many friends and neighbours who were as shocked as we were at her sudden death, so her loss was the topic of conversation for a long time in our home town of Swords.

In March 2003, we decided to get Dad away from everything. Mandy and I agreed that we all needed a holiday. I remember it was a cold, wet time of year and we were all absolutely living for a break, needing to get away from the harsh reality of what had happened, even if it was only for a week. As I was working in a travel agent's at the time, Abbey Travel in Sutton, on the north side of Dublin, I knew the popular resorts that year, and I knew where to bring a man in his 60s to relax – and where not to!

Cyprus seemed to be the perfect destination for everything we needed: peace and relaxation, beaches and sunshine. I was suffering at this time from chronic depression and I just felt that everything was getting on top of me, so this was exactly what I needed: some downtime and to feel the warmth of the sun on my bones. We booked a beautiful hotel in Paphos for a very good price and we headed off. We were only there for a week, yet I knew that Cyprus was where I wanted to live. I absolutely loved the island and, in particular, Paphos.

Dad totally chilled out that week, although we knew that he would have loved nothing more than to have my mam beside him. I knew on the day we left the island that I would be back. I told Mandy that I needed to get away and that I felt I had to do it sooner rather than later or I would never go. Mandy was heartbroken by my decision, but she knew that once I made my mind up there would be no stopping me. I was always very strong willed, and if I got something into my head, I had to do it.

I was very similar in looks to my mam, and people always commented on how identical we were. I knew that Dad saw that too, and, although it was nice, I felt that me being around all the time was making it harder for him to move on, because when he looked at me he saw my mam. I knew that he would be in bits when I broke the news to him that I would be leaving Ireland, but I wanted to sort everything back home first, with work and so on, before saying anything to him.

When I arrived back into work on the Monday, I was so unhappy. I kept thinking of Cyprus, that beautiful, idyllic island, and I wanted nothing more than to be back there, away from everything. After a couple of weeks back in the office, I asked to speak to my boss, Aisling. I explained to her how I felt very disillusioned with life and I needed to get away. She was very understanding and she told me to take a career break for three months, then come back and let her know what I wanted to do. She offered to keep my job open for me until I had made my decision. I was the top salesperson in this branch of Abbey Travel at the time and I loved my work, but I felt like I was under immense pressure after my mam's death and I constantly had a horrible feeling, as though I was imploding, and I couldn't cope. The break, I knew, would do me good.

I told the girls in the office of my big plan to escape, and another girl, Jenny, decided that she wanted to go with me to see what life was like in Cyprus. We decided that we wouldn't leave until the beginning of the summer. I had started a photography course at night in a college and I loved it, but I knew that if I didn't leave Ireland then, I would probably never go, and I needed to get out as soon as possible. I thought that I could use my new skills with a camera while over there, as I'd already bought the perfect piece of equipment, a state-of-the-art Nikon camera, and I had planned to spend some time going around the island snapping away.

I started to research Cyprus on the Internet and I found a lovely place called Kissonerga. We got a great deal in a self-catering apartment for just 20 euros a night. It was perfect. We flew out in May, and although we were only going for three months I knew that if I loved it enough I wasn't coming back to Dublin. I think all of my family knew this could happen, because I was obviously looking for the perfect place to escape to. However, as I left the departures hall of Dublin airport that day I was worried about my father. I could see he was heartbroken to see me go, but Mandy had assured me that she would be there for him and I wasn't to worry. God forbid, should anything should happen, I was only a few hours away on a plane.

Jenny and I absolutely loved the apartment when we arrived. It was a five-hour flight from Dublin and we were shattered when we got there, but we were also so excited at the start of something totally different. It wasn't just going away for two weeks in the sun; it was a chance to chill out and do nothing we didn't want to do for three whole months. We spent our days lazing around the lovely hotel pool and watching the gorgeous sunset at night from the hotel restaurant, and we got very friendly with lots of local people, which was great.

In July, I met a lovely Welsh family who were living in the

area. They were from the Welsh Valleys, and one of the girls, Rachael, was a qualified stylist. I had always been fascinated with hairdressing, as a lot of my family were involved in the business, and so we became good friends almost instantly. I had basically made my mind up by then that I wasn't going home, and Rachael said that she was going to open up her own little hairdressing salon, so we chatted about it and I decided that I would get involved with the business. I would invest some cash and be her partner and we could run it together.

We were so excited, making all these plans for a new start, and as we were both very business orientated we decided that we would open up a cleaning company called Scrubbers on the side. The area was very popular with tourists, so we would offer to clean privately owned apartments and villas at a good price, and we would have people working for us so that we could concentrate on the hairdressing side of the business. I felt my depression lifting every day, and it was a great feeling. We were friendly at the time with another girl called Debbie, who was originally from London, and she became the third partner in the business.

We went to Limassol, a town not too far away, and we applied for our business licence for the hairdressing salon. We decided to open the business in premises back in Paphos that suited us perfectly. We called the salon Freckles. It was a lovely little shop. We painted it luminous pink and had it all 'girly', and we were over the moon when it took off from literally day one. It was really small, and we only had one sink, two mirrors and two seats, but it was hugely popular with the expat community and we had plenty of work. Fridays and Saturdays were manic, and we thrived on the adrenalin rush of it. We loved people coming in and having a chat with them, and within weeks it became a lovely little hub in which the English-speaking community could meet up and be pampered. We had more space upstairs that we weren't using, so we let these rooms out as a nail bar and beauty parlour, and the rent we were getting from subletting was basically paying for us downstairs as well. It couldn't have worked out any better. It was a great life.

We worked all day and partied at night. We were enjoying the sun, the sea and the craic and were bringing in a very good wage, too. The cost of living was very low, so most of what I earned I managed to save. It was a no-lose situation.

We, the girls, were well known on Bar Street, a street famous in Paphos for obvious reasons, and one night we went into one of our regular haunts, a nightclub called Rainbows, for a few drinks. We knew the owner of the club, and he always looked after us. On this particular night I was standing at the bar ordering a drink when I saw this guy at the other end staring over at me. I knew he was foreign, not Cypriot, and I swear to God I fell in love on the spot. There and then. My stomach had that feeling they say you get as a teenager when you fall for a guy: the 'butterflies' were fluttering away. I had never really been in a serious relationship before, other than my first childhood sweetheart and husband, but there was an instant attraction here. I knocked back a few drinks for Dutch courage, and after a while I decided to get up on the dance floor. I told my friend how I was feeling and she agreed that he'd been staring over at me all night. So, with the drink on me, I signalled to him with my hand to come over and dance with us.

He totally ignored me. I was gutted. It had taken a lot of courage for me to make a pass at him, and I had been dismissed. I felt like a right fool.

I continued dancing, and later, as I walked off the dance floor, I felt someone tapping me on the shoulder. I looked around, and there he was standing right there, with the most gorgeous eyes I had ever seen. He asked me in very broken English if I would like a drink. His English was so bad that he could only say the typical phrases that you would expect from a foreigner trying to chat up a girl who spoke a different language, like, 'You are beautiful.' Cheesy, I know, but he won me over none the less! We had a drink at the bar that night and he dropped me home, and that was it. I was in love.

Mandy was due to arrive into Larnaca airport the next day with Josh. She had visited me when I had first come to Cyprus, and when she saw the salon she actually invested some of her own money into it as well. So she was coming over to see me and to see how things were going with the business. I was so excited to see her, and I couldn't wait to fill her in on the new love of my life. I was genuinely head over heels in love. I must have talked the ears off her in the car on the journey back to Paphos, but I was bubbling over with excitement. I remember telling her how this Adonis was handsome, charming and the man of my dreams. I told her that he didn't have much English, and I jokingly said, 'But who needs him to talk?' I was smitten. Mandy thought it was hilarious, because she had never seen me like this before over any man. She was delighted that I was so happy and that in just a few months my depression had started to lift.

The next night, I headed back to Rainbows with my little sister. I was so excited, knowing that he would probably be there, and lo and behold, when we walked in he was standing there with his cousin. He came over to us and started to chat, and I was flirting and all smiles, but Mandy hated him. From the first minute she was introduced to Mostafa, she disliked him.

I remember feeling shattered when she said to me that night, 'Louise, I don't like him. There is just something about him that I don't trust.' I was distraught. But, looking back on that night now, two nights after I had first met him, he was already showing signs of being controlling and suspicious. He acted as if we had been going out as a couple for years. But I couldn't see it. I thought he was just jealous over who I might be with because he loved me. I realise now that even then he was actually following my every move. If I went to the toilet, he was standing outside the door when I came out. If I got up to dance, he would stand at the nearest pillar watching me or would walk up behind me.

Even on that very first night when Mostafa dropped me

home, I was naive. Despite working in a travel agent's, I wasn't aware of the Muslim culture, and when I asked him where he was from and he said Syria, I was wondering what part of Russia Syria was in. I admit, embarrassingly, that I was very innocent. So his behaviour wasn't worrying to me, because I didn't know anything about Syria, Islam or how some men from these countries treat women, especially foreign women.

Mandy was staying with me for two months, and over that time frame she saw a lot of Mostafa and nothing could convince her that he was genuine. As sisters, we went about together a lot at night. Most nights it was just for dinner and a few drinks, as we had Josh with us and he was only five years old at the time. But Mostafa always knew where we were going, and without warning he would arrive at the bar or restaurant to watch us. Again, I thought he was jealous in case other men tried to chat me up. To be honest, I was delighted that he was so caring, as I saw it, but Mandy saw through him. No matter what she said, though, I was in love with this man and that was that.

In autumn, Mandy, Josh and I headed back to Dublin. The plan was to get more funds for the business. We were there for just over a fortnight, and my dad said he and my aunties would look after Josh if Mandy wanted to go back to Cyprus to give us a hand in the salon for a few weeks, as he knew it was to be a busy time for me. During my two-week break in Dublin, Mostafa hounded me with phone calls. The phone was ringing up to ten times a day, sometimes more. He wanted to know what I was doing, who I was with, where I was going. He kept asking what date I was coming back. The calls were non-stop, one after another, and the conversations were pointless because his English was so bad. I could see that both my dad and Mandy weren't happy. It wasn't normal behaviour, as they saw it. But I still couldn't see through him.

When we got back to Cyprus, he was at the airport to meet us. I knew he wasn't happy that Mandy was with me, because I think he realised by then that Mandy wasn't his biggest fan.

He got even more possessive at this stage, and because Josh wasn't with Mandy, we had more time to go out at night, and this wasn't going down too well with him either. He wanted me with him 24/7. I remember how on one night Mandy and I decided to go to Ayia Napa, a very popular resort on the island with a big nightclub and bar scene, and we would just have a girls' night out and hit the clubs. It was a two-and-a-half- to three-hour drive away, but we planned to stay overnight in a hotel. I told Mostafa what the plan was, and I knew he was unimpressed. As myself and Mandy sat in a nightclub on our rare night out alone, I suddenly spotted Mostafa out of the corner of my eye. I thought I was seeing things. He made no excuse; he simply walked over to us and sat down. I wasn't happy, he knew that, but there was nothing I could do. This was getting to be too much of a regular thing. Looking back on things now, I believe that from day one he was either following me himself or he had one of his friends or his cousin doing it for him and reporting back. He always seemed to know where I was and who I was with. The Ayia Napa incident is the best example of this, as there were more than thirty nightclubs in that town back then, and there was no way he could have just walked into one and spotted us.

I was in an awful situation, though. I could tell that Mandy was disgusted by this because it was happening all the time, but I could do nothing about it. Yes, I could have ended the relationship, but I loved Mostafa. I just couldn't see through him.

Back then, he was extremely loving towards me, apart from the controlling element of his personality. He also drank alcohol, which was contrary to Muslim beliefs and convinced me that he wasn't actually a strict Muslim. I had been reading on the Internet about fundamentalist Muslims and hearing stories at first hand from some of the women I knew in Cyprus who were in relationships with very controlling Muslim men, and it all seemed so far removed from the man I knew. Yes, the possessiveness and desire to control me rang a bell. But Mostafa wasn't beating me or ordering me about, he was enjoying life, alcohol included, and not visiting mosques or praying every few hours on a prayer mat. To me, he was born Muslim but was not practising, and he definitely wasn't one of these extremist Muslims. I had nothing to fear.

There were times when I would ring him during the day and he wouldn't answer his phone, telling me later that he was too busy to talk. But if I didn't answer the phone to him, he thought it was because I was up to something suspicious or was talking to a man. I was never just 'too busy' to take a call.

At the time, he was working in construction and earning good money. There was an economic boom in Cyprus in the building business, as foreigners were investing a lot in holiday homes, so work was plentiful for him. But he never really had lots of money. I found out much later that he would send most of his money back to Syria, but I didn't know why.

Once Mandy went home and was out of the way, Mostafa asked me to move in with him. I had been living in a villa with my friend from Ireland, Jenny, but she had decided to go home, and so I was delighted that Mostafa seemingly cared for me so much that he wanted to live with me. To me, this was another sign that he was not like these fundamentalists that I had been reading about.

He had been living in an apartment down at the harbour in Paphos with members of his family: his uncle, who was the same age as him; his cousin; his sister, her husband and their two children, all in the one flat. I had met them all on a few occasions, but I only found out years later that the woman he had introduced as his 'friend' was in fact his sister. I don't know why he felt he had to lie to me about this, but he did. In fact, a few times when I was at this apartment, this woman would come out to the balcony with a tray of tea or a cold drink, but she never said much to me, she would just serve the beverage and walk away. It was very odd.

Not knowing anything other than the caring side of Mostafa, I agreed to get a place just for the two of us. We found an apartment that was very cheap and yet very nice. I was lucky to have sourced it through a friend who worked in a bar. It suited us both, and we settled in. But, right from the start, he became distant to me. He was very independent and he wanted me to see this from day one: living together clearly didn't mean going out at night together, as a couple, for meals and drinks. No, it meant Mostafa going out every night for meals and drinks with his friends. To make it worse, he would take my car, leaving me no means of transport if I wanted to go anywhere. I was driving a nice car, a sporty one called a Toyota Levin, and Mostafa would come back in at three or four in the morning without batting an eyelid or making any excuses to me. I never thought of checking my mileometer to see how many miles he had been driving. This would have given me an idea of where he was going each night, as the island is very small and everything is a couple of hours away, at most. At first I thought that he was just finding it hard to settle down, to be in a 'serious relationship'. He would tell me that he was only meeting his friends for coffee, but I should have known better. He was obviously still enjoying the single life in the clubs and bars of the island. Taking the car was part of his plan to keep me inside, I know that now, but at the time no amount of arguing changed the situation. I wasn't thinking straight back then, and even if I had challenged him, he wouldn't have told me anything different other than he was meeting friends for coffee. And who was I to question that when I had no proof of anything otherwise?

This went on for months: him coming and going and doing his own thing. We had moved into the apartment at the end of September, but he never mentioned paying any of the rent or bills. I paid for everything from day one, and he never offered to help. In fact, just weeks after we started to date, he'd sold his car and begun using mine every day to get around. Once again, these were all warning signs that I somehow chose to ignore. I said nothing and just accepted it.

The following March, six months after Mostafa and I had moved in together, Mandy was due to come over with her friends Sonya and Jackie for a break. They were to stay with us in the apartment, but I knew Mandy wasn't too happy about being around Mostafa and that he didn't like her. I, on the other hand, was living for their visit. The only worry I had was that I didn't want Mandy to see him going out every night and coming home at all hours of the morning. On the night before they arrived, he came home in the middle of the night, as usual, and I finally flipped.

I asked him what he was up to. I challenged him as to whether he was seeing another woman, and in the end I told him that I'd had enough of him.

He lost his temper. I was sitting up in the bed trying to have this conversation with him, trying to make him realise that he was in the wrong, when he went into a total rage. As he was shouting and screaming at me in English and Arabic, he pulled the belt off his trousers and, as I tried to cover myself with the duvet cover, he lashed out at me, beating me violently until he was too drained to continue.

I lay on the bed, curled up, sobbing. I felt immense agony everywhere, but I couldn't move. I was screaming uncontrollably with the pain, and as I looked down I could already see that I had a thick welt right across my stomach, across my hips and down my thigh.

I couldn't stop crying, and then, all of a sudden, he came at me with the ugliest, most terrifying face, and he dragged me from the bed and pulled me by the top of my nightie down the stairs, with my legs and back taking the brunt of each and every step. My head was hitting off the wall, and I had no way of protecting myself or my dignity. In a fit of temper, he said, 'Right. We are going for a drive.'

I had somehow managed to pull on my flip-flops as I was dragged off the mattress, because they were right beside the bed, but I was petrified, not knowing what Mostafa was going to do next. He roughly bundled me into the car in just my little nightie and shorts, and despite my cries he drove the car erratically to a place called Coral Bay in Paphos. He was clearly agitated by my cries, and he pulled the car in and dragged me back out and over to the cliff tops. He made sure I was standing right at the cliff edge, and he said, 'Right. If you ever do anything like this again I am going to throw you over.' I looked up at his face and I thought, 'This man is insane.' I thought at that very second he was going to throw me off the cliffs and that would be that.

I knew I had to beg for my life. I looked up at him and I said, through tears, 'I am very, very sorry, Mostafa.' And after about a minute's silence, he let me go. We drove home and neither of us said a word. I crawled into bed, silent and sickened and in agony, and I tried my best to sleep with the uncontrollable, evil monster lying beside me.

The next day when the girls arrived, I carried on as if nothing was wrong. I was in pain all the time, but for the whole week I covered myself up as much as I could. I wore sarongs and made sure that they didn't blow open on the beach. But one day, as I sat beside the sea with my friend Sally, Rachael's mum, the sarong blew open and Sally immediately said, 'Oh my God! What happened to you? Was it him? Did he hit you?' I knew she was well aware of what Mostafa was like, so I admitted what had happened, but I told her that I had to keep it from my sister. Sally told me that I had to get away from him before he killed me, and I reassured her that I would, but that I couldn't do anything to upset him until Mandy had gone back to Dublin.

Sally had told me on numerous occasions before that she believed Mostafa was violent towards me, despite me arguing in his defence. All of my friends in Paphos had witnessed how possessive he was and how aggressive he got if he found me talking to other men, or to anyone he didn't know, man or woman.

In fact, that had not been the first time he had beaten me. I remember only too well the very first time. It was early in our relationship, and he was living in the apartment with his family. He had gone back to Syria on holiday for two weeks and a person that he knew very well, a close associate of his, made a pass at me and tried to kiss me. I pulled away immediately and fended him off, but I was worried sick that it could happen again, so I told Mostafa what had happened when he got home. I told him that this man had tried to kiss me a few times and I didn't know what to do. I could see the fury in Mostafa's face, and he screamed at me, calling me a liar, and with that he swung his arm and slapped me full force across the face. The pain was horrible; it stung so badly. I was totally shocked. I was really upset and crying, and I remember saying to him how sorry I was and maybe I was responsible for this man coming on to me. Maybe I had flirted with him without realising and given him the wrong signals. I was terrified of what Mostafa was going to do to me next unless I said I was sorry and took the blame.

By the time of Mandy's visit, Mostafa's English was very good. It had only taken him a few months to become nearly fluent in English, and he was using every word he knew. His favourite words for me were 'cunt' and 'Western bitch'. These terms were ones he used all the time, and I just took it and said nothing.

I think that early in the relationship I was still very vulnerable. I loved my life, but I was still very upset over losing my mam, and I was in a strange country without my family to support me. I didn't want to burden them with my problems, as they had things to deal with at home. Mostafa was the only person I had at night to rely on, and I think, more than anything, I feared being without a man in my life. Even after the terrifying drive to the cliff, I tried to tell myself that he had only hit me a couple of times and it might never happen again and that I could make it work, but I was only kidding myself.

Thankfully, while Mandy was over, she didn't notice the marks on my body and I never mentioned them.

When Mandy and her friends flew back home, I tried to just get on with my life. Nothing changed. I worked all day, and Mostafa carried on in construction. He played all night and I mostly stayed home. I was coming to accept this pattern as the norm for us, and I said nothing to upset him. I just carried on living in the same space and tried not to do anything that would make him angry.

Over time, things seemed to get back to normal. There was never a mention of the abuse he had put me through, and we tried to get back on track. We would both work during the week, and I would come home and cook dinner. He would still do his own thing most nights, and on the odd night I would go for a drink with the girls, making sure to come in early to avoid any confrontation. At the weekend, we would go down to Bar Street, just the two of us, and have a few drinks. He loved vodka and Red Bull, and he loved to sit outside watching everyone go by while he had a few cigarettes: definitely not traits of a practising Muslim.

He didn't eat pork either, which I knew that from day one, but he didn't insist on halal meat either and would eat chicken and other meat from the supermarket. He ate lamb if we went to a barbecue, and I respected his choice. I would never have ham in the fridge or anything that I knew would offend him; that just became a part of my life and I accepted it with no concern. If we ordered a pizza, I just had to make sure that it had no ham on it. His religion wasn't a big deal for me at all.

Then, one day, over a cup of coffee, a partner of a friend, a Lebanese man, asked me if I knew that Mostafa had a wife and two children in Syria. I thought he must have got it wrong; maybe he'd overheard something about another Mostafa and put two and two together and got five. There was no way that Mostafa was married. No way. I would have seen some signs, heard him on the phone to his wife. And why would he not tell me, given that we were living together as husband and wife, even if it was under common law? I couldn't accept or believe this. Mostafa's outright denial of any such thing when I challenged him made me believe that this man had got his wires crossed. He just got mixed up with someone else. Mostafa even went as far as to say that whoever this man was who had told me these 'lies' was obviously only trying to cause trouble between us because he fancied me. I remember thinking, 'If Mostafa had children wouldn't he want to visit them, or have pictures of them in his wallet?' Yet, despite my questioning of this man's accusations, something wasn't right. I wasn't sure that Mostafa was telling me the truth. There was just something about his denial that didn't sit comfortably with me.

Bit by bit, I began to doubt his innocence. I felt that I had somehow caught him out and it was eating him up. He was demanding to know all the time who had made up these 'lies' to tell me. Over the next few months, I found myself doubting him more and more. I brought up the allegations time and time again until, one day, he broke.

He admitted that he was married. He told me that it had been an arranged marriage and that he didn't love his wife. Yes, he had two children, a boy and a girl, but he didn't see them often because his life was in Cyprus.

I was gutted. I kept asking myself, why did I not see through him? Why did I not believe my friend when he had tried to warn me that Mostafa was a liar? Why did I fall for every lie this man had ever told me?

I listened as he claimed to tell me 'everything'. His story was that his family set up the marriage when this girl, who was his cousin, was just 15 and he was 23. He said it was a marriage of convenience and he had no choice in the decision. He said he had been in the army, because all men in Syria have to do two years in the army, but, being the coward that he was, he bought himself out, as they can do, after six months. He claimed that because he came out after six months, his family made him get married.

He said he had two children, but he rarely saw them. That was why he had gone to Syria some months before, to see his daughter and his wife, who was pregnant at the time with their second child, their son. This meant that his wife had been pregnant when he was dating me. Yet he claimed he didn't have any relationship with his wife and, in fact, he wanted a divorce.

I hated him for not telling me the truth. I hated him for living a lie, and I hated him because I still loved him. And, once again, I agreed to forgive him. He promised me that he would make me happy and he would never lie or keep anything from me again. And, of course, I believed him.

At this time, things were going really well for me. The salon was thriving, and Mostafa was happy to see the money rolling in and happy for me to keep paying for everything. I put everything behind me and tried to move on. But very soon he started to arrive unannounced at the salon and I would suddenly spot him, maybe across the road, staring over.

I got on really well with our clients, and, as we all do in Ireland and the UK, and in many other countries, I would hug people on meeting them or when they were leaving and think nothing of it. On a few occasions, a client's husband or partner would arrive to collect them and I would give them a peck on the cheek or a hug as they left, but Mostafa spotted this and I was screamed at and abused and called a 'cunt', as usual, and was warned that I was his property and I was not allowed to even shake a man's hand, never mind hug him. There was no point in complaining. It got me nowhere.

But, on a number of occasions, when things got really bad, I left him. It would only happen following a bout of beatings or emotional abuse.

I had a very good friend who lived in Cyprus who was separated with two children, and she was a huge support to me in Paphos. Rachael was a medium and had given many very accurate readings to our friends over the years, and to this day I genuinely believe that she is gifted. On many occasions she literally begged me to leave Mostafa, believing that one day his beatings would go too far and he could kill me. She couldn't understand why I kept going back to him. No one could, but she never gave up trying to make me see sense.

There were many times when, after a fight with Mostafa, I would pack my clothes and run to Rachael. She always welcomed me and always stood up for me when he would inevitably come banging at the door demanding me to return home. He often literally dragged me crying from her home, with Rachael struggling in the middle to free me from his tight grip.

On one occasion, having been gone from him for two or three days, I decided that I would head back to the apartment to pack as many of my personal belongings as I could. Rachael came with me, as we knew he would be in work around that time. When I walked in I spotted a cake baked by him, something we both did regularly, sitting on the counter. In my stupidity, I remember thinking, 'Ah, bless, he made me a cake.' For a split second I felt guilty enough to go back to him, believing yet again that he actually loved me and he didn't mean to hurt me. But, thankfully, I reminded myself very quickly of the beating he had given me just days earlier – yet another beating – and I quickly grabbed what I could and ran.

As I got back into the car, with my friend's two children in the back seat, Mostafa pulled up behind us in his work van. When we spotted him we started up the car to drive away, but he chased us down the road in the van. He followed us at speed for about half an hour, and at every opportunity he pulled up alongside us and tried to ram us off the road.

The children were screaming in the back seat, absolutely hysterical. I thought we were all going to be killed. Rachael was terrified as well, but also fuming at the nerve of him to keep trying to ram us, especially as he knew that we had the children in the car. There was no way he could have missed seeing them as he pulled up alongside us. So, in a fit of rage, Rachael slammed on the brakes and jumped out of the car. She screamed at him, asking him what the hell he was playing at. She told him to back off and leave us all alone. She said, 'Louise doesn't want to be with you. Just leave her to live her life and stop harassing her.'

But Mostafa pleaded with her to make me 'see sense' and go back to him. He said he loved me and he was sorry for everything. He was like a broken record at this stage, I'd heard it so many times before, but for some reason the guilt set in again, and days later, after numerous calls from him, begging me to forgive him, I once again went back.

I know Rachael must have been sick of me leaving and going back all the time and frustrated with me for not listening to her, but I cannot explain how much of a hold Mostafa had over me. I always felt in some way compelled to go back to him, as he was the first real relationship I'd ever had. I didn't know anything else.

Once I was back with him, and as things seemed to settle down a bit and the abuse became less frequent, he started putting pressure on me to marry him. We were still only a few months into our relationship, and those months had been horrendous for the most part, but he told me that he would feel much better if we were husband and wife, as we were already living like a married couple. He told me that he would get a divorce and everything would be fine. Despite the abuse and the control he had over me, very weirdly I still loved him, but I didn't want to marry him, because I secretly feared the situation could get a lot worse if I did. I knew my family didn't want me to be anywhere near him, never mind vow to be with him for the rest of my life, and that was also in the back of my head. And so I put it off and put it off until I was basically forced into it.

In 2004, I booked a flight home to see my dad and sister. Things had been bad with Mostafa, yet again, and I needed to be around my loved ones, away from it all. We were still sleeping together, but I was only doing it to keep him happy, to stop him getting agitated.

Mandy and Josh had been over on holiday to see me, but it wasn't the same as seeing them in my family home and so I decided to go back to Dublin on the same flight as them. Mostafa wasn't a bit impressed with me leaving and tried to make me change my mind every day before I left.

But I couldn't wait for the break. I spent the first few weeks in Dublin, and then I went to stay with my cousin for a few days, who has a lovely big house in the countryside, just to chill out. One morning I went up for a shower and felt a sort of fluttering in my stomach, and I knew instantly that I was pregnant. I knew it could only be very early on, but a woman knows the signs. So I went out and bought a pregnancy test in the chemist, and I went up to the bathroom in my cousin's house and did the test. I was shocked when I saw the blue line appear, but secretly I was also actually very happy.

My life wasn't great in Cyprus, I knew that, and although we had only been together a few months Mostafa's control over me had become quite strong. He chose our friends, he told me what I could and could not wear, and on some occasions he actually went as far as to grab me as I walked out the door, ripping the clothes off my back, insisting that I wasn't going anywhere in the clothes I had chosen to wear. I remember going out with him for a drink one night when I had put on this beautiful flowing top that was off-the-shoulder on one side and had a wide sleeve on the other, and I felt great. I loved this top. But when Mostafa saw me heading down the stairs, he grabbed me so fast that the sleeve ripped to pieces and came away in his hand. He demanded that I put on something to 'cover up' and so I did exactly that. I would have done anything that night to keep the peace. He said if I wore anything like that again, he would kill me. And I still went out with him that night and pretended that nothing had happened.

I was leading a double life, really. I was bubbly Louise who loved a laugh and a joke at work, I was a businesswoman who drove a big sports car, and yet at home I was a subservient female who was controlled by her partner and terrified of saying or doing anything to upset him. I was living a lie.

But, despite all this, I was about to hit 30, and I was actually delighted that I was about to have a baby. I never for one minute thought of the consequences of having *his* baby, I just loved the idea of becoming a mother.

When I told my family, they were delighted for me, but without saying it to me they knew that this was not good. They were happy that a new baby was on the way, just not at whose baby it was. They had no idea of my life as it really was, because I told them only a fraction of the truth, so that they wouldn't worry, but they knew enough to fear the worst. Mandy can never keep her emotions hidden, her face says it all, and I remember her expression so clearly when I broke the news. As usual, her face didn't let her down. My family knew, even more than me, that this would mean I would feel obliged to not just live with Mostafa but to marry him.

I knew that I had to ring Mostafa to tell him he was to become a daddy. I didn't know how he would react, but it had to be done. When I broke the news to him on the phone, he sounded elated. He said this was 'fantastic' news and that he loved me more than ever and had missed me so much. He begged me to come back to him, saying he would look after me for ever.

He said he knew already that it was a boy and he didn't want a girl. I, on the other hand, wanted a girl. I didn't want a boy, because I didn't want a carbon copy of Mostafa, and I knew that if it was a boy he would try to mould him into a 'mini me' version of himself.

I rang Rachael and broke the news to her. Like everyone else, she was delighted for me, just not delighted at who the father was. I told her I would be flying back to Cyprus the following week and asked if I could stay with her and the kids for a while, which I did. But as soon as Mostafa heard I was in Paphos, he called over and told me that he had got a lovely apartment for us, with a pool, and he wanted to take care of me.

Despite Rachael's pleas for me not to go, I went. And to be honest, Mostafa was actually like a different man throughout the pregnancy. He still went out to meet his friends for 'coffee' at night and did his own thing, but he didn't beat me up and he wasn't as aggressive towards me as before. In fact, I remember at times thinking he had somehow changed and maybe he would continue being that bit nicer to me. During the pregnancy I had a craving for fruit, and he would often come into the salon during the week with a fruit basket and give me a kiss on the cheek. It was a totally different Mostafa to the man I had known before this.

When I was six months pregnant, I had to fly back to Ireland for a scan in St Michael's Hospital in Dun Laoghaire. Mandy's son had been born with an illness that affected his kidneys and the illness was hereditary, so I needed to have my baby checked to see if he or she was affected. As the girl in the hospital did the scan, I told her that my partner hoped I was having a boy, and she said, 'You're not having a boy, love, you are having a girl.' I was absolutely over the moon when she said that. It was like having all of my dreams come true. I had always dreamed of having a little girl, and I used to think that if I did have a daughter, I would call her May, after my mam. But I knew that Mostafa would be disgusted when I told him, as he had convinced himself and everyone else that he was about to father a son. It was a big deal to Muslim men to bear a son who would carry their surname into another generation, and I was about to scupper that plan.

I remember leaving the hospital and actually talking to my little girl, saying, 'Oh, May, I always knew you were a little girl and already I love you so much.' When I got back to my dad's house I rang Mostafa straight away. I couldn't wait to break the news to him that he wasn't having a son. It was probably very mean of me to think like that, but I knew that he would never have the same power over a little girl as he would over a boy, and that made me so happy. I would have been happy to have a baby boy for any other man on the planet, just not for this man, a man who would have tried to poison our son into believing that his mother was, as he always said, a 'Western bitch' and a 'cunt'. I knew that he would have a harder job persuading a daughter, and for this I was so grateful to God. When I told Mostafa, he waited for about 20 seconds before he replied, 'Are you sure? They might not know for certain yet. We will see.'

To which I smugly replied, 'Oh, they do. It's definitely a girl.'

He paused for a few seconds and then said, 'Damn it.'

I tried not to laugh, but I was struggling to hold it in, as his reaction made my day.

I knew that no matter what happened in my life, I would always have my daughter beside me. He could do whatever he wanted to me, but he would never harm my little girl. I would make sure of that.

My baby was due in April 2005, and the business was flying. Mostafa would drive around in my car while I was in Ireland, picking up the takings from the salon every evening, but he never lodged a cent into my bank or gave me a euro. He came to love it when I had to go home for a check-up, because that was when he could rip me off for every cent that was due to me from my little company. No excuses, he just felt he had a right to do it, and the girls in the salon were afraid to question him. And they were right. It just wasn't worth the bother.

Once back in Cyprus, I carried on working, but I was getting tired very easily, and I would just come home at night after work and flop onto the sofa and chill out. So, on New Year's Eve in 2004, I was in no humour to go out to the pubs to drink, I just wanted a quiet night in to have a nice dinner and a chat and think about what the new year was going to bring us. But Mostafa had other ideas. He asked me if I minded if he was to go out for a drink. I said that I didn't mind, but I hoped that he would come home to be with me at midnight, just to share the moment.

But midnight came and I didn't even get a phone call from him. Shortly after all the excitement on the street outside had died down, the phone rang, but it wasn't Mostafa. It was a friend of mine who used to run the beauty parlour upstairs from the salon. I knew she was in a pub, because I could hear all the screaming and shouting and clinking of glasses behind her. She asked me if I was OK, to which I replied I was. She told me to sit down, as she wanted to tell me something. I didn't know what to expect. She said that Mostafa had just walked past her in a pub and he was holding hands with another woman. I remember sitting on the bed as I heard her tell me that he was also kissing this woman, in full view of everyone. I was gutted. Before I rang him, in a temper, I packed my bag, got dressed and I ran out to my car.

As I sat in the car, I rang Mostafa. It rang and rang, and after about five minutes of non-stop redialling, he eventually answered the phone. He asked me what was wrong, and I demanded to know where he was. He said, 'I'm fine, don't worry, I am on my way home.'

I screamed down the phone, 'My friend saw you walking into the bar with a girl, you bastard. How could you do this to me? I am pregnant with your baby.'

He made all the excuses under the sun. He told me that she was 'nobody'. He had just been wishing a stranger a Happy New Year! He did everything he could to make me believe that my friend was a liar and that she hadn't seen anything. And he could always be quite persuasive. But I knew this time that he was a lying bastard.

I drove to my friend's apartment, but she was worried in case Mostafa found us, so she said we would go for a drive. With that, I looked in the rear-view mirror and there he was, following us. We pulled up outside a kebab shop and we went in. I thought I had lost him, but within minutes he was there, standing in front of us.

In the kebab shop he pulled me out of my seat, and, despite my friend pleading with him to leave me alone, he dragged me all the way out to a car, which he must have borrowed from a friend. He threw me into the front seat and said, 'You are coming home with me and that's that.' He shouted back to my friend, saying that we needed to talk and he was taking me back to the apartment. There was no point in arguing with him. I knew I had to go. I was more worried about my baby and I feared that if he beat me up I might lose my child. One good thump could knock me out, and I knew the power of his smacks, so I just went along with him to protect the child. I listened to all of his lies about this woman and his pleas for me to stay with him. To be honest, it wasn't worth responding. I just wanted peace and quiet and to spend the next few months looking forward to the birth of my little girl. I hated him at this stage, but I didn't want to annoy him, as I knew what he was capable of.

The lease was up on the apartment around this time, and, as always I was paying the rent, so I found a small holiday apartment in Paphos and I decided to rent that until it was time to go back to Dublin to give birth. Mostafa knew I wanted my little girl born in Dublin and he didn't argue. My plans were already made.

Just days before I was to leave, I took money out of the bank to bring home with me. I left more than 2,000 euros, maybe a bit more, on the bed as I was tottering around packing my clothes. Mostafa spotted the money and asked me why I was bringing all that cash back to Ireland. It was suddenly dawning on him that I was going away and that he had no access to my money. It must have been like a light switch going off in his head, because suddenly the person paying the rent and all the bills and buying the food was about to leave. It was around early February, as I needed to fly before the last eight weeks of my pregnancy, and Mostafa had very little work because it was 'low season' in Cyprus. It had just dawned on him that once I was gone he would have to fend for himself. He never said to me directly that he wanted money, but I could see his temper rising. I tried to explain to him why I needed so much cash, that I was going home for at least three months and I wanted to have money to spend on our baby. But he was furious.

A massive row broke out and he started to scream and shout at me. He dragged me by the shoulder and threw me around the room, and he gave me such a punch in the back of the head that my earring actually came out of my ear. He knocked me unconscious onto the bed.

I remember waking up in the shower, fully clothed and absolutely soaking wet, with the water still running down on top of me. He had obviously dragged me from the bedroom into the bathroom. I woke up to see his cousin trying to hold me up in the shower and Mostafa on his knees in the bathroom praying to Allah in Arabic. He kept saying he would never hurt me again if Allah let me live. He honestly thought that I was dead.

His cousin told him in Arabic that I was OK, that I was coming round. They put me into bed, still soaking wet, to let me sleep, and as I lay there I remember hearing his cousin asking him what the hell he was playing at. He was speaking in Arabic, but I could understand exactly what he was saying. His cousin was really annoyed at him.

When I woke up, I was terrified. I didn't know what was going to happen next. I had the worst headache I had ever had in my life. I honestly thought that day that I would lose the unborn child in my womb. I was seeing stars when I went to stand up, and I remember thinking to myself, 'If I haven't lost my baby today it will be a miracle.' And I waited and waited, sick with worry, for the innocent child inside me to give me a kick to let me know that she was OK. I prayed for my child to move, to reassure me, and when she did, I was overjoyed with relief.

It was possibly the scariest moment in my life up to that day. That evening, Mostafa came up to me and apologised for what he had done. It was the first time in his life he had ever said sorry to me, and I was absolutely shocked. But I knew that he hadn't changed his ways. It was simply a moment of remorse, as he knew that he could have killed his child that day. I think he could have dealt with killing me, but his conscience would not have been able to cope with his murdering his own flesh and blood.

I rested for a few days in the apartment, but I could not wait to escape. I monitored every movement in my stomach in anticipation. If I felt nothing for more than an hour, I panicked. I prayed to my mam that my little baby would be born healthy and that the beating I had endured would have had no effect on her. I didn't care about myself; the only thing that mattered was my child.

One week after the attack, I flew home to my family. They knew nothing of what had happened and I wanted it to stay that way. They hated Mostafa anyway, and I didn't want to give them any more reasons to detest him, because I knew that as the father of my child he would have to be in my life in some way, and to have my family beside me, not questioning me as to why I was having anything to do with him, was very important. The less they knew of what I had to endure with him, the easier it would be for me to let him see his child once she was born. I had enough worries without making any more unnecessary problems.

Looking back, I think the only reason I stayed with Mostafa was because I was brought up by my mother to believe that if you made your bed you had to lie in it. I was a very loyal person, and Mostafa was my first real love. It was a stupid way of looking at life, but I knew of no other, so I just endured what I had to, as long as it didn't affect my child.

I went into labour in Dublin in the Holles Street Hospital on a Thursday. I spent all day and night in agony on Thursday, Friday, Saturday and Sunday, and after those four days I was absolutely exhausted. Mostafa knew that the baby was on her way because I'd rung him on Thursday, so he was plaguing all the family with phone calls, awaiting an update.

May was what they call a 'lazy baby', and when they brought me down on Monday morning to induce me, I expected it to be all over in minutes. But at 8 p.m. they told me I was only a few centimetres dilated. Yet minutes later I was whisked down for an emergency section, and thank God May came into the world a healthy, beautiful black-haired child with big brown eyes and a button nose: a carbon copy of her daddy. And I was delighted.

Because she was an emergency delivery, it took a few hours before I was allowed to hold her. That moment was the best moment of my life. There is nothing that will ever compare to it. I rang Mostafa immediately after I'd held May for the first time to tell him we had a healthy, beautiful baby girl, and he said he was delighted, but I could sense his disappointment.

He said he wanted to see me, but, more importantly, he wanted me to tell him where the papers were for my car, as he was selling it. I couldn't believe it. This was just hours after I had given birth to his child. I didn't want to sell my car; he just decided that he was getting rid of the car and that was that. I was in Ireland and he could do what he wanted.

I knew I had to go back to Cyprus, because my life was there and I had a business to run. Also, I didn't know what Mostafa was up to with me out of the way. But I also wanted to stay for a couple of months in Dublin until I knew that May had had all her needles and was given a clean bill of health. But, for some mad reason, I missed Mostafa. I don't know why, maybe it was simply my hormones acting up, but, despite everything, I actually wanted to see him. And two weeks after I gave birth, I headed off on a flight to Larnaca.

Mandy said she would mind May, as she was too young to travel, and although Mostafa wanted to see her, I agreed with Mandy. I didn't want to take May anyway, as I didn't know how he would react to me. And if a row broke out, I didn't want him hitting me in front of the baby.

I decided that I would only go for a weekend, but as soon as I got to Heathrow airport, having taken a flight from Dublin, I was pining for May. I almost cancelled the connecting flight and headed back to the house, but I knew I had to sort some stuff in the salon as well, so I carried on.

I was still struggling physically, having had a Caesarean, and it was sore to walk, but I had to keep going. When I arrived at Larnaca airport, Mostafa was there to greet me in a horrible cheap car that he had rented. He didn't seem too happy to see me – there were no big hugs and kisses, no flowers and champagne for the mother of his newborn child – but as soon as we got to the apartment he wanted sex.

I told him that I was too sore to do anything, and I explained to him how a Caesarean affects you, but he basically raped me. He insisted we had sex, and he forced himself onto me. I was in tears when it finished. And as soon as he got off the bed, he had a shower, got dressed and went off to meet up with his friends.

I was left in the apartment, inconsolable and in agony. About an hour after he left, I got up to get dressed, because he'd told me to be ready by a certain time to go for dinner. As I went over to the sideboard I found an open packet of condoms. I knew immediately that he was having sex and cheating on me.

That night we had a huge row. He denied he was seeing anyone and claimed that the condoms belonged to a friend of his who had been staying with him. All lies. I decided to go home the following morning, back to Dublin, and we fought in the car all the way to the airport.

He kept insisting that he wanted to see May, and I kept insisting that it would never happen now. Finding the condoms just confirmed everything I had suspected anyway. I told him that I was going to be returning to Cyprus within three months, but myself and May would not be staying with him. I had arranged to move in with Rachael. He ranted and raved at me and told me that I would live with him and no one else. I dreaded coming back to Cyprus because of him, yet my life was there, my business was there and my friends were there.

Rachael was still running the business singlehandedly, but Mostafa was still taking my money and I was getting nothing. I was sick of the way he was abusing the fact that I wasn't around, and I remember wishing that I could be stronger and that I had the courage to fight this man. But I knew in my heart he would always control me. I was just too weak to fight back.

When May was three months old, I finally made the journey back to Paphos. But not before I did something that to this day Mostafa knows nothing about. I went down to my local church in Swords in Dublin, and I had May christened into the Catholic Church.

It was my way of life, and a way of life I was proud of, and I wanted May to be christened. I wanted to know that, God forbid anything should ever happen to her, she had received the blessing of the Church. We had a great day. All the family arrived and all of our friends, and May was the star of the show. She looked beautiful. But I never told Mostafa, and I vowed that as she got older May could make her own decision about religion. If, later in life, she decided that she would convert to Islam, then so be it. She was half Syrian, and I had no problem with that: her religion would be her choice, and I would never force Catholicism on her, but for now I wanted to know that she was protected by God, as I saw it.

I said nothing to Mostafa about this, and days after the christening I started planning to go back to Cyprus. I was excited about going back to the lovely warm weather and the beaches, but I was also very nervous about how Mostafa would react to my return, considering I wasn't returning to him. The plan was to move in with Rachael in her lovely villa and pray that he would just leave us alone. It was a good plan, but I knew in my heart that it wouldn't work.

I arrived into the airport to be met by Rachael, who was thrilled to see me, and me her. We drove to her home, and as we pulled up Mostafa jumped out of a car, ran over to me and grabbed May out of my arms, saying how beautiful she was. He kept repeating over and over again, 'Oh my mother, she looks like my mother.' I felt sick that he was there.

He followed us into the house, knowing that he was not welcome but also that there was no man in the house to stand up to him. Rachael had no choice but to make him a coffee, as there was no sign of him leaving and we were dying for a drink.

He was cooing and cawing over the baby and trying not to pay attention to us. He knew we were both fuming. I told him that he had to leave, but he refused to go and said he was staying just for one night. He said I was his family and I was holding him back from his child and that he had rights to his child. He said that he would get an apartment the next day and insisted that I was to go with him, as I couldn't take his child away from him.

Poor Rachael was in a situation that she couldn't get out of now, and it was all my fault. I felt so guilty for bringing all this trouble to her door. I felt physically sick. That night, he came into the bedroom where I was sleeping and he got on top of me and insisted on having sex with me. I told him that I was still very sore and we weren't a couple any more. I told him that our relationship was over and I did not want to be with him, but he ignored me and I lay there on the bed nearly in tears as he did what he wanted to do.

After that assault, as in my mind it was an assault, I just wanted to cry myself to sleep. I wanted him to die and to leave myself and May alone to live our lives without him. But I also knew it wouldn't be that simple: for as long as I was in Cyprus, he would be around. I just had to accept that.

The next day, Mostafa told me that he would be staying that night as well. There was no use in arguing. I knew that I couldn't bring this stress on Rachael any longer. It was her home and she had two young children and this was not her problem. It had only become her problem because I had brought it on her. I knew I had to leave, but I was determined to fight him until the end.

On the third day, after Mostafa had argued with Rachael when she challenged him over how he was treating me, he left, saying he was getting an apartment and I had to be ready to leave when he got back. And that's exactly what happened. He went off and came back to the villa to get me. Rachael had gone to the salon and her mother, Sally, was in the house. As Sally cleaned up the kitchen, Mostafa arrived at the door and said that he had found somewhere for us to live and I was to leave with him immediately.

I told him that I wasn't moving, and with that he grabbed me by the neck and pushed my head against a pebbledashed wall. As I put my hand to my head, I noticed that it was covered in blood. Just at that moment, Sally came running out of the house shouting at him, saying that she had seen what he had done and demanding that he leave the house. He denied it to the hilt, saying he hadn't touched me, and she screamed at him that he wasn't going to 'pull the wool over her eyes'.

He finally left, but he came back that evening, stormed into the house and into my room and started to pack my bags. Rachael threatened to call the police and ran for the phone, but I knew what I had to do: I couldn't keep bringing trouble to my friend's door. As my mam would have said, I'd made my bed and now I had to lie in it. And that was what I did.

That day I left my friend's beautiful home, heartbroken at how my life had ended up. I watched them as we drove away and saw the fear in their faces as they envisaged what lay ahead for myself and my new baby. But it was too late now to run. I had given birth to Mostafa's child. I hated him. I saw him as a monster, but he was also my little girl's father, something I suddenly regretted more than anything in my life. My child was the best thing that had happened to me, but unfortunately her father was the worst.

Mostafa and I moved into yet another apartment, and from that day we started to live separate lives. I hated him more than I could ever explain. That first day when I arrived in the apartment, he told me to unpack my suitcase, as we would be staying there for a while. He headed into the shower, and all of a sudden his mobile phone rang. I picked it up and noticed that it was a private number. When I answered, the phone went dead. It rang again and again, but each time the person put the phone down when he or she heard my voice. So when Mostafa came out of the shower I told him about the calls, and just as the words came out of my mouth his phone rang again.

This time he answered, and I realised he was talking to a woman as, in Greek, he told her that he wanted to be left alone, that his partner was back and he didn't want to see her again. I couldn't believe this was happening. I asked him what the hell was going on and he told me that he had been seeing this Cypriot woman from Limassol who was in her 40s and married with four children. The husband was not aware of their relationship, obviously, and Mostafa claimed she wouldn't take no for an answer and was continuing to hound him with calls, begging him to meet her.

I was devastated. I had just walked back into this man's life and here he was, on day one, telling me that he had been seeing someone behind my back and then finishing the conversation by saying, 'But it was only for sex.' In his mind, if it was only for sex it wasn't so bad. He 'didn't love her'. I didn't know what to say. But one thing I did know was that I wasn't going to stay in a relationship with this man for any longer than necessary. At my first opportunity, I was getting out.

We barely spoke from that day, and we hardly ever had sex, thank God, unless he forced himself on me. We only went out together when he insisted.

Then, when May was about six months old, I was forced to take her to Paphos General Hospital, as she was constantly getting very bad infections. While we were there one day I noticed a very large woman standing at the door as we walked in. It turned out that this was the woman whom Mostafa had been having the affair with. She started shouting at him, and all of a sudden the two of them had a massive argument, screaming at each other in the hospital corridor. He told her that he never loved her, and I remember standing staring at them as they had this huge row and thinking, 'Am I mad'? Why am I putting myself through all of this with this man?' I knew that if there was one woman there were probably many more, and yet here I was living with him and, at times, having sex with him.

I knew, though, that I was in this for a while, and so to keep the peace I tried to be nice to him, but it was killing me. However, Mostafa was good with May. He would take her out for walks and he helped me to dress her and feed her. He was actually a good father in the early days, and it was for this reason that I stayed with him for so long.

My days were spent swimming in the pool with my little girl and shopping. And when Mostafa wasn't working, he would either watch me at the pool or follow me when I left the apartment. I knew what he was doing, but it wasn't worth arguing over. Even though we weren't married, in Mostafa's eyes I was the wife of a Muslim and he 'owned' me. I had to just accept this.

When I started to go back to work, I had to take May with me. Despite Mostafa being good with her most days, he refused to mind her for me, even if he had no work. May was a great child, but it was much too difficult keeping everything going and so I made the heartbreaking decision to give up the business. I absolutely loved my job, more than anything and it broke my heart to have to call it a day. But I was getting no support from Mostafa. And while I was stressing over having to give up my part in a business that I had helped build up from scratch, a business I was so proud of, he was once again pulling the wool over my eyes.

What I hadn't realised, as he never told me, was that he had been illegally in the country for some time because his visa had run out. I only found this out because he wanted to go to Syria and for me and May to go with him. He eventually told me that the apartment where he had been living months before when we had just started going out together had been raided, his friend had been arrested and his own passport had been confiscated by the police after they found it under his pillow. Mostafa knew that I was selling my business and therefore I had money coming in, and he wanted me to pay for us all, as a family, to go to Syria. He wanted us to start a new life there, with his family around us.

However, to do this he had to hand himself in to the police and they would have to deport him. He begged me go to the police station with him and to stand by him. He asked me to tell the police that I was his partner and May was his child: this, he said, would ensure that they would let me go to Syria with him. As a family.

And, of course, I did exactly what he asked me to do. Stupidly, very stupidly, I felt slightly sorry for him. I felt that, despite everything, May was his child and I couldn't say no, I couldn't stop him from seeing her. If he went to Syria and I didn't follow, then I was denying him the right to see his daughter. I couldn't do that. I wasn't too keen on going to his home country, even though back then, in 2005, the country was not at war. I had read about Syria, and the rights held by a mother were few and far between, but I felt I had to give it a try.

When we got to the police station they did, as Mostafa said they would, arrest him immediately. They took us all to the airport to deport him, but when we got there I was told that I couldn't fly into Syria with May as I had no visa, but Mostafa told them that I was his 'wife' and somehow they agreed to let me go. The police were delighted to be deporting him, as he was just another illegal immigrant to them. They didn't care about myself or May.

I remember praying that everything would be OK, as I hadn't told my family where I was going or what I was doing. Only a handful of my friends in Cyprus knew; I was too terrified to tell people because I didn't want to hear their opinions. I knew exactly what they would say.

We flew into Damascus that night, and Mostafa booked us into a hotel for the first two days. It was a bit of a shock to me, arriving into this country where all the women were covered up from head to toe and where I was the only Western person visible and, to make it worse, a Western woman. But he assured me that I would get used to it and it would all be fine.

On the third day, we drove to a city called Aleppo, near his village. Mostafa booked myself and May into a hotel and told me that I was to stay there and that he would be back in a few days. He told me not to leave the room, as it was too dangerous. He organised a cot for May and for us to have breakfast, dinner and tea in the hotel so that we didn't have to venture outside. I begged him not to leave me, but he said he had to tell his family about me, and once they knew all about myself and May he could then take us to his home town.

I was distraught when he walked out the door. May was just eight months old at the time, and I had to keep her locked up for days with no fresh air. Mostafa was gone for more than 24 hours before he even made contact with me, and that was only because I kept texting him on the mobile phone and hounding him with calls. I had sent a text asking if he was all right, and he replied, 'Yes. But big problems here.' I hadn't a clue what was going on. It transpired that on the night that he arrived home, they threw a big party for him in the village. His wife and kids were there, and he actually went back to his home with his wife that night. But he told her that he didn't love her and that he was with another woman, had a child and wanted to marry her. He told her that we were in Aleppo. She seemingly went berserk. They went to the mosque the next morning, and his wife told his mother everything. His parents were disgusted with him. Mostafa rang me 48 hours after leaving me and he said that he was coming back. I was relieved, as I was stuck in this place with my baby and I couldn't move.

But I could never have imagined what was to happen next. Out of the blue there was a knock on the hotel room door, and when I opened it, standing in the hallway was Mostafa, his wife and his two children. I was left standing there with my mouth open, wondering what the hell was going on.

They all walked into the room. Nothing was said to me, but his wife, wearing a hijab and a full-length dress, typical Muslim clothing, walked over to my baby in her pram, picked her up and in Arabic kept repeating over and over again how gorgeous May was. What freaked me out the most about the whole situation was that this young woman was the absolute spitting image of Mostafa. You would have sworn that it was actually Mostafa in a dress; that was how identical they were. She never spoke to me and hardly looked in my direction, and I wondered what the hell she was doing there. With that, though, Mostafa told me to get ready, as he was taking us all out for dinner. This was the weirdest situation I had ever been in.

We all got into a car that Mostafa had got from his home town and drove to an Arabic restaurant in a town between Idlib and Aleppo. I remember the smell as we drove along the streets: it was a mixture of sweat, dirt and sewage, and it was everywhere. It turned my stomach as we made our way out of Aleppo. The city was thronged with people, more people than I had ever seen before.

When we got to the restaurant, we were seated with me facing this strange woman, Mostafa's wife. Despite what he had done to her and how he had broken the news of his new family to her, she still appeared to love him. Everyone in the restaurant was staring at us, staring at this Muslim with three children and two women. Yet Mostafa wasn't at all fazed by it. At one stage I went to take May out of her pram to change her nappy when his wife jumped up from her seat, grabbed May and ran into the toilet with her. Minutes later they emerged, May in a fresh nappy and a whole new set of clothes. I don't know where she got them, but they fitted her perfectly.

When the meal was finished we were packed into the car again, and, to my shock, we were driven to Mostafa's home town. We were heading to the home he shared with his wife and children. It was late at night and pitch black, but I could clearly see that there were no walls or pathways anywhere, and the smell was woeful. It was a horrific sight and I didn't know why we were even there. I couldn't wait to get out, away from this weird situation, away from this town. When we got to Mostafa's house, at the bottom of a long road, I was surprised that it was a bit better than other houses I had witnessed along the way.

Mostafa's wife had it nicely decorated. I was, as I saw it, a guest in her home – in very unusual circumstances. If it had been me I thought I would have killed Mostafa, or just packed my bags and left with my children, but she endured this weird situation. And, oddly enough, so did I. I had a very bad migraine by the time I got to the house, probably brought on by the stress of this totally unnatural situation. I told Mostafa that my head was throbbing, and he told me to go to bed and rest. In front of his wife, he told me that this was my home now and I was to relax.

He took me into his bedroom, *their* bedroom, and he tucked me into their marital king-size bed. I was looking at him in total shock. He was acting as if there wasn't a problem, and while it might have been normal in his world, it was far from normal in mine. His wife, this strange woman, took my child and brought her into the kitchen to feed her mashed banana and milk. She clearly adored her, but I felt very uncomfortable. I got out of the bed to check on May, and I remember walking into the sitting room to see this poor young woman helping Mostafa to put on his coat, holding it out for him to put his arms through the sleeves. She then bent down and put the shoes on his feet. It was a shocking scene watching this girl still displaying her love for her husband despite the situation she had been put in by him. I went back into the bedroom and tried to act as if nothing was wrong.

I knew that Mostafa was dressing to go to his parents' house, but I didn't know what was going on or why I hadn't yet met his parents. I finally fell asleep, and when I woke the next morning he told me that I would have to go back to Cyprus, just myself and May. He said his parents wanted nothing to do with myself or my child and that he had been told to get me out of the village immediately.

I was absolutely shocked. It seemed that Mostafa wasn't coming back to Cyprus with us, because he had no passport, but he was sending myself and May back on our own, after all I had given up and left behind in Paphos for him. I didn't care for what I felt my life would be like in Syria, especially as there was another woman and two other children on the scene when I thought that they would have been living somewhere else, so I was somewhat relieved. But I knew that Mostafa was basically getting rid of me because I was unwanted and an embarrassment to his family.

I packed what I had unpacked the night before for myself and May, and I was ushered out of the house and into a car. He told me that he was taking me to a hotel. He explained that things were not going to work out for us in Syria, but he was doing his best to sort things with his family.

He left me alone with May in a hotel room again that night

and went back to his wife and children. Somehow, I built up the courage to ring Mandy. I told her where I was and what had happened. I told her that it looked like his family didn't want me or May, and I was probably coming back to Dublin. She couldn't believe that I had put myself in that situation, but, in fairness to her, she wasn't judgemental. She just wanted us back safely.

When Mostafa arrived the next day he said what I had expected, that he needed to get me on a flight home. He said his family wanted him to live with his wife again as a family and they wanted me out of the country. So, once again, he packed me and May into a car and drove us all the way back to Damascus, a five-hour drive, with May crying all the way and me begging him to try to sort things out so that I wouldn't have to go back to Dublin or Cyprus on my own. I felt such a fool.

He promised me that he would be with me soon. Once again he insisted that he didn't love his wife and he wanted to be with me and May for ever. But, although I wanted to believe him, and despite everything that had happened over the previous 72 hours, I felt gutted. In my heart, I felt as though this was the last time I would see him and the last time he would see his little girl.

This man had treated me badly for years, and I still don't understand why he had such a hold on me. I loved him and I hated him all at the same time. And I hated myself for that.

We had a very tearful goodbye that day, and he assured me, 'I will see you soon. Please trust me.' He left us on our own in the airport, and I was devastated. I was crying and trying to stop May crying, and then I was told by the staff at the departures desk that they couldn't let me out of the country without Mostafa's permission in writing. I couldn't believe it.

We were ushered into a room and left there for more than an hour. I was worried sick about whether we would actually manage to get out of the country that day and wondered if this situation would force Mostafa to let us stay. The airport staff told me that they would ring him on his mobile phone to inform him that he would have to return to the airport to give his permission for our departure. He eventually arrived, signed the forms and left with not a word said to me.

I was heartbroken. That night we had to fly to Milan, myself and my baby girl, and then get a connecting flight to Dublin. I was absolutely shattered when I arrived in Dublin but delighted that I was safe and that I had the support of my family: a loving, truly caring family.

I heard nothing from Mostafa for a whole week, until I finally managed to get through to his phone, after hundreds of attempts to get him to answer. When he finally decided to accept my call, he told me that he was back with his wife and he had slept with her the night before.

I couldn't believe it. Again, he told me that he didn't love her, he loved myself and May, but my life was in a million pieces. I looked down at my beautiful baby, sleeping peacefully in her pram, and decided there and then that it was time for me to move on, without him. We were free from his control, free from his bullying and his domination. We had our own lives and we didn't need him there.

It was something I had been waiting for for so long, and now I finally had it.

I decided that day that it was finally time to reclaim my life. And, this time, for good.

CHAPTER FOUR

———◆———

Always Going Back
for More

When I arrived back in Ireland, my family were absolutely delighted to have myself and May home. I knew that they were secretly annoyed with me and obviously frustrated by the fact that, despite everything, all the abuse and the lies, I always forgave Mostafa and returned to him. Even though Dad never actually sat me down and said he was annoyed, because that wasn't his nature, I could see it. Yet, more than anything else, I could see that he was hurt: hurt because it wasn't just his daughter caught up in all this now but his granddaughter as well. He didn't want to see his child upset, which I clearly was. But he knew very little of the abuse I had gone through. Mandy and I had kept this from him, as we didn't want to distress him. He wasn't aware of the real story.

We never really discussed what had happened, any of us; we simply got on with things. I busied myself over the following six or so months. I went back to college to study photography, and I had decided that I would try to get some work in the travel business, too, as I had loved it before I fled to Cyprus. I started working from home, booking holidays and flights for individuals and companies through a business called Travel

Counsellors. It was the ideal set-up, because it allowed me to be with May all day as well as work. It was the perfect job.

Then Mostafa rang me one day out of the blue, and the vicious circle started again. The phone calls began to get more frequent. Mostafa would ring the house three or four times a day, sometimes more, begging me to bring May to meet him. Again and again I told him that I had moved on with my life and I was never going back to him. And again and again he informed me that his relationship with his wife was over and he would never hurt me again. He said he wanted to see May and that as a father he had that right. He said he would go to Dubai and meet me there. He told me that it would cost me nothing, as his brother was working for a major airline and he would get flights organised.

At this stage, I had already made my mind up to go back to live in Cyprus. I was missing my friends and my life in the sun terribly, and in my mind Mostafa was in Syria and so wrapped up in his family that he would never return to Cyprus. I hadn't told him, but I had decided to invest in a property in Paphos and I had already bought a little maisonette online. I hadn't actually seen it with my own eyes, but a friend of mine had gone to look at it when it went on the market and she said that it was a bargain and I would love it, so I bought it over the Internet. She had warned me that it would need a bit of work done to it, but that didn't put me off, as I loved decorating and putting my own stamp on things anyway. So I was already making plans to move back.

I still had feelings for Mostafa, despite our history, and I honestly didn't think I would ever meet another man, especially now that I had a child.

And so I agreed to meet him in Dubai. Despite all the promises of his brother getting me a cheap flight, I ended up booking and paying for the trip myself, but when I arrived at the airport Mostafa was nowhere to be seen. He knew I was worried about arriving into this strange country on a night-time flight with May, yet he ignored my concerns. I tried to call him, but when I eventually got through to him he said that he couldn't make it and his brother would pick me up. He didn't arrive either. Luckily, I'd had the forethought to book into a hotel and it wasn't until the next day that Mostafa's brother turned up.

When Mostafa eventually showed his face, I was shocked by how different he looked. He had put on weight and he seemed as if he had the weight of the world on his shoulders. But he seemed genuinely delighted to see us, especially May. He kept going on about how much he missed us being in his life and how, if we stayed with him, everything would be different to what it had been in the past.

This was my first time meeting his brother and he seemed like a lovely man, very different to Mostafa. He was very friendly, and he thought May was beautiful. But very oddly, on the second night, he took me aside, and I was shocked when he told me that I had to leave and get away from Mostafa. He said he loved his brother and that his family was the most important thing in his life but that he knew that Mostafa was 'crazy'. He said Mostafa was the black sheep of the family. He had excellent English and said, 'You are a lovely girl and your daughter is beautiful and you don't need this. Mostafa has a wife and family in Syria and he will never leave them. You need to get away from him. He is my brother and I love him, but for your sake and her sake get away from him now.'

I was totally shocked at his outburst, but I listened to him, because I felt this was a man who had known Mostafa all of his life and who loved him but did not trust him, and if ever I should listen to someone it was him.

I asked him if he would book me flights to Cyprus, which he agreed to do, and I began to walk away when Mostafa arrived. An argument broke out between the two brothers, and next thing I knew May and myself were in a car with Mostafa and his brother. They were arguing non-stop and Mostafa cried all the way to the airport.

Funnily enough, that day I didn't feel as upset as on other

occasions. In fact, looking back, I think I might have actually felt a bit of relief. I think Mostafa's brother got through to me somehow, more than any other person had in the past, possibly because I knew that he knew Mostafa better than anyone.

I rang my friend when we landed in Larnaca airport. She couldn't believe that we were back in Cyprus. She told me that it would take a few days to make my new house habitable, so she invited me to come to her house until things were sorted. It was great to see her again and to feel a sense of belonging.

I absolutely loved Cyprus and my life there, and I was thrilled to be back. I felt that this new start was exactly what May and myself needed, and I was more positive than ever that this time we would be fine. It was our opportunity to start afresh, just the two of us.

I told Mandy what had happened and that I was back in Cyprus, and although she was worried that Mostafa would follow me there, she was glad I wasn't with him. We were on speaking terms, myself and Mandy, but just barely. And that broke my heart, because, in my mind, we weren't just sisters, we were best friends. She was the one person I trusted with every bone in my body. We were more like twins with an unbreakable bond than just sisters – well, that was until Mostafa Assad came into my life and tore us apart. She was happy that I had my own place, but I could also sense her annoyance and I knew that she felt that no matter what she said I would just do my own thing anyway. And, unfortunately for me, she was right.

When I eventually moved into my new house, I was happier than I had ever been. I turned my home into a little palace, and it was great having all my friends over for dinner and drinks and not having to worry about Mostafa. I felt totally free for the first time in years.

I began to use my travel-agent skills and started working for two different companies, Topflight and Skytours. I was making lots of money and I had met a new man. My life was perfect.

The new man on the scene could not have been more

different to who I had left behind. His name was Al. He was Lebanese and he was the most loving, caring man I had ever met. In looks he was very similar to Mostafa. He was tall, dark and handsome, but he genuinely cared for me and May and wanted to protect us. He was shocked at what I had gone through in my life and promised that he would always be there for both of us. He had no problem with me going out with my friends, and he was extremely sociable. He had lots of friends himself, and he got on with all of the girls and their partners. Life was great.

Al knew that I suffered because of my hips and that I loved swimming, so he would pick me up from the apartment and take me off for a swim as a surprise. During our albeit short relationship I dislocated my knee – another symptom of my osteoarthritis, which results in loosening of the joints – but he was so caring that not only did he do anything and everything I needed, but he also cared for May and made sure that she wanted for nothing while her mammy was stuck in bed.

I even remember one day that Al collected us and took us for a drive. It turned out that he had rented a villa for a day, and when we arrived at around 6 p.m. he placed candles all around the swimming pool and we swam in the pool until midnight, all three of us. It was such a romantic thing to do, and I was delighted that he hadn't left May out; he included her in everything, which I loved him for.

Mandy was delighted for me. Because she felt Mostafa was gone for good and I had moved on, we started to talk more, and it was great to know that I had my sister back in my life.

I had been in Cyprus for about seven or eight months when, out of the blue, my life was thrown into disarray yet again. I was sitting in a bar one night with my girlfriends, their partners and Al when out of the corner of my eye I saw Mostafa Assad walking in the door. He stood there for a few seconds staring over at me, and then he just walked towards the loo. I remember as clear as day nearly choking into my drink. I still vividly remember how he was wearing a white and blue Diesel shirt

and a pair of dark jeans. When I saw him, at first I thought it
was an illusion, that it was someone who looked exactly like
him. It couldn't be him. I actually blinked a few times, trying to
refocus my eyes to see if it was actually the one person I dreaded
seeing more than anyone else. It was my first night out in a bar
in a long time as well as my first night out without May. We
always socialised in other people's homes at barbecues and
dinner parties, so I never really went to pubs, but this night I
had got a babysitter, an older lady recommended by a friend,
and it was a treat to be out alone, even though I was worrying
about May and whether she would be OK if she woke up to see
a strange lady in the house. Never in my wildest dreams did I
expect my night to be ruined by Mostafa.

When I'd seen him stare back at me, I was gutted. I turned
to Al and I said, 'I have just seen Mostafa.'

He said, 'Don't be silly, Louise, you are imagining things.'

But suddenly Mostafa appeared again, this time outside on
the road. I started to shake. My teeth were chattering. I was
terrified.

Al went out to him, and Mostafa was insisting that he wanted
to see May. He was being an absolute gentleman to Al, begging
him to ask me to allow him see his child. Al was totally fooled
by him that first night. He walked back up to me and said,
'Louise, he is a very nice man. He just wants to see his daughter.
He is being very nice about it, but he just misses his child and,
in fairness, it is his child.'

I couldn't believe that Al had been so taken in by him, but no
amount of explaining could convince him that Mostafa was
acting and that he had an ulterior motive for arriving back in
Cyprus.

I point-blank refused to let Mostafa see May. He had moved
back to Cyprus, although to this day I don't know how he
managed it, given that he had been deported as an illegal
immigrant. It turned out that he was living in Limassol, and
that night was the start of another nightmare for me. Mostafa
was disgusted that I wouldn't let him see his child but even

more disgusted that I was with another man. In his mind, I was and always would be his property, and despite Al being fooled by him, Mostafa was about to prove to this man that I would never be another man's woman. It was that simple. I was hysterical with worry. I knew that Mostafa was not going to sit back quietly and accept the situation. I knew he would be plotting a way of getting his revenge on me, but when I approached the authorities they didn't understand why I was so concerned. From the evening I first saw him in the bar, I got nightly visits from Mostafa. He would bang on my door, demanding that I let him in. I could see the hatred in his eyes, but I wasn't giving in to his demands, as I had done in the past. I really liked Al and I didn't want to lose him, but I knew that Mostafa would have something up his sleeve. I knew he wouldn't take to this situation kindly, and I was about to find out just how evil he could be when he wanted to.

One night as Al, May and myself arrived back at the house with a cooked chicken for dinner, a group of Syrian men ran at us throwing bricks and sticks at the car windscreen. Al, who had just got out of the car before the attack began, jumped back in and somehow managed to reverse out of the car park with this gang running after us, pelting the car. As we drove away, I looked behind and saw Mostafa slap bang in the middle of this raving gang with a look of disdain on his face. With that – though I don't know who threw it – a rock came through the back windscreen, just missing us but smashing the glass into a thousand pieces. Poor May was in a baby seat in the back of the car, screaming hysterically. She was only about 18 months old at the time.

I grabbed my mobile phone from my handbag and somehow managed to dial Mostafa's number. He was furious. I said, 'How the hell could you do that, you bastard, with your own daughter in the car?'

He said, 'I didn't ask them to smash the window; I just wanted to frighten him. You are my woman and I wanted to teach him a lesson, to get away from you.'

We went straight to the police station to lodge a complaint. I didn't care what they did to Mostafa; I just wanted him out of my life and away from us. But the police weren't interested. They said it was 'a domestic'. I was disgusted with their response. I had been to the police station many times before lodging complaints about Mostafa, and each time they had dismissed me. It was as if they couldn't have cared less what happened to me because I was a European woman in a relationship with an Arab man: I was basically asking for trouble.

I remember driving away from the police station, with shards of glass everywhere, and thinking how unfair it was to put Al in this position. I knew that what had just happened had terrified him, but he didn't want to show me just how worried he was about future attacks. What Al saw that night was the other side of the man he, just days before, thought was 'very nice' and a 'caring dad'. He was shocked that a father could have put his own daughter's life at risk with such a stupid and uncaring act.

On another occasion Al had decided to stay overnight, and at some stage late that night there was a knock on the door. As I went to open it I heard men shouting, saying it was the police and they had a search warrant for my home. With that, before I had a chance to open it, the door was kicked in and my house was flooded with members of CID and the local police. They pulled my house apart, bit by bit. I was hysterical and little May was screaming. Al didn't know what was going on. They told me that they'd had an anonymous tip-off from someone in Limassol to say that my home was being used as a bomb-making factory. I couldn't believe what I was hearing, but I knew exactly who had made that call. They even knocked over all my full tins of paint onto the veranda while looking for bomb-making material, destroying the place with paint.

Al's name had been given to them by whoever tipped them off, and they arrested him. I was so upset. They held him overnight and right up until 7 p.m. the next evening. They held him for longer than normal because his papers weren't in order. He had claimed asylum, and I knew there were problems with his paperwork, but this wasn't unusual in Cyprus and so I thought nothing of it. But it was a reason to detain him for a longer period of time and so they did. I remember how gutted I was that this innocent man was in a prison cell simply because he was my friend. And I was equally gutted at the condition the police left my house in.

After that, my relationship with Al started to go downhill rapidly. Mostafa began to send death threats to Al and even got his friends to ring him regularly, warning him that he would be killed if he didn't leave me alone. Mostafa's plan was working. I could see how nervous Al had become when he was with me. He was even more scared when we went out in public. I hated seeing him like this.

Al knew what some of the Syrians were like in Cyprus and how they would do anything for each other. And so after a few weeks I decided to tell Al that we would have to go our separate ways. I was upset and so was he, but I couldn't risk losing him some other way. I knew what Mostafa was capable of and I genuinely feared that he would either kill Al himself or arrange for someone else to do it for him. It broke my heart to let him go, but I didn't really have a choice. It was bad enough that Mostafa had such control over me, but I knew that I couldn't risk anyone else's life either. This was probably the first time that I realised that Mostafa Assad would never allow me to be another man's partner. He would follow me to the ends of the earth if he thought that I was with another man. And this terrified me. This was simply how it was going to be for the rest of my life, no matter where I lived.

I didn't go into too much detail with my family back home. They knew something had happened but didn't really know the full facts. My dad decided that he would come over for a visit for two weeks, and I was so excited to be seeing him again.

When Dad arrived, I told him that Mostafa was back on the scene. He didn't realise how bad things were, but he advised me to meet up with Mostafa just so that he could see his daughter. Dad said it would keep the peace.

I decided that I would do it if Dad came with me, which he did. We met in a place called Orphanides in Limassol, and Mostafa was on his best behaviour that day, laughing and joking, playing with May, telling us both that he loved us. He spent three hours with us, and my dad was totally taken in by him. He thought that Mostafa had changed and that he genuinely seemed to love May. I didn't want to upset my father by telling him the whole truth and so I agreed that I would let Mostafa back into May's life. I knew at the time it was possibly the biggest mistake I was to make, but I felt pushed into a corner.

When my dad went home, Mostafa came to the house and said, 'So. When are you coming to Limassol to live with me? I want you back.' I told him that I needed time, as I had my little apartment now, which I loved, and I didn't want to leave it. I had a lovely life in Paphos and a home with views from both balconies on to the sea and the beautiful beaches, and I loved my life as it was. I was biding time and hoping that he would get fed up asking and just agree to me living in Paphos while he lived in Limassol, and that I would allow him to see May.

That very same evening, I answered a knock on my door, and standing outside was Mostafa and a friend of his. They simply walked in and started to pack my clothes, May's clothes and some of our personal items. Mostafa even took my TV. No matter how much I argued, he continued to pack the car. He told me that I could rent out the maisonette but I was going with him whether I liked it or not.

I cried all the way to this apartment he had found in Zakaki. I couldn't believe what I had left behind me. Mostafa had rented a very old-fashioned apartment on the third floor of a building, and it was absolutely horrible, but I knew that there was no coming back from this. My life would never actually be my own, because I had his child, so I thought I would just do my best to make the most of a bad situation. At least if I was with him, in the same apartment, he wouldn't be banging down my door in the middle of the night causing mayhem or following me around. If I was with him, I was under his control. I was too exhausted to put up a fight. I was emotionally and physically drained by trying to escape from him all the time only to be dragged back kicking and screaming.

And so we simply got on with things. He did his thing and I did mine. As before, I stayed in at night and he went out. When I first moved in he was paying the rent, but within weeks he insisted that I pay, so it was back to the same routine all over again. I knew if I didn't pay we would have nowhere to live, so I just accepted it, again.

Luckily, I found a good playschool for May fairly soon after we moved in, and I started to work in the Limassol branch of Olympic Holidays. Myself and May went for walks along the beachfront in the afternoons and spent our days off in the park and in the sea.

When I got offered the job, Olympic told me that it was a full-time position from 11 a.m. until 7 p.m., but I told them there and then that I was a mother and that I couldn't do those hours because of my child. I asked them if they would agree to me working until 4 p.m. for part-time wages instead of a full-time employee's rate, which was a bit higher. Thankfully they agreed, because they knew my sales record from other companies. The pay cut didn't bother me because I knew that I could make up that loss in commission with my sales. We were all happy.

I made a large circle of friends very quickly. Most of the staff were expats from the UK, and they were a great bunch of people. I went to their homes all the time for parties, but I was too mortified for many months to ask them to come to my home. I hated the place with a vengeance. It just looked like a cheap holiday rental, and no matter what I did I couldn't improve it. I used to make excuses all the time as to why I couldn't ask them round. The first time my friend Nicola came around to the place to collect me to head off to another friend's house, I spent all of my time apologising for the state of the place. Thank God she never made me feel bad about how I was living. She just laughed it off.

Things were going really well for me at work, and I was bringing in good money. Mostafa was working all week as well, including Saturdays, in the building trade, but I never saw a cent of what he earned. And, to be honest, I wasn't bothered, because I knew that he would never be able to throw anything at me about me being 'a kept woman'.

The truth was that I loved him being out all the time. In fact, his one day off was Sunday and he always lay around the apartment then. I hated Sundays. In fact, it's something that still affects me now, because every Sunday ended up in a screaming match and a big fight and little May would be there to witness it all. I actually hated going to bed on Saturday night, knowing what lay ahead. Mostafa was very strict with May and he liked to push his fatherly authority on her, especially at weekends.

He knew that myself and May had a great relationship, but when he was around he liked to let her know that he was the leader of the family. He liked to smack her: a little girl. He would hit her on the bottom and he would regularly make her hold out her hand so he could strike it very hard. I hated this, and we fought constantly about how he asserted his authority so heavy-handedly over our little girl, but he would always scream at me, saying that he was the man of the house and we would all do as he said.

For example, I loved tucking May into bed at night and reading her a bedtime story. We would have a chat and a laugh and a joke about things that had happened that day, but when Mostafa was at home he controlled everything, and once he told her to go to bed she wouldn't move from it. She was terrified of him, as he would go crazy even if she got up to go to the toilet. If I heard her getting out of the bed to go to the toilet I would race out to help her, protect her, but he would race at us both, screaming and shouting, and he would smack May, demanding that she got back into bed. Then he would scream at me and push me, telling me that I would not have a say in how he controlled his child.

He knew that I was comfortable moneywise and that I didn't actually need his income. He insisted that I sold my apartment, which, of course, I gave in to. The sale went through very quickly, which meant I had a nice sum of money in the bank. He was delighted with that, even though he knew that technically it was my cash and not his.

Then one day he told me that he was in trouble and could be deported at any time unless he got married quickly. He told me that his divorce had come through in Syria, although he never showed me any documents to prove it and he had never told me that before. He simply led me to believe the relationship was over and that he had told that poor girl he didn't love her and that he wanted to be with myself and May. He said that he would be devastated if he was deported, as it would mean that he would never see his child again and he believed that a father should always be in his child's life – although he didn't seem to think the same about his two children back in Syria. Then he proceeded to tell me to get dressed, as we were going to the registry office to plan our wedding day.

I was totally shocked by this, as it had come completely out of the blue. As we drove along, I told him that I needed some time because I wanted my family with me on my wedding day, and they would need to organise flights and holidays back in Dublin, but he just ignored me and we carried on driving.

Once we were at the registry office, the lady there took all of our details. She asked what dates were we thinking of, and as I went to say, 'In a month or so,' Mostafa butted in and said, 'Tomorrow.' I turned to him in total shock, and I could clearly see the look of surprise on the woman's face. I think she was waiting for a reaction from me, but I knew there would be no point in arguing with Mostafa, so I simply nodded in agreement. And that was it. It was to be a 'quickie' ceremony simply because, once again, Mostafa had clicked his fingers and I had, yet again, said nothing.

I simply agreed because I knew that if we were married he would have the papers he needed to be legitimately in May's life. I didn't think about the consequences; I just went along with his plan. I wasn't fooling myself. I knew he had his own motives for wanting to marry me, and they didn't involve love. It was, as usual, all about Mostafa.

That afternoon, I rang my friend Nicola, who I had only recently met, and I asked if she and her husband would act as our witnesses at the ceremony the next day. I was embarrassed to ask her. I'm sure poor Nicola thought that I had gone mad, because there had been no talk of a wedding, it had never been on the cards, and now, all of a sudden, I was getting married in less than 24 hours.

Mostafa didn't even buy me a wedding ring; nor did he buy himself one. We actually had to borrow the rings from Nicola and her husband. It was mortifying. In fact, I never got a ring from him. I didn't even have a new dress to wear on my wedding day. I wore a pair of black shorts and a black and white top tucked into them. I was heartbroken that day. I wanted to run away and never come back. We had no photographer, no video, nothing. I know that Mostafa never loved me the way I wanted to be loved and that it was nothing more than a marriage of convenience for him, a way of stopping him being deported, and I was nothing more than a fool.

After we received our blessing from the registrar, the poor woman we had met the day before, who I knew was wondering why the hell I was doing this, we simply headed down to the beachfront and had our wedding feast of scrambled eggs on toast.

That was the start of married life for me with a man whom I had once loved but whom I hated more and more with every day. But I knew that one day I would escape from his grasp. I just had to wait for that opportunity to raise its head.

In the meantime, I asked Mostafa if we could move out of the apartment. He knew that I hated the place we were living in, and he agreed to move if I found a place myself and I agreed to keep paying the rent, which, of course, I did.

After only a few weeks I found a lovely house with three bedrooms and a lovely garden. It was near Orphanides supermarket, where I had met Mostafa with my father that day when he acted as the perfect loving dad. The house was unfurnished, but I told Mostafa that I would pay for furniture if he agreed to move. I told him that the current apartment wasn't healthy for May, as she was cooped up all day and needed to have a garden where she could wander out for fresh air. He agreed, and so we moved into our new home and I started to make it our little nest. I was beavering away buying a new settee and comfortable chairs, a lovely dining-room suite and new curtains: the works. I loved it.

I started to bring all of my friends round for dinner and coffees, and May had all her little friends round. We were really comfortable, myself and May, and we basically lived a separate life to my husband, but we were only too well aware that he was around when he was there. However, Mostafa wasn't too bad when people came around and he was there. He ate with them and spoke to them, but he watched me like a hawk and made sure that I had no skin-to-skin contact with my friends' partners. In fact, I had to ask my friend one day to beg her husband not to come near me to kiss me when Mostafa was around. I explained to her how I had to act as a Muslim wife in his company, and I told her how embarrassed I was to have to even say this to her, but I explained that it would keep the peace and stop Mostafa from starting a row. She thought I was mad for staying with someone like that, but she accepted that it made life easier for myself and May, so she agreed to have a word with her husband.

Certain times of the year were always worse than others, and Christmas was one of those bad times. I love this time of year, but Mostafa hated me celebrating and was against me decorating the house or having any festive cheer. I knew he wanted May brought up in the Muslim faith, but I suppose I got away with putting up holly and mistletoe and decorating the tree because

I explained to him that Christmas wasn't a religious festival to me. I believed the opposite, of course, but if Mostafa had known about my beliefs I would never have been able to enjoy the best ceremony of the year. And so we got to enjoy our Christmas dinner and have some festive fun. Halloween was the same: all the kids in the street came to our house, and we played games and had a laugh and May loved it.

But I knew Mostafa wasn't happy with how my life was going. He started to allow me to go out with my friends, but I could only go to dinner, not to a pub for a drink. It was very embarrassing, but he would arrange a time to pick me up once the meal was finished and I would have to go straight home. He would meet me at the restaurant door and I would be mortified. But I was glad that I was at least allowed out in the first place. I became grateful for small mercies.

I got my first real taste of Islam when the son of a lovely woman I knew died suddenly. This woman was also married to a Syrian man, and the loss of her little boy absolutely shattered her world. She was so distraught that she couldn't even go to his burial. This little mite was only one year old when he left this life, and his death taught me how quickly Muslim people deal with a loss. In Muslim funerals, when someone dies they are buried as soon as possible, certainly within three days and often within twenty-four hours, before the body decomposes. This is a way of life for Muslims, but it is just something that I, as a Catholic, am not used to, and I found it very hard to cope with what I had to witness.

This little boy's death tore me apart. His mammy, unable to cope with the heartache of it all, asked if I would go with her little boy as his father prepared him for burial and then be with him as he was laid to rest. I hated the thought of it, but I knew that I had to be there for her, as she just wasn't able to go herself.

I walked into a room as a group of men laid this little child on a white muslin cloth and proceeded to wash him down. They cleaned every section of his tiny, frail body and then simply wrapped him in a clean cloth and prepared to take him for burial.

His father was in an awful state and was being comforted by a group of men. I was the only woman in the room and I could see that most of the men gathered were not impressed at my presence, but I was there for the little boy's mammy and I didn't care what they thought. I fought back the tears as I watched a Muslim preparation for burial for the first time, and I thought of May and how I would feel if this was me, if I was this little boy's mammy. And I could hold back my tears no longer. And once I started I found it very hard to stop.

When the men's work was done they wailed and cried, and then Mostafa told me that it was time to go to the burial ground. As they left, I got a call from the baby's mother, who begged me to take a lock of her first child's hair before they laid him to rest. I don't think even she knew what happened during a Muslim burial, but I told her I would make sure that I got some of his hair for her and then she begged me to put a piece of his comfort blanket in with him.

I called to Mostafa and told him that no matter what was to take place, we had to carry out her final wishes for her child. He went mad, trying to explain to me that once the body had been washed and prepared it was sacred and couldn't be touched again. But I didn't care; I wasn't letting this baby go to his final resting place without allowing his mammy to have her final wish granted. This little child had not been ill and the family had no time to prepare for his death; he had just died and they'd had no time to grieve.

I could see that the others were not happy when Mostafa told them that not only did I need to get a lock of his hair but they needed to put some of his favourite blanket in beside him as a comfort to him. They all started to scream and shout and said that the body was cleansed and there was no way that they could 'infect' the body with any impurities, as it was ready to go to its final resting place.

None of the men wanted the body to be touched, but

somehow the baby's father must have convinced them. They finally allowed me to cut a tiny lock of his limp hair and they took a piece of his blanket from me and placed it on top of the muslin, not inside where it could make contact with the body. Then they placed this tiny little child in a hole in the ground, placed slats of wood on top of his little body and then poured wet cement into the freshly dug grave.

I found out later that this little tot was laid six feet below ground on his right side with his face to what they call the *qibla*. This is the direction of the Kaaba (the sacred building at Mecca), to which Muslims turn at prayer. This is customary.

I was standing looking on from a distance, as I wasn't permitted to stand beside the men, and I have to be honest and say that I was shocked by how it all happened and how quickly it was all over. As I watched the men lower the baby into his final resting place that day, I burst into tears and clutched the hair of this innocent child who came into the world and died just a year later. And I wondered if he had been older, in his teens, maybe, if he would have been buried the same way. Would he have chosen the Muslim faith? Or would he have had any choice in his religion?

It was the huge cultural difference that made me so annoyed that day, so confused, but I was glad that his mammy was too ill to attend, because no mother should have to bury her baby, never mind bury him in this manner when her own culture is so different. I admit that at the time I knew nothing of why the Muslim faith buried the dead in such a way, but it was a world away from my culture and I just found it very hard to understand.

I knew that Mostafa was annoyed at me interfering, as he saw it, in his religion's burial rites, but it just widened the gap between us even further and made me realise that my life was very different. God forbid, if something were to happen to May, I didn't want that ceremony, or anything like it, for her. I still wanted her to make her own choice when she was older as to what religion, if any, to follow, but I also feared for her if she chose the Muslim way of life and maybe ended up living in Syria.

I wanted her to be proud of her heritage and her multicultural parentage, though, and for her to be fluent in Arabic. I was determined never to have her say I stopped her doing anything in life. I continued with my Arabic cooking and told May all about Syria. I even started to learn the language myself. When I went to enquire about Arabic lessons I met a lovely girl called Justine. Her husband was also Syrian, and when I started the class with May she was there with her two children, and all three kids became really close friends.

I thought Mostafa would be delighted that I had met a woman who was married to a Syrian, but I was wrong again. About six months after Justine and I became really close friends, Mostafa came home one day and for some reason a big argument broke out. He started screaming abuse at me and pushing me, and I ran out of the house and down to Justine's home.

She knew I was distraught and I told her that I couldn't take any more abuse. The day after that I got a call from Justine. She said that Mostafa was outside talking to her husband and he had told her husband not to allow her to talk to or contact me. Her husband agreed. I was devastated. Not only had I lost a good friend, but May, who was only four years old, had lost her two best friends.

I didn't see Justine for nearly two months after that episode, until one day we met in the park and she meekly approached me, apologising for what had happened. I was delighted that she was back in my life and we agreed that we would be as secretive as possible. But I didn't have to worry about hiding from Mostafa for too long, because, within weeks of me renewing my friendship with Justine, he put the nail in the coffin of our relationship himself.

He had started to go out every night again, doing his own thing, and I would stay at home with May. It was nothing unusual, but one day he arrived home at about 5 a.m., his hair all messed up and his clothes stinking of perfume. I knew instantly that he had been with another woman, as I could actually smell that distinctive smell of sex off his body. But despite my screaming at him, demanding that he be honest with me, he denied it to the bitter end.

Nothing, however, could convince me that I was wrong, and my fears were confirmed not long after that night. This particular day was lovely and warm, and even Mostafa was in good humour. I put May to bed and he went out for his usual 'coffee' with his friends, leaving me alone to watch TV. I decided to go onto the Internet and I took down the laptop. As I opened up the laptop, a little pop-up appeared in the corner of the screen saying, 'You have a new message from Tagged.' I hadn't a clue what Tagged was, but as I opened the page of this website it showed me pictures of women. In fact, it showed me the 120 women Mostafa had been 'socialising' with for more than a year: all living in Cyprus; in fact, all living in Limassol or nearby.

There was a chat history still open, and I discovered that he was talking to four women very regularly and a fifth on and off. He was sending messages saying things like, 'I really enjoyed last Saturday. See you the same time this week babe.' I felt nauseous reading through these messages, and then I clicked onto another area of the website only to see dozens of photos of these women posing naked, some in the most explicit poses I've ever seen, which they had sent to him.

I was furious. Without thinking for a minute, I picked up the phone and I called Mostafa. He answered with, 'Oh, what's up, babe?' I remember screaming at him, 'I found your Tagged account.' He just hung up. I tried to get back to him, but he just wouldn't answer.

I went to lie on the bed, and after a few minutes the door opened. Mostafa totally ignored me as I jumped up, grabbed the laptop and shoved it into his face to show him what I had found. Eventually he screamed that it was just for extra fun, nothing else. He said it was just a game. I wanted to kill him. I asked him how could he do that to me when I was sleeping with him, cooking and cleaning for him, trying my best to be a good Muslim wife. But he wasn't interested in apologising or explaining. I had always suspected that he was still cheating, but this was the icing on the cake for me. I screamed at him that I had obeyed all the rules he had forced on me, not even shaking a man's hand, and yet he had done this to me. But he didn't seem in the least bit bothered. He kept ignoring me and then he just walked out. For him it was yet another Friday night of drinking and doing whatever it was he did at weekends. I was distraught. But what could I do? I had made my bed, as my mammy would have said.

The next day I awoke with a sick feeling in my stomach. I hadn't heard Mostafa come in at whatever time he had managed to get home, but I knew that it was Saturday and, according to one of the messages on the website, he had a date that night. I tried to put it out of my mind as best I could, because I realised that I couldn't change him. I took May off, as usual, to her horse-riding class, which was given by a friend of mine just outside Limassol. I tried not to give anything away to May.

I told my friend what had happened. She advised me to get out now that I knew for a fact that Mostafa was still cheating. I knew I had to go, but I carried on as normal with May, and after the horse riding we headed to the beach, as we always did, and we had a lovely swim in the sea and did our body boarding for about three hours. To be honest, despite everything that had gone on with him, I felt so happy with my life in Cyprus, so privileged to be able to spend my weekends with my little girl, swimming in the sea all year round and enjoying the sunshine. Mostafa was the only thing I hated about my life, but everything else made up for that.

As we laughed and splashed about, I suddenly looked up to see Mostafa in my BMW in the car park on the beach. I was sick. This was something he would regularly do: search for us until he found us and then sit in his car, or *my* car, rather, staring out at us. I got May out of the sea and we dried off and headed back to the car. He was parked right beside me, as I had taken the second car. As we rushed to put our stuff into the boot, he lowered his window and said, 'Right, if you promise to forget what happened last night I will never do it again.'

I replied, 'I can't do that.' I had finally found the courage to say, 'No more.' I just felt at my wits' end. We both drove off and I knew that I had to get out for ever.

That week we argued non-stop. I moved into May's bedroom and made the decision to leave as soon as possible. Mostafa knew that it was over as well. I was probably stronger than I had ever been with him, and he could sense that. We argued at home, we argued on the phone, it never stopped. In one argument on the phone he screamed at me that he hated me, I was a cunt, I never gave him sex. I screamed back that I'd had enough of him and that I didn't have sex with him because there was a possibility I could get a sexually transmitted disease. I told him that our marriage was over and that he would find his clothes outside the door. And that's exactly what I did.

I bagged them and I threw them out onto the path. Within minutes, I heard a car screech to a halt outside and in he came with a face like thunder. I ran into the main bedroom, as May was asleep in her room and I didn't want to wake her, and he threw the bags back into the bedroom. He said that he would leave when he wanted to and not when I said. He told me if I did anything like that again, I was dead.

I went to a solicitor and asked for advice on what to do. I had spent a night with a friend of mine who lived in the mountains and she had told me to get out before it was too late. But I loved my home and thought, 'Why should I leave?' It appeared, though, that I had no other option. The solicitor informed me that because it was the family home and I was married to Mostafa, despite him not laying out a cent for it, I couldn't throw him out: I would have to leave. I was disgusted with how the law worked, as I loved my little home, but I knew that I would have to go, as Mostafa was obviously not going anywhere.

That night he came in acting like a maniac. He started to throw furniture around, smashing a table against the wall and throwing a chair at me, and I screamed at him that it was over and that I wanted him out. I threatened to ring the police if he didn't go, but that just made him worse. I told him that if he didn't leave I was going, to which he screamed that I wasn't to go anywhere as he wanted me where he could watch me at all times.

I had always loved my plants and spent a small fortune on plant-pots. I had this beautiful big white ceramic plant bowl with a lovely flowering plant inside it, and Mostafa ran over and kicked it repeatedly, smashing it to pieces. For me, this was the last straw, as I knew that he must want to destroy everything I loved, whether it was human or not. He just hated me and wanted to make sure that I knew that he would stop at nothing to destroy everything I had: even a worthless plant-pot.

I started to cry, and poor May woke up and ran down to me. She jumped onto my lap while I was sitting on a chair, and I picked up the phone and rang Nicola and asked if she would come down and pick us up. Mostafa went to grab the phone, but I pushed it out of his reach. This really pissed him off. With that he kicked out at me, but he actually managed to kick poor May full force in the stomach, and she crumpled over in agony, crying.

On realising that he had hurt May, he just shouted something in Arabic and ran out the door. With that, Nicola and her mum, Irene, arrived. The house was destroyed: broken furniture was flung everywhere and there was soil from the smashed plant-pots littering the floor. Their faces said it all. Poor May was sobbing uncontrollably, and they took her up to her room and put on a DVD, trying to take her attention away from what had just happened.

Irene walked over to me and said, 'Right, Louise, enough is enough: you have to leave him. I have no doubt in my mind that if you stay here he will kill you.' I knew this myself. Every attack got worse.

She rang the police and eventually they arrived at the house. They were their usual unhelpful selves. They probably had very good reason to be uninterested in domestic-violence cases amongst mixed marriages, to be honest, although back then I wasn't thinking like that. They were so used to taking on cases of domestic violence between a European woman and an Arabic man and spending weeks working on a case and getting it to court only to find out that the woman had dropped the charges. Whether or not the charges are dropped out of fear of what might happen after the case, it must irritate the police. And so they seemed to me to treat every domestic-abuse case between Arabic men and their European partners with scepticism, knowing that nine times out of ten any work they did to make the case stick would fall down at the last hurdle.

And this time their scepticism was high. They could clearly see that the house was wrecked. I told the police officers that Mostafa had kicked May but that he had intended the kick for me and not our child. They put out an APB for the car, but I could see they were annoyed because it looked like just another one of the cases they were used to seeing dropped at the last minute. They told me that it wasn't safe for me to stay at my house, so I agreed to go to my friend's home after I was checked out by a doctor.

Myself and May had to go to the hospital to make sure that everything was OK. I was sent for a head scan, and they also saw all the bruising and scratches on my body from Mostafa's previous attacks or from where over the last few days he had grabbed me violently during an argument. The hospital staff noted all this.

I then went to the police station in Limassol with the hospital report. I said that I wanted to press charges and they put a warrant out for Mostafa's arrest. They were ringing me all the time, updating me, but said that they couldn't find him anywhere. It later emerged that he had locked himself in our house and wouldn't open the door.

On the Monday morning, Mostafa left the house and went to a solicitor. Within an hour of the visit, he walked into the police station and handed himself in. I was shocked. They kept

him overnight and released him on bail on the Tuesday after an
initial court sitting.

He was told that he would have to hand in his passport and
report to the police station to sign on every Wednesday until
his next court appearance. He was also told to stay away from
myself and May.

It emerged that he had asked his solicitor to put May on a
stop list so that I couldn't leave the country with her, as he
wanted to start fighting for access. I was disgusted with this,
because he was a dreadful father who had little or no time for
his child and yet suddenly he wanted to be seen as a caring dad.
This stop list prevented me from even bringing May back home
to Ireland on holiday without him giving his approval, which I
knew he would never do, and I was devastated. I couldn't
understand how the law could work like this, but I had no
choice but to accept whatever was being dealt out to me. I was
also worried that if Mostafa took May to Syria then he, as a
Syrian, would hold all the parental rights as a father, and I
would have none, because Syria is not signed up to the Hague
Convention. The Hague Convention on the Civil Aspects of
International Child Abduction, to give it its full name, provides
legislation to protect existing child-custody arrangements and
to prevent parents involved in a custody dispute from crossing
international borders to find a more sympathetic court. But no
one listened to me. However, the legal profession reassured me
that this would never happen, because Mostafa could never
take May out of the country either, without me signing in
agreement. How wrong were they?

I moved back into the house with May, and I decided that I
would start divorce proceedings immediately. Mostafa came to
the door on a number of occasions begging me to let him in,
but I even surprised myself and I stuck to my guns all the time.
I was terrified of what might happen if he got annoyed at my
continual refusals, but I wasn't giving in.

May was just five years old at this time, and access rights
were being looked into by Social Services. They paid me regular

visits. The social worker told me that she was against Mostafa having May on overnight visits, as his apartment was not suitable for a little girl, which gave me some relief. In my mind he was an unfit father and should have had no right to see May, but who was I to say anything? I was only her mother.

Within weeks, the court date came for the assault charge. Mostafa and I were on talking terms, at least, but looking back at it now, in the cold light of day, I realise that he had been manipulating me even then, because he obviously wanted me on his side so that I would feel obliged to help him get a lighter sentence. And, of course, he won. On the day of the case, I was asked to take the stand, and I told the court that I had been assaulted by Mostafa. However, I asked the judge to be lenient on him. I only did this because if I was responsible for him being sent to prison I was scared of what he would do to me when he was released. Mostafa had warned me immediately after his arrest, before he had started to be nice to me, that if he was jailed I would pay big time. And I had to remember that he had May on a stop list, so if I was bad to him he would continue to be bad to me.

I was just like all the other European women I knew who lost their nerve at the last minute. I'd always wondered why they gave in to their partners after suffering so much abuse, yet I didn't realise at the time that I was one of those very women. I was just too caught up in the situation to see clearly.

And so, because I asked the judge to be lenient in sentencing Mostafa, he released him with a warning and told him that if it ever came to the attention of the court that he had assaulted me again within a two-year period, he would be imprisoned for a term of four or five years.

Mostafa was released that day. Although he never actually thanked me for pleading on his behalf, I think he was grateful in his own way, because he agreed to let me take May back to Dublin for a two-week break that Christmas. I had begged him to lift the stop list for weeks, and he knew that I needed to see my family badly. So, after a lot of pressure and begging, he got a designated signatory provided by the court to witness us signing the agreement that would allow me to leave the country for a fortnight with May.

The relief I felt that day was immense. It seemed slightly surreal; in fact, I was actually still in disbelief when I went to Larnaca airport to fly home. Although I had the letter in my hand overriding the stop-list stamp on May's passport, I was still terrified that Immigration wouldn't let me leave. But I was absolutely shocked when they didn't even ask for the letter. They disregarded the stop-list stamp completely and let me walk straight through into the departures area. I remember at the time thinking how easy it would have been for me to have walked away with my daughter before now.

I had just witnessed how the stop list meant nothing. Looking back, having had my daughter taken from me on a cancelled passport, I realise how easy it was for Mostafa to kidnap May. But, at the time, I was just so grateful to be getting away from him for a two-week break to the peace and quiet of my own family home. My divorce was being dealt with and soon I was to be free of Mostafa for ever. 2010 couldn't have come quickly enough for me.

CHAPTER FIVE

Life in Idlib

I learned very quickly while in Idlib in the suburb of Nairab, to be nice to my ex-husband. I had always tried to keep him calm and relaxed in Cyprus, but it was even more important here in his home town, because I had absolutely no rights in Syria. I was aware of that, and at any stage he could have beaten me to death and claimed that I had been unfaithful to him. I had to obey everything he said, as he could and would take May away from me in a flash and I might never see her again. I had to play the game to keep him calm, but it was killing me.

On the day after I arrived, Mostafa told me that he wanted to get May a Syrian passport. I asked him why he wanted to do that, and he replied, 'Why would you ask such a stupid question? She is half Syrian and I want her to go to school here.' He said that he had got a solicitor and had been told that the government would not allow him get May a passport unless he showed them an official marriage certificate. He said that he needed May's birth certificate and a copy of my passport and that we needed to get married in Syria to make everything happen.

I had no intention of doing this, but I had only just arrived and there was no way I was leaving without May, so I played along. I reluctantly gave him my passport, and he rang his cousin and they chatted away in Arabic. After they'd finished talking, Mostafa said that he would need to get my passport translated into Arabic and that he would do it in Idlib that day. He took my passport, did what he had to do and gave it back to me the next day.

I knew that he would bring up the marriage issue again once all the paperwork came through for him, but I decided to say nothing and do nothing about it until the time came.

I was extremely depressed though from the first day I arrived in Idlib: not just because I was a prisoner in Mostafa's home but also because he had everything thought out so well that I could not see an escape from this hellish scenario. I was absolutely horrified that he had thought everything through so in depth in such a short time and that he had every intention of ensuring that May stayed in Syria indefinitely. I found a schoolbag with the local school uniform rolled up inside it, and I felt sick to the stomach. He had no intention of ever letting me take May out of Syria again, but I had to put those thoughts to the back of my mind and take one day at a time.

I prayed day and night that the Turks would come. I prayed that they would manage to get through the strict armed checkpoints and make it to the house More importantly, I prayed that Mostafa would not be here when they came, or, if he was, that he would be fast asleep.

The house we were in was a million miles away from what I had considered a home back in Cyprus. There were no luxuries, no comforts – no food, even. We lived on yogurt and rice, and when Mostafa's cupboards were empty sometimes, his mother, whom I had never met, sent food over for us. I wasn't allowed to leave the house, even to go and buy food.

The house itself faced a tall cement wall, so we were not overlooked, but neither could I see if we had many neighbours, if any. Behind this wall lay the local primary school and a mosque. Waking to the sound of the prayers each morning at

5 a.m. terrified me and just heightened any fear I already held about this strict, religious country. The sound was alien to me and hearing it never got easier during my time there. I dreaded prayer time. I just had to try to block out my fears every day. It was the only way I could get through this ordeal.

On my second day in Nairab, May went to her aunty's nursery. I hated seeing her walk out the door, and once she was gone the horror of the situation hit me yet again. Mostafa knew how upset I was that he had sent her to the nursery, and I begged him not to let her go again. I think he simply did it to appease me, knowing that I wouldn't be around for long, but he didn't send her after that.

There was nothing for me to do each day but think. I would call Mandy as soon as Mostafa left to see if there was any news on the people smugglers arriving, but each time we spoke the news was never good. Mandy was also frantically contacting all the Irish newspapers and radio stations, as well as local and national politicians, and she was trying to get the Department of Foreign Affairs back home to intervene to get May and myself out, but nothing seemed to be working.

It was only when I eventually got back home that I realised that my story had been all over the front pages of every newspaper for days on end. Thankfully, Mandy and Yvonne, a journalist and now very good friend of the family, managed to keep the story from the UK press and foreign TV stations. They did this to prevent Mostafa discovering the coverage, knowing that he could become volatile at any moment and could even run away with May, leaving me abandoned in Syria. They were well aware of the dangers to my life and May's, but they were making calls to anyone and everyone in a position to highlight our case. I was totally unaware of exactly how much was being done back home; I was simply spending my days locked up in a horrible house with no air conditioning and little food. The minutes seemed like hours, and the days seemed like weeks. I lived for little May running through the doors each day so that I knew she was safe.

Her brother and sister clearly hated me, and I didn't realise until some time later that their mother lived just a few doors away on the same street, but they were forced to live with their father: it was just customary. I think they despised me for being with their father, probably believing that if it weren't for me they would all be a family living together in one house. They had no idea how much I wished they were.

Every day I would struggle to look through the windows to the outside world, but it was hard to see anything, as there were bars and wire mesh on each and every window. I don't know whether Mostafa had put these up himself either for my benefit or for security purposes, but it only enhanced the prison-like surroundings I was already in.

Even going to the toilet was a horrible chore in that house. There were two markings on the floor, where you placed your feet, and then you literally crouched over a hole in the ground to go to the toilet. Instead of toilet roll, there was a hosepipe coming out of the wall, which you used to wash yourself down, although there was no way you could dry yourself. The smell in the toilet area was horrendous – and it was right beside the kitchen. However, Mostafa also had a proper bathroom with a real toilet, as we would know it, but there was still no toilet paper, and a hose was used here as well.

In the kitchen there were two big sinks and lots of presses with no doors, which were filled with pots and pans but no food. I remember when I first turned on the tap in the kitchen sink, filthy brown-coloured water flooded out. Even leaving it running for ages didn't make a difference. There was no way I would drink the water, even if it was boiled first. There was also a big fridge, which didn't work, and an old Aga-type cooker. If there had been food around I would have used it, but there often wasn't, so it simply stood there like an ornament.

In some areas of Syria it is customary to eat food with pitta bread as opposed to cutlery. Families sit on a carpet and enjoy a meal served on a large shared plate. Although to me it was an unusual way of eating, I devoured every morsel when Mostafa's mother sent food over.

I remember seeing about fifty big black bags filled with black tea in one of the bedrooms. The smell of it was disgusting and would waft through the house all day, so I made sure to always shut the door as tightly as possible.

One day, as I walked around the place aimlessly, I noticed that there was a back door with no bars or locks on it. As I gently pushed it, it opened. I couldn't believe it. I made my way outside, sheepishly, in case I was spotted, and saw that there was a staircase that led to a top floor, on which you could actually have built another level of the house. I saw a hole cut out in the shape of a window, which I reckoned they had intended to put glass into, but it had just been left open instead. When I stretched out of it to look outside, I could see what looked like a twelve-foot drop to the ground. There was no way that May could survive a drop like that, and my immediate thought of using it as an escape route if the Turks came was scuppered. As I sneaked up the staircase, with no hijab on, I realised that I could see all the houses in the area for some distance and so, in case I was spotted, I quickly made my way back inside.

That afternoon, Mostafa came home and left just as quickly. It gave myself and May another chance to chat. She told me that she had met her grandmother and grandfather, and that her granny was a very cross woman but her granddad was 'OK'. She said that her father's sister, her aunty, also lived with her grandparents. She described her as having 'really long hair' and being 'very nice'. She said that her aunty had minded her before I came. I was trying to find out who lived where and which relatives were around us.

Later, Mostafa came in with food from his mother's house, rice and lentils, but I found it very hard to look at him that day. I remember bursting into tears and begging him to let me go home with May. I actually felt a pang of compassion for him, because I knew that this life was so different to what he had been used to back in Cyprus. I was surprised at how he seemed to regard it as normal. I even told him, and at the time I genuinely meant it, that if he let us go he could come and live in Dublin and I would look after him financially. I meant it, because on that day in particular I felt that he had been brainwashed into believing that this life of bombs, gunfire and murder in Syria was normal. I knew he loved his life in Cyprus and this was a million miles away from what he had been used to. I'd found it hard to understand why he would rather be here, in a country caught up in conflict, when he so clearly loved the good life in Cyprus. But I'd had time to think that day, and I felt that Mostafa might simply have come back to Syria because he felt he had to be near his family during wartime. I actually felt sorry for him having to live like this, because I believed that he was torn between the great life he had in a Western country with myself and May and what was expected of him in his own country.

I begged him to let me leave. I told him that I had sat all day listening to bombs exploding and gunfire all around me and I was terrified. It was a million miles away from what I was used to and what our child was used to. I was losing it in this house, where the only thing I had to do all day was watch TV and the only stations were news channels showing me what was happening right on our doorstep. But his only response was that he would take me out that night into Idlib.

I tried to explain to him that I didn't want to go into this town. I wanted to go home. He asked the kids to go to their grandparents' house for an hour to allow us to talk, and I think he believed that once I'd had one outburst that would be it: I would accept things as they were and carry on. But he was so wrong.

Once the kids left, a huge row exploded and I picked up a chair and flung it across the room. And, for the first time since I had met Mostafa, he just stood there and accepted it. And all he would say was, 'What's done is done. I can't change it. May will never leave Syria, never ever, so get that into your head.' I told him that I couldn't live like this, I wanted my family, to which he replied, 'Sure, they can come here. They can have holidays here.' I remember thinking, 'Is he mad? Has he finally lost it? How the hell can he think this is a place for a holiday?'

I knew there was no point in arguing. That evening, we didn't go out, as he had suggested. I acted as normally as I could, for May's sake. We all watched TV. Mostafa had European and American stations, as did most people in Syria, despite their government's hatred of the US and the West. Yet in the back of my mind, as the call for prayer went out yet again, I secretly prayed that the smugglers would arrive quickly and save us.

I remember thinking that Islam was Mostafa's and his countrymen's sole reason to live, and I reflected on how different Catholicism was. We go to Mass and tell a priest our sins through choice, but with Islam there are set times to pray and Muslims must pray at those times. In Idlib, the calls to prayer went on for about 15 minutes each time, and whenever they started I yearned more and more for home. And once the call started, any conversation with Mostafa stopped. He didn't have a prayer mat, even in his house, yet he acknowledged the calling and respected those 15 minutes with silence. He wasn't outwardly religious, yet he seemed to be totally torn by Islam in other ways. I knew that I was fighting a losing battle early on. Mostafa would never give in to me. I was there for the long haul unless I made my own escape. Eventually I went to bed, feigning sickness.

The next day I actually did feel sick. I was so thirsty. But I couldn't bring myself to drink the water, no matter how many times I boiled it. I knew if I did I would feel twice as sick. I asked May if she would wake her daddy, as I needed him to go to the shop, but it took him so long to get up that I had no choice but to boil enough water to make a cup of coffee. I drank it very reluctantly, knowing that it could actually make me feel even more nauseous, but between my lack of fluids and the heat I was getting weak from dehydration and so I had to take the risk. When Mostafa eventually got up he drove to the shop, but instead of buying water he bought little cartons of juice. I didn't care what they were; I just wanted to know I could drink them and wouldn't die of cholera as a result.

That evening Mostafa told me to dress up, as we were going to meet his cousin and his wife for dinner. I didn't want to leave May alone because I always worried that something would happen to her when I was gone, but I wouldn't take no for an answer. Finally he agreed that May could come with us.

I knew that I would have to wear the black hijab that he had given me that first night when I arrived. But when it was time to go, in the pitch dark, so that no one would see me, Mostafa ushered me into the car, telling me to hold on to the hijab tightly around my chin until we got to his cousin's home, as I just couldn't close it properly. The fact that I couldn't put on my own hijab was really frustrating him.

As we drove along, about two hundred metres up the road, Mostafa pointed to a big ten-foot-high wall and he told me that his parents' house was behind it. We carried on down a long dirt track into a filthy area stinking of sewage and littered with dirt, yet Mostafa didn't even seem to notice.

We arrived at his cousin's house, and it turned out that it was the same cousin who had lived in Cyprus: a man I had socialised, eaten and drunk with, and the same man who had helped Mostafa to get me out of the shower on the night he knocked me unconscious. And here he was standing in front of me dressed in Arab clothing, a million miles removed from the person I had known in Cyprus, a person who drank whisky, danced all night and loved life. He too had become a changed man once he crossed the border into Syria. It was shocking to see his transformation. But he welcomed me in with open arms.

It turned out that the house had been left to him by his parents. Previously he had been penniless and living in a hellhole of an apartment in an area ravaged by poverty, and so for him having a proper house was like winning the lottery. He was so grateful to have a home he could call his own. That night he brought me into his home to meet his wife, whom I had met once before, when Mostafa brought us to Syria so that he could take May to see his parents, very early on in our relationship. I had actually been to Syria twice before May's abduction. The first time was to Aleppo, when myself and May stayed in a hotel and Mostafa went to his home town of Nairab in Idlib. The second visit, which was just for two or three days, was after Mostafa had divorced his wife and we had married in Limassol. It was the only time in our marriage we were in any way happy. We went to stay in Latakia, where his cousin lived. That time, I was actually left on my own with his cousin and his wife in a dilapidated apartment block until the next day, when Mostafa brought May back. I vividly remember looking out of Mostafa's cousin's flat window and seeing old food and piles and piles of rubbish lying all along the roadside and a big red truck driving by, spitting out something as it drove along. It turned out that it was spraying some sort of poison that killed mosquitoes, as the area was ravaged with them.

I was shocked that neither Mostafa's cousin nor his wife was at all surprised at me being there in Idlib. It was as if they were unaware that Mostafa had kidnapped May and that I was in Syria against my will, simply because it was the only way I could be with my child. It seemed as if everyone was acting normal. Mostafa asked his cousin's wife to fix my hijab, telling them that we were all going into town. She was wearing a house hijab; women always had a garment for the house and very elaborate clothing for going out. Unfortunately, I didn't have the latter. Once she had fixed my headscarf she went into a room to dress herself and her daughter, who was about 15 years old. Within minutes they both appeared in the most beautiful clothing, black full-length robes with sparkling jewels all down the sides, and their hijabs were stunning. I felt like the poor relation this time.

We all bundled into the car, looking up to the rooftops as we left in case there were snipers around. We made our way towards a checkpoint. This one was manned by a local group wearing casual clothing, like jeans and sweatshirts. Mostafa pulled the car in to the side of the road before we got there and he asked his cousin to drive. I was to learn why later. We carried on towards the group, which was heavily armed with sub-machine guns, and thankfully they just signalled for us to keep going. The relief I felt was unreal as I spotted more men hiding behind sandbags.

We got into town after passing another checkpoint, this time an army one, and we parked on a shopping street. All around this filthy street were stalls selling school uniforms, as the school term had just started in Syria. Mothers were walking around with young children, rummaging through these street stalls. As we started walking around, I asked Mostafa how he was going to pay for anything we bought, knowing full well he had no money. He told me to give him any euros I had with me and he would go into a currency-exchange shop to change it into Syrian pounds. When he came out, he handed his cousin some of my money and started to walk off. I had May's hand firmly in my grip, because it was obvious that it wasn't a very nice or safe area. As we walked along, little May suddenly screamed at me to look down on the ground, and as I did a number of cockroaches ran across our feet. They were crawling out of the drains and running blindly everywhere. I was hysterical, yet no one else seemed bothered at all. This was life as they knew it.

Then, within minutes of our arrival, we heard gunfire and people started running left, right and centre. I told Mostafa that I wanted to leave immediately. He tried to convince me that the gunfire was a good distance away, but I didn't care how far it was: I was terrified and so was May. Her little startled face said it all.

I looked up and saw snipers or spies, I'm not sure which, crouched down on the roofs. I was terrified, knowing that at any second they could just open fire on us, for no reason. Thankfully, Mostafa saw them as well. He finally agreed to leave and said we would go to a restaurant to get off the street.

We went back to the car and drove off to what they called a five-star restaurant. It was the type of place we would never go into at home, but it was obvious that this was considered a nice place for local people to go. The restaurant reminded me of a bingo hall, and it had horrible tables and hard chairs, yet the people there were very well dressed and obviously had money. We ordered food, and as soon as we were finished we headed off. We went back to Mostafa's cousin's house for a drink, and I remember looking at my ex-husband sitting in a big armchair as if he hadn't a care in the world.

We drove back home, and the next morning, as usual, I woke to find him gone and the doors locked to keep me in. I rang Mandy to see if there was any news or any help coming, but she once again had nothing new to tell me. I could hear the exhaustion in her voice and the lack of positivity. She was trying to be upbeat, saying, 'It will happen, don't worry,' but I knew her well enough to read between the lines. It wasn't looking good from where I was sitting, that was for sure.

I told her how bad things were in Idlib and that Mostafa was still thinking of sending May to school. It was a nightmare scenario for me, because I didn't want her in school speaking Arabic and chanting from the Koran. In my mind, every day she was there she would be brainwashed into conforming to a religion she knew nothing about. He took her to playschool one day, which was run by his sister, but May hated it. Yet every morning he would take May with him when his two older children left for school, and I never knew if she had been at school too until she came home and told me about her day. It seemed she was always left with her grandparents. I think Mostafa just didn't want May around me at all. Her school uniform still sat alongside her schoolbag, and I worried every night in case Mostafa decided to go against my will and take her to school. I prayed and prayed that this would all end soon and we would escape in one piece.

My biggest fear about May being away from me all day in her grandparents' house was that a protest might take place in the village, or it might come under attack, and what then? How would I get to my baby? When she came back in that day I had never been so relieved to see her.

While I'd been waiting for May, I remember hearing goats out the back and going to see them: funny-looking goats with big, bulbous heads, but I was fascinated by them. It turned out that a herder would take them by the house every day, and after that day I would look out for them, waiting to hear their bells ring as they came towards the house. Under normal circumstances it would be a stupid fascination to have, but for me, in that boring house, it was a treat each day to spend 20 minutes or so having a cigarette and watching the goats make their little journey. I was very careful not to let the herder see me, though, because I knew that if he did, Mostafa would kill me. For sure.

On the Saturday after I arrived in Idlib, Mandy told me that I would need to put some sort of marking on or near the house in case the Turkish guys came to find us. I remembered that the door to the roof was left open most days, which was the only access to the outside world available to me, so I thought I would put a white towel up there, where they would be able to see it clearly.

Mostafa had gone out, so I ran out and up the stairs just as it was starting to get dark, and I placed the towel where it would be visible from the street. I wasn't wearing the hijab, as I had planned on getting up there and down again as quickly as possible, but just as I arrived on the roof I heard a woman's voice say, '*Marhaba*' ('Hello' in Arabic). I looked down on the street and recognised the woman: I had seen her before, walking up and down with her daughter. I knew that she was aware I was in the house because they would both strain their necks to look in every time they passed. I didn't know if she was part of Mostafa's family, but she had seen me, so I couldn't run. I replied to her in Arabic, and she was delighted. She was surprised that I spoke her language, but I explained that I only had a little Arabic. She asked me over for coffee. I refused and said I couldn't go right then, but I would call over another day. She seemed pleased, but I was sick with worry because I didn't know who she was or who she was related to, and I knew that Mostafa would beat me severely if he ever found out that I had been on the roof, and with no hijab covering me. I rushed back in, having placed the towel in the best spot I could find so that it would be visible to anyone coming along the street.

I called Mandy and told her that I had been caught outside. She told me not to panic. I had to just sit tight until Mostafa came home and pray he knew nothing.

When he came in, everything was as normal. He told me that we would be going out again that night and that I was to cover up. I flipped. I screamed at him that this was not how I lived. I said I was sick of seeing women covered up and that I didn't believe that was their choice. He screamed back at me, 'It's not about, you, Louise; it's about my honour.' I was disgusted with him. I didn't even want to go out anywhere because I was terrified of the protests and the gunfire. I was also hoping against hope that the Turks would come that night. Mandy couldn't guarantee it, but she was hopeful too. However, I knew that I had to do everything I could not to raise any suspicion, and if that meant going out then it had to be done. I had to just hope they didn't arrive while I was gone.

We all bundled into the car, including May, and we headed into town, where Mostafa bought some bananas. Within minutes of leaving the shop, the gunfire started again and I could hear what sounded like bombs exploding, but he wasn't perturbed at all. Once again we got into the car and drove to the same restaurant we'd been in the night before. We met Mostafa's cousin and his wife there, and after eating we all headed to a local park. I was terrified that we would get caught up in a gun battle or that a bomb could go off at any minute, but none of them seemed at all bothered.

As we got to the park, Mostafa's phone rang. It was Mandy, asking for me, because my phone was back at the house. I'd decided to leave the phone at home that day, because I knew that Mostafa would feel like he was in control if Mandy had to ring his number. It would take away any suspicions he had about me and my mobile phone. I had already told Mandy that I would leave the phone at home that day and that she should phone Mostafa if she wanted me. I thought it relaxed him a little, knowing that I didn't need to have my phone with me day and night. I acted very calm and said that we were having a great time and that everything was fine. In the middle of the conversation, May asked me to go to the toilet with her. She was grabbing my hand and pleading with me to take her, but thankfully Mostafa told me to carry on talking to Mandy and he would take May. I was relieved. I told Mandy that it was OK, Mostafa had taken May to the toilet, and I casually let her know that I was with his cousin, who at this stage was staring at me, listening and hanging on to my every word to report back to Mostafa.

Mandy started talking in code, saying Sean was still off the drink, which meant the men were coming. She said it would definitely be that night. I felt butterflies in my stomach, but I had to stay calm. I said, 'That's great. I will talk to you later,' and I clicked Mostafa's phone off.

All of a sudden a text arrived. It said, 'Oh babes, thinking of you so much and love you so much. Please let me know you're OK,' followed by about ten kisses. I knew the sender's name: it was an English woman Mostafa had been with in Cyprus – one of his many conquests. As soon as he came back, I turned on him to take his attention away from the fact that Mandy had rung me on his phone. I asked him what the hell was going in with him and this woman, to which he simply replied, 'Oh, I can't help it. She is just mad about me and keeps texting.' I knew I had rattled him by finding this text, so it lifted any suspicion he might have had about my conversation with Mandy.

I turned to his cousin and I said, 'Do you know he has taken May? He kidnapped his own daughter. I looked after you in Cyprus, and I respected you. How do you think I feel about being here against my will?'

The cousin tried to calm me down, saying Mostafa was getting annoyed. He said, 'Come back to my place and let's talk about it.' Poor May didn't know what to do. I felt so sorry for her. Mostafa looked livid.

We drove back to his cousin's house and the whole argument started again. We had been quiet as mice in the car. When Mostafa was in the toilet, his cousin asked me what was going on. I told him that Mostafa had snatched May from Cyprus and that neither of us, myself or May, wanted to be there. He simply looked at me and said, 'Look. May will have a good life here in Syria. She will have good schooling and a good upbringing with her father. You two are always arguing. You need to sort it out.'

I couldn't believe his reaction. I looked over at his wife, who was standing by the door, and I could see the shock on her face at my revelation. But, as a good Muslim wife, she said nothing. She knew her place only too well. I could see that she felt sorry for me but was unable to do anything about the situation. She obviously hadn't even contemplated the possibility that Mostafa had abducted May.

We left their home that night, and although we had argued I genuinely felt pity for Mostafa. In my mind, May and myself were going to escape that night with the help of the Turkish guys, and I knew that once we were gone Mostafa would be distraught and would have no hope left. I remember thinking how hard it would be for him to live in Syria without us, but then I realised that on many occasions during the six days I had been there I had given him the chance to let me go. I had begged him to let myself and May leave, promising him that nothing would happen to him, giving him my word that I would even look after him financially if he wanted to leave too. But he had made his mind up.

As we drove along, he got a phone call. I could see a change come over him almost instantly. His face froze, and he turned to me with a look of hatred and bewilderment in his eyes. He said, 'That was my cousin. He has told me that there is an international arrest warrant out for me for kidnapping May and that you are in all of the newspapers in Ireland.'

I was in total shock, but knew that I had to stay calm if I was to get out of this one. I played the game as usual, feigning disbelief at what he had said. I said, 'Who did that?' I played it very cool, even though I was sick inside. I said, 'You mean to tell me that I am in the paper with my daughter? What paper?'

He seemed to fall for it. He said, 'Don't panic. I'll find out which one. I'll ring him back.'

I said, 'Why the hell is there an arrest warrant out for you? If this is true, Mostafa, this means that you can never go back to Cyprus, and if you can't go back, that means May and myself can't go either. This means I am stuck here, Mostafa, for ever.' I really played it up, pretending to be totally oblivious to whatever had apparently happened while I was in Syria. I was aware that at any time he could cop on that I was well aware of what was going on in Cyprus and Ireland, and if that happened I knew I was dead. He could turn nasty in a split second, and I knew that the consequences would be horrendous.

Mostafa's phone rang again, and this time it was a friend of his who read out a newspaper article from top to bottom: 'Louise stated on national TV that she was distraught over her daughter's kidnapping. Her ex-husband had rung and told her to sell all their possessions and her cars and go to Syria if she wanted to see her child again . . .'

I had been on RTÉ's *Prime Time* via Skype the night that myself and Mandy stayed in Turkey, before I walked into Syria. I felt my legs turn to jelly, but I had to hold my nerve. Plead total ignorance. I wanted the ground to open up and swallow me. He turned to me, looking like an absolute madman, and, grinding his teeth, he said, 'You have been on national television in Ireland telling people that I kidnapped May. What the hell are you playing at?'

I very calmly said, 'Mostafa. How the hell could I have been on national television in Ireland? I was in Cyprus when you took May, then in hospital on the Saturday, and then I made my way from Cyprus to here. Your friends even saw me in Cyprus, because they were all bloody following me everywhere I went. So how the hell did I get to Ireland to go on television and then get back here? And I can hardly walk with the pain in my hips. Are you mad?'

Somehow, though I don't know why, he believed me. He calmed down. I could see his mind working, but he said no more.

I would have to get to ring Mandy, to warn her that Mostafa knew something was up, but I was terrified in case communications had been cut off in the village. It happened quite a bit; I would be on the phone and suddenly the line would drop. At first I thought that perhaps my calls to Ireland were being monitored as part of a security check, but I soon realised that all mobile signals would be blocked as soon as the government heard even a sniff of a planned protest. They did this to stop any communication between groups of protesters, hoping this would scupper any protest. It never did.

I remembered how I had gone into a total panic one day in Turkey when I was trying to get through to Mostafa, as the line just kept going *beep beep beep beep*. I honestly thought that he had gone on the run with May, or worse. I rang his cousin and somehow managed to get through to him, and he told me that phones had been useless for hours because of trouble in the area. That was when I first realised the government messed with the phones. Within minutes of that call, a friend of Mostafa's who was still living in Limassol rang me back and asked if I was in Hatay Province. I told him that I was and that I was desperately trying to get through to Mostafa. He told me the same story about the phones but explained that it was only mobile numbers that were blocked, so he would call Mostafa on a landline.

Mostafa later told me that this same guy had been arrested by the Cypriot police shortly after he had spoken to me on the phone, and because he was an illegal immigrant he was immediately deported back to Syria. I felt terrible about this, because I had no ill feelings towards this man and yet he was sent back to a country in the depths of war. But, in fairness, that was the chance they took, staying illegally in a country. It wasn't my fault, but I still felt bad over it.

But the day that Mostafa's cousin told him about the media coverage of the kidnapping, I just prayed that I could get through to Mandy to warn her that things might be very different now that Mostafa suspected there was a warrant out for his arrest. I knew he must have been thinking that it was Mandy who had alerted the police to what he had done, or one of my aunties. For now, he seemed to believe it wasn't me. Thank God.

I now had to concentrate on escaping, and tonight was to be the night. I remember thinking all the way back in the car, 'What if they have come already and I'm not there?' And, 'What if they are already there and are sitting outside in a car and Mostafa sees them?' Every scenario was going through my head. But when we finally turned the corner onto the road and I saw no sign of anything, I was petrified. I kept thinking they might be hiding in the olive trees to the side of the house or around the corner, waiting to see a sign of life in the house, but my gut feeling overtook me, even though I tried to blot out the feeling that maybe they wouldn't come at all. But I knew that I had to keep that thought to the back of my mind and plan ahead in the hope that a better scenario took place.

When we got into the house, Mostafa was complaining of a headache he'd had most of the day. It was the best thing that could have happened, because it gave me an excuse to give him a 'painkiller'. Little did he know that what I was actually giving him was Xanax, tablets Mandy had given me, which were basically a heavy sedative. If I was in luck, they would knock him out and leave me time to escape with May when the men arrived. I suddenly got excited again. Maybe it would happen in an hour, two hours. I just kept telling myself that this was it; myself and May were going to start our journey back home tonight. It was finally going to happen.

Within ten minutes of giving Mostafa two Xanax and a bottle of water, he was conked out in front of the television. He woke up briefly and said he was going to bed.

The three children were fast asleep in the main sitting room, and I remember suddenly panicking about how I would get May out of the room during the night without waking her siblings. It was something that hadn't occurred to me until that very moment. May was positioned on the mattress closest to the door. I had put her there from day one, thinking ahead to the night when we would escape, and luckily she was still in this spot. I just prayed that the creaky door wouldn't make too much noise when I did go in to get her, because I knew that the other kids could wake up and get their father.

I checked on Mostafa a few times, and each time he was snoring. So, after about an hour, I started to pack my clothes and some for May. I put on my hijab and a full-length dress and I waited, watching out of the window for any sign of life. I didn't know what these men would look like, but I knew that they would most likely be armed and speak Turkish. I had given Mandy the best directions I could to the house, so it was all in the hands of God now.

It was a very hot night, and I was keeping one eye on the bedroom door and one eye on the road outside, and in between looking at these two I was also trying to watch my mobile phone in case they rang. I waited and waited, terrified that Mostafa would wake before they arrived and see me in full dress and know immediately what was happening. For some reason I went to the front door to see if he had locked it, and, to my shock, it was open. This was the first time this had happened, and it convinced me more than anything else that this was it: I was going to be saved with May that night. The door being left open was fate intervening. Mostafa had conked out before he'd had a chance to lock it.

But as I waited the minutes felt like hours, and the hours dragged on, with my sense of dread increasing all the time. I had no fear of the strange men who were due to arrive; I didn't think twice about them. I was simply terrified of Mostafa waking before the plan could be put into action.

Then, just after 3 a.m., I got the text message I was dreading. It was from Mandy. She simply said, 'It's off tonight, love. Don't get disheartened. They are going to try tomorrow.' I wanted to break down and cry, but what could I do? It was out of my control.

I quietly walked into where May was sleeping, kissed her gently on the head and carried on into the bedroom, being careful not to wake my oblivious husband, sleeping peacefully in our bed.

I put away all the items I had packed, hung my clothes up in the wardrobe just as they were before and climbed into bed. I felt weak with desperation and disappointment. But I had to try to carry on as normal. No matter what, I had to make Mostafa believe that nothing had changed. The charade had to go on. I had little hope that the men really would come the next day, but I had to stay positive. I dozed off after a little while, but within two hours I was woken again by the call to prayer from the nearby mosque.

I went on with my day as usual, washing clothes, cleaning and sitting around with a cup of coffee and a cigarette. There was no sign of Mostafa waking, which panicked me slightly. I remember thinking, 'What if he is unconscious for much longer, what will happen then?' It would mean that he would have to go to hospital and there they would realise that I had drugged him. Thank God, after checking on him every ten minutes or so, he eventually woke at around 2 p.m.

He was in a very bad mood and looked very groggy. He told

me to get May ready, as he wanted to take her out. I hated it when he did this, which was every couple of days, because I never knew where he was going or if he would come back. Every time he did it I begged him not to, to leave May with me, but, of course, he didn't care how I felt. On this day it emerged that one of his sisters was coming back home from Dubai, where she had been living, but May had to tell me that, as Mostafa would never give me the satisfaction of informing me of anything he was doing or people he was seeing. It was just another way for him to torture me. He had threatened me a few times over the previous few days, telling me that if I wasn't happy I could go, but I would never see May again. I never knew how his mind worked.

That afternoon, I watched at the window for May's return. Eventually I spotted her, running ahead of her father, and she ran into the house and into my arms. I remember thinking how desperate a situation we were in but also how lucky I was to actually be with her at all.

Mandy had texted me to say that she'd had no word from the traffickers all day and not to build my hopes up. And, despite staying awake all night with my phone on vibrate in the hope that they would just suddenly arrive, nothing happened. I had planned to just leave everything if they rang or texted; there would be no planning, like the night before. I would just grab May and we would escape via the roof if need be, but that opportunity never came.

Over the next day or two I got very sick. In fact, by Tuesday I was so sick that I begged Mostafa to call a doctor. He refused point blank, not wanting anyone to know that I was there, but I became so ill that I couldn't even put my feet to the floor. He could see how bad I was, but he showed no emotion. I was vomiting and had severe diarrhoea, and my head was spinning. The pain in my back was horrendous, and it was made worse by my hip condition. Every bone ached, and although it was baking hot I was shaking with the cold. But he still didn't budge on getting a doctor.

By Thursday I honestly thought that I was dying, and I suddenly realised what the problem was. Mostafa's daughter had been taking my bottled water from the fridge and filling up the bottle with tap water. Mostafa and his family were all immune to whatever parasites or bacteria were in the water, but I wasn't, and it was the source of the extreme gastric bug I'd picked up.

Eventually, when he saw me getting no better, Mostafa said that his sister was a pharmacist and he would ask her to come round. Later that day, in she walked, covered with a hijab and a long, flowing dress. She said nothing to me. No eye contact was made. She simply directed me to turn on my side and produced a massive needle. As she jabbed me in the bum, I thought, 'This is it, he is killing me,' but I was too sick to care or to do anything about it. All that went through my mind at the time was, 'If this is it, let it be quick.' I fell asleep afterwards.

I woke hours later and felt so much better. I couldn't believe it. I looked in the mirror and saw that I was green in the face but was definitely on the mend. That night, Mostafa came in with some food his mother had prepared, rice stuffed in aubergine, and I managed to actually eat some of it.

I had never met Mostafa's sister, the pharmacist, before. I knew that he had three brothers and five sisters, but I had only ever met one sister and one brother. I remember thinking, 'What must they think of this situation? They know I am here yet they have stayed away.' I couldn't make it out at all.

The very next day, poor May was struck down with the same virus. It broke my heart to look at her shivering and vomiting. It knocked her for six. She was on the toilet screaming in pain, and because there was no toilet paper she had to keep using the hose to wash herself down. She was in a really bad way.

Mostafa took the other two kids out of the house for a while, but as soon as they came back he would leave again and they would beat each other up, biting and pulling each other's hair. They behaved like animals, but even though I wanted their father to chastise them, especially as May was so sick, I was also hesitant about telling him about their bad behaviour most of the time, because he would beat them with a belt regularly, leaving them in agony. Although he hadn't actually started this with May yet, I knew it was coming, and it was yet another reason for us to get out as quickly as possible. Poor May had to witness all this as she lay on the bed in agony, but there was nothing I could do. She got better bit by bit, but Mostafa refused to get her help. The only option he gave me was for him to take her to hospital, without me, but I was terrified of letting her go, so I had to just try to care for her myself as best I could.

I remember when she was really sick one morning, Mostafa and myself had an argument about the fact that we didn't even have any air in the house because he was so determined to keep me a prisoner. I told him it was also a fire risk and that he would have to do something about it. But it all went over his head. There was no way he was giving me an inch. I lost it with him that day. I screamed at him, calling him a bastard and telling him that I would never have been there if it hadn't been for him kidnapping our child. I told him I hated him and that I wanted to kill him, and with that he screamed at me, saying I wasn't in Cyprus now, and he dragged me into the bathroom and punched me repeatedly. He punched me so hard that I fell and banged my head on the tiled floor.

He continued to beat me, smashing into the back of my head, and then he punched me in the side. I felt myself losing power, but he grabbed me as I fell and dragged me across the bathroom into the bedroom, where he threw me across the floor.

I saw May trying to crane her head from her bedroom to see what was going on. She was screaming, 'I want my mama, I want my mama.' I was devastated. He simply shoved me and said, 'Die, you bitch.' I was in agony and my head was pounding, but I was worried sick about poor May, as she had seen everything.

I shouted at him to please get me help. I said, 'Mostafa, I need a doctor, my head is throbbing.' But he simply walked over to May's bedroom, took a glass of 7 Up off the table and flung it over me.

Poor May started crying, asking why he had done that to me. She said, 'Baba, why did you throw 7 Up at Mama?'

And he said, 'I am just cooling her down to make her feel better.'

I could feel the stickiness of the Seven Up all over me, and I hated him so much at that moment.

CHAPTER SIX

Our First Steps
Towards Freedom

In the days that followed the allegations over the newspaper articles, Mostafa had said nothing of what had happened. I had tried to make conversation with him, but, although he knew that there was absolutely no way I could have gone to Ireland after he abducted May and got back so quickly, he still doubted me. I could see it in his eyes. He simply ignored everything I said or did, and acted as if I wasn't even there. Any trust he'd had in me was gone, and I knew it.

It was coming close to my time to go back to Cyprus, as he knew that I was due to have my operation within days, but there was no way I was going back, no matter what. On the eve of the assault I had pleaded with him to extend my visa. I did everything I could to make him feel that I wanted to make our relationship happen again.

The day after Mostafa assaulted me, I picked myself up and tried to pull myself together. I hated Mostafa, but I knew I had to try to get him back on my side. I cleaned the house vigorously for two hours. I remember sweeping out the house with the typical straw brush all Syrian women use, which almost looks like a witch's broom. I swept all of the floors, making sure that there wasn't a sign of dust, and then I hosed them all down with a hosepipe that extended from the hallway all around the house. In each room there was a drain into which you would sweep the water away. Again, this was typical of all Syrian homes.

Afterwards, I dusted everywhere with a wet cloth. I wanted the place to look lovely for Mostafa. I was drained at the end of it, but I still made the effort to cook him a lovely dinner: egg fried rice and one of his favourite dishes, tzatziki, a Greek dip made of natural yogurt, finely diced cucumber, garlic, salt and olive oil. I put on what make-up I had, dressed up in my long white dress and white cardigan, and washed and styled my hair. I was willing to do anything to make him agree to me staying on for longer.

When Mostafa came in, he was red-faced and seemed very uptight. His hands were in fists by his sides. I think he didn't know what to expect from me when he came back. I could see him looking around at what I had done, but he didn't acknowledge all the hard work I had put in despite being in absolute agony with my hips. He simply sat down to watch TV, and I brought his food in and placed it in front of him on the floor, and we both ate quietly without saying a word. He had brought the two older kids back with him, and they went into the bedroom to play with May.

I casually mentioned that I had seen the news earlier that day and that the situation looked particularly bad in our area. They had been reporting on the weekend riots, and it was shocking to see people being shot dead and bodies lying on the ground so close to where we were living. I made him a cup of chai, and I ate humble pie and apologised for my behaviour. I explained to him that I was only worried about May and that we might all be killed in one of these bomb blasts or gun attacks. I also made it clear that May would never have become sick if he hadn't taken her to Syria in the first place.

I pleaded with him, but he continued to stare at the TV, saying nothing. I told him that I knew my visa was nearly up.

He had screamed that at me that very morning saying that it was going to be up the next day and I was going back to Cyprus whether I liked it or not. In fact, he had said that if I didn't go, if my family didn't pay for a flight back for me the next day, he would personally go to the police and have me arrested. I knew that one phone call from him once my visa had expired would have seen me dragged from the house and locked up in a Syrian prison, no questions asked, and I knew that I was at his mercy.

I told him that May would really miss me if I left now and it would be better for me to stay, at least a bit longer, before I went to Cyprus for my operation, so that she could get used to the idea that I would finally have to go. I begged and pleaded with him, saying I wouldn't be able to travel the next day in any case, given the pain I was in. When I saw that ranting on about my illness was having no effect on him, I used Mandy as my bait and said she hadn't sorted the money for us yet and it would only take another few days. He still thought that Mandy was selling everything belonging to me back in Cyprus and was going to forward the money to us in Syria. I basically told him everything I knew he wanted to hear. I said that if he let me stay for another 15 days, as that was the maximum amount allowed to foreigners on visits, I would make sure that he was financially comfortable until I came back to them.

I said, 'Mostafa, please think about it.'

He suddenly turned to me with a face like thunder and said, 'Right. I will think about it.'

And I meekly answered, 'Well, that is all I can ask of you.'

I knew that the money had swayed him. Nothing else.

I then went into the bedroom and got May ready for bed, and the three kids settled down in the room on their mattresses. When I walked back into the sitting room, he stood up and walked into the hallway and out the front door. I climbed into my own bed. All I could do now was wait.

The next morning, I woke once again to the call to prayer from the nearby mosque. No matter how many times I heard it, I just couldn't get used to it. I could sense a very uneasy air around the house, as if Mostafa was in a foul mood. We would have to tread very lightly that day in case we pissed him off.

I was worried about the fact that my visa was up, as there was no flight back to Cyprus booked for me. I also knew that if I outstayed my visa Mostafa would be in serious trouble – he had brought me into the country, and I was his responsibility – and so would I. In fact, as a foreigner the consequences would probably be much worse for me, and I dread to think what could have happened.

I didn't want to bring up the subject in case he started to rant and rave again. I went into the kitchen and made myself a cup of tea. I asked him if he would like a cup. He said he would, and he walked into the sitting room to watch TV. He said nothing more, and nor did I, but when he finished the tea he stood up and said that he was going out and would be back in an hour. He told me that I was to be ready to go out with him when he got back. I didn't know whether he had arranged a flight back to Cyprus or not, so I decided not to pack anything, just to get myself and May dressed.

I rang Mandy, and the first thing I said to her was, 'Happy birthday, Sis.' I could tell that she was upset, but I told her that her birthday was still very important to me and to May, despite the circumstances. I told her that Mostafa had left the house but that I was hoping that he was going to extend the visa for me.

With that, her voice became very serious. She said, 'Louise, there is no one coming for you. Everything has failed. The Turkish guys have gone AWOL and it looks like the government have no powers to do anything in Syria and no one will risk going in for you. It's just too dangerous. I hate to say this, Louise, but you are on your own now. No matter what, you and May have to try to get out or you will be stuck there for ever. I wish I had better news.'

At this stage I was unaware that Mandy had paid the Turks 5,000 euros to get us out and that they had absconded with it. I just thought that they were too terrified to come in. The situation was absolutely dire in Idlib, and I thought that they didn't want to risk their lives.

Hearing her words, I was devastated. I had been holding out hope all along, but I knew that now more than ever I needed to escape. I said, 'Mandy, I will do my best. I am going to pack a little bag now and I will update you on what is happening.'

I always had my mobile phone fully charged, and I made sure that it was OK in case I needed to use it later that day. I put the hijab on and my full-length black dress. I knew that I couldn't take the book that I was nearly halfway through reading or my clothes in the wardrobe. I had to try to escape with as little as possible. I took up my handbag and only packed it with little things, so that Mostafa wouldn't notice anything out of the ordinary. I put in underwear for May and myself, some Motilium tablets, my passport, May's Nintendo DS, the mobile-phone charger and all the money I had. I was about to put my make-up bag into my handbag but noticed how bulky it looked and realised that it would raise Mostafa's suspicions, I left it out, knowing that even if I did somehow manage to escape I wouldn't be needing any make-up. Not in this country. I remember at that very moment thinking how important simple little things were to me, like my make-up, or a perfume that Mandy had bought me the Christmas before that I couldn't now take with me.

I wished to God that I'd had a passport for May, but Mostafa had that in a little bag he had kept around his waist from the day I had arrived. He even slept with the bag beside him at night in case I tried to grab it while he was asleep. He was a clever man. There was no way that I would ever get access to it.

Mandy's words were rolling around and around in my head, and I decided that even though I didn't know exactly what was going to happen when Mostafa came back for me, I would make the most of being outside with May. I don't know why, but I had a very weird feeling that I would escape that day. But I also knew that if I did, it would be a miracle.

When I heard Mostafa's car pulling up, I called May. We

stood in the kitchen together, and when he walked in he just said, 'Right. Come on, we are going into Idlib for your visa.'

He told me to get into the back of the car, so I guessed that he must be leaving the front seat free because someone else was coming with us. We drove to his cousin's house and picked him up. He got in, and I remember thinking that Mostafa must have been bringing him with us so that I wouldn't be left alone at any stage. This terrified me, because I knew that if he was with us all the time there was no way that we could try to escape. It just wouldn't work.

We drove into the town and through the checkpoints. As we went by one street, the smell of sewage floated into the car. I tried to make a joke about it with Mostafa and his cousin, and I remember that he actually smiled. Somehow, Mostafa seemed a lot calmer than he had earlier that morning. He seemed very self-assured. I knew he had some plan in his head; I just didn't know what that plan was.

We drove past the immigration office but couldn't find a parking space anywhere. Mostafa had to go up and down the road twice until eventually he came across a space about 300 metres away. He asked me for my passport and grabbed his little bag, which I knew contained May's passport. He gathered all the paperwork for the visa, and he and his cousin got out of the car.

I couldn't believe Mostafa was actually leaving us on our own in the city. Then I realised that he thought there was absolutely no way that I, as a woman, and a European woman at that, would be able to go anywhere with a Syrian-looking child. But he underestimated my need to escape and my determination to get May away from him, back to a normal life, back to safety.

As he walked away from the car, he suddenly turned back and said, 'I will leave the keys in the ignition and the car running as it is so hot. It will keep the air conditioning on.'

I was in shock. Yet not for one second did I think of trying to use his car to escape. If I did that I would be caught within minutes.

When he was out of sight, May said that she was bursting to go to the toilet, but there was nothing I could do because I wanted to do whatever I could to get away right there and then. I pulled out my phone and sent a text to Mandy, saying, 'I have a chance to run. No passport.'

A text came back immediately: 'Fuck it. Run.'

I turned to May and said, 'May. We are going. I know you want to go to the toilet, but please hang on and be brave.'

And the poor child just said, 'Yes, Mama, I will.'

I knew that she was as eager to run as I was. I remember as I grabbed the door handle thinking that this small action would change the outcome of my life for ever, for better or for worse, and pushing the door open took all the strength and willpower I had.

We fled from the car and I hailed a taxi. We both jumped in and immediately, without me saying a word to her, May jumped down onto the floor to hide. Sometimes I think she is much older than her tender six years because she is such a clever child.

We drove straight past the immigration office, and my heart sank. We hit emerging traffic at a roundabout right outside the door of the immigration building, and I saw the taxi driver staring at me through his mirror. He knew something was wrong. He turned and said to May, 'Where is your father?'

Again, without prompting, my little girl said, 'He is dead.'

The taxi driver asked in Arabic where we were going.

In Arabic, I said, 'I am going to Aleppo.'

He said nothing, but I feared that he was going to do something, so I rang a contact of mine back in Cyprus who knew a lot of Syrian men whom she could trust and asked her to get someone who spoke Arabic to help me out by talking to the taxi driver. I told her whomever she chose she would have to trust 100 per cent, because our lives were at risk. She already knew about the whole situation, because she had been around when May was abducted and I left for Syria. She didn't ask too many questions; she could tell that I was in immediate danger by the panicked tone of my voice.

Within a minute someone called me back. His name was Tariq, and he was a man that I had seen before, when I lived in Cyprus, though I'd never spoken to him. My contact had given him the low-down on my situation. I thanked him and asked him to help me by interpreting between myself and the taxi driver. He was fine with this, so I passed the mobile phone over to our driver and prayed. After a minute or so of conversation with Tariq he handed it back, and Tariq said, 'Listen, Louise, he is not going anywhere with you. He is definitely not going to Aleppo.'

With that, the driver pulled into the bus station, and poor May said, '*Yalla, yalla, yalla*' ('Move, move, move'). We kept looking out of the back window, convinced that Mostafa would see us and run after us. But Tariq was right: this driver wasn't taking us anywhere. He turned to us abruptly and said, 'No. I will get you bus tickets.' But I knew there was absolutely no way that we could get on a bus, we would be caught in minutes, so when he got out of the taxi we ran. He started to shout, 'Tickets, tickets. *Massari, massari*,' ('Money, money'). But I kept running.

As we were running, the phone rang and, thinking it was Tariq again, I answered and said, 'This is not a game, this is not a game. We have to get out of here.'

Then Mostafa's voice said, 'Louise. Where are you?'

I just hurriedly switched the phone off and put it back in my bag. I thought there and then that there was no way we would make it out of there. Mostafa was literally around the corner and I knew that he would look for us in the bus station before he looked anywhere else. I ran towards a taxi rank where three or four yellow cabs were waiting. A young girl ran over to me and started begging, saying, '*Massari, massari*,' but I just pushed her hand away, holding on tightly to May. As I approached the first taxi I noticed that the driver was a young man, and for some reason I got a bad feeling, as if there was no way he would drive me anywhere. He reminded me so much of Mostafa.

I looked at the next car and I saw that the driver was an

older man in his 50s. He had a kind face. I decided to take my
chances. I had no choice really, because I knew that time was
ticking away; any minute now Mostafa could come around the
corner and that would be it. If he caught me I would be dead. I
might as well just kiss my child goodbye, because I knew that
he would beat me so badly I probably wouldn't survive. This
was my only chance, and if this driver refused me then it was
game over.

May and myself jumped into the back seat of the taxi. I said
we were going to Aleppo, and the driver asked me about money.
He kept saying, 'Dollar, dollar,' (which was worth more to
Syrians than their own currency) and I said, 'No, euro, euro,'
and I showed him the contents of my wallet. He carried on
driving, passing a checkpoint leaving the city. There was a sign
on our left saying Aleppo, and then all of a sudden we pulled
into a petrol station. The driver turned around to me and,
rubbing his fingers together, he said, '*Massari, massari.*' I had
more money tucked away safely in my bra, and I reached inside
my clothes and I showed him what I had. I once again took out
my wallet to show him that I wasn't hiding anything. He smiled
and seemed happy enough, knowing that he would definitely
get paid at the end of his journey. He started up the car again.

I immediately rang Tariq, and he agreed to speak to this
second driver to explain the situation and ask him to take me
as far away as possible, to safety. As we sat there waiting for
Tariq to finish talking to the driver, I looked at May and she
had a horrible look of fear on her face. Like me, she was staring
around her, looking for Mostafa's car. He was driving his father's
car that morning, which was maroon, and it was as if every
maroon-coloured car there was in Syria had come out that day,
because everywhere I looked there was another one.

The driver turned around and handed me back the phone.
Tariq said, 'You are in luck, Louise. This man will drive you all
the way to Damascus, and we can sort him out there. It is a
five- or five-and-a-half-hour drive and it is very dangerous. Do
you have a hijab on?' I told him I had put it on that morning so

I was well covered up. He seemed more relaxed then. He wished me luck and told me to ring him if I needed him again.

I couldn't believe the driver was taking us all the way to Damascus. I was just so relieved. I didn't know what exactly we would do once we reached the city, but I was hoping he would take us straight to the Irish consulate, wherever that was.

All of a sudden the driver got out of the car, and he kept beckoning to May and asking her to go with him. I was terrified. I didn't know what the hell he was doing. I immediately thought that he might know Mostafa and that he somehow knew that May was his child and that he was trying to take her away from me. May refused point blank to go with him, and he finally gave up and walked into the petrol station alone. I remember sitting in the car, thinking, 'Why is he so anxious to get May out of the car? Why does he look so anxious? Is he waiting for Mostafa to come and get us? Did he ring him?' All these thoughts were racing through my head.

After about 15 minutes, I said to May, 'OK, love, we are going to have to go. We can't trust this man. He is up to something.' The next thing I knew, the car door opened and he was standing at the door with two bottles of orangeade and two cakes and a packet of cigarettes for me. I felt so bad for being suspicious of this man. I had lost trust in everyone.

As we drove away I kept thanking him, and he kept looking back at us in his rear-view mirror, smiling. He was a very genuine man, I realised, and yet I had thought the worst, simply because he was Syrian. I felt very guilty for my thoughts. My paranoia was clouding my sense of compassion and my intuition.

We carried on driving on dirt roads, going through areas I had never heard of and some I had, mostly from the news coverage on TV. I knew some of these areas, like those around the cities of Hama and Homs, which we drove through, were very volatile areas and that people there were being killed on a daily basis for rising up against the government. Driving through places I'd seen on the news terrified me, and I was extra careful to ensure that my hijab was covering every single hair on my head and that I made no eye contact with people as we drove by.

After a few hours, we started to see signs for Damascus. One of them said it was 108 kilometres away, but it might as well have said a million miles for how far away it seemed at the time.

May and I spoke to each other in whispers. We also prayed and said the Hail Mary, a prayer we always recited together. It gave me some sort of comfort many times on our journey.

Every so often the driver would light a cigarette, and each time he gave me one too. I was very grateful, as it seemed to calm my nerves a bit. I was still very anxious, though, constantly thinking that Mostafa was behind us, catching up with us, and I kept asking the poor driver to go faster.

All of a sudden he pulled the car off the road, and he picked up his mobile phone to make a call. I didn't know what he was doing. Then he handed the phone to me. Tariq was on the other end; I had given the driver his number earlier in case he needed him to interpret. Tariq said, 'You keep asking the driver to go quicker. Why?'

I said, 'I just want to get to somewhere safe quickly.'

And poor Tariq said, 'I know that, Louise, but he has asked me to tell you that there are speed cameras everywhere, and if he starts going fast then he could be stopped by the police, and that will be the end of it.'

I felt awful. We continued driving at a slow speed in the taxi, which was so old; it must have been manufactured in the 1970s. But as soon as we got out of the area that was littered with speed cameras, the driver put his foot to the floor and we were once again speeding along.

We were stopped along the route a number of times, and each time armed men would briefly look in and just say *yalla* and wave us on. It was so unusual. I knew from travelling with Mostafa that we nearly always got stopped. I felt very strongly that we had an angel along with us on this journey. There was definitely someone watching over us, and I firmly believed that it was my mammy. I prayed that if it was her she would stay with us until we were safely out of this hellhole.

I rang Tariq again so he could check where we were. He asked me to wait for the next road sign and read it out to him. Within minutes, we came to a sign indicating that we were near a city called Douma, and he said to me, 'You are nearly there now, Louise. About one more hour to go. Well done.'

Just as I put the phone down to Tariq, we came to another checkpoint. This one was very big. There were many soldiers, heavily armed, holding their guns upside down, the butt resting on the floor. Most were dressed in full uniform, but some were clearly special forces and were dressed in shirts and jeans. They mostly sat at either side of two trucks, The men were very militant. They were checking every single vehicle and making each car approach very slowly and in a single line.

As we got closer, I could see a soldier staring in at me and May in the back of the car. I tried not to look tense, though I was very anxious. But he casually waved us on.

I just exhaled a sigh of relief and clutched May closer to me. I saw the driver look in his rear-view mirror and smile. It had been such a terrifying journey for all of us. I knew this poor man could have lost everything, perhaps even his life, if he had been caught helping illegal immigrants like us to escape, but he had put everything on the line for us since talking to Tariq. I owed the driver our lives.

We had only driven a few yards away from the checkpoint, not even a hundred, I'd say, when the car started to choke. I noticed smoke coming out of the gearbox. I couldn't believe it. I kept saying to the driver, '*Yalla, yalla, yalla,*' and as I looked back I saw one of the soldiers start to walk over to the car. I thought, 'This is it. We have come to the end of the road and all of this has been in vain.'

But the driver somehow kept going, very, very slowly and as the car turned a corner I watched through the back windscreen, seeing the army drop out of the sight. We rolled onto a sandy road with mountains all around us, and the car just stopped on a hillside. Dead.

I couldn't believe it. I immediately texted Tariq and said, 'We have stopped. The car has broken down. Please help us.' I then sent a text to Mandy and told her the same thing. I got a text back from her and I could tell that she was sick with worry. She just said, 'Oh my God, Louise!'

I started to look around to see our surroundings, and I spotted a massive rock at the side of the road. If we hid behind it, Mostafa wouldn't see us if he drove by. I was terrified that if he went past a taxi with an Idlib registration plate he would know that it would more than likely be us.

I could see the look of horror on the poor taxi driver's face when, despite his best efforts, the car just wouldn't start. Not only would he be in trouble if he was caught with myself and May in his vehicle, but now his taxi, his only form of income, had broken down. May and I stayed in the back of the car, but after a few minutes I got out and lit a cigarette. The driver told us in Arabic to stay where we were, not to leave the car, and he walked up the road a bit.

When he came back, he lifted the bonnet, had a look inside and put it back down again. He came to the back of the car, and I asked him what was wrong. In Arabic he just said, '*Khalas*' ('Finished'), throwing his hands up into the air. I felt distraught for myself and May, and so sorry for him too. He had risked everything for nothing. We were doomed.

The driver made some phone calls, and I told May that we were going to get the car fixed. Poor May said, 'No, Mam, that's it. Grab your bag, we're walking.' I told her that we couldn't do that. I said it was an hour's journey by car and it would take us hours on foot and it would be a huge risk to walk anywhere. I tried to explain to her that our only way of getting to Damascus was to wait until we got the car fixed.

She saw a bus approaching, and the poor child put her thumb out to hail a lift. I couldn't believe it. Of course the bus didn't stop, it just beeped and passed us, but even if it had we could not have risked getting on public transport.

Shortly after that, we saw an army truck approaching. I

immediately went back to the car and climbed inside. As the truck got near it slowed down, and the driver stared over. Fair play to the taxi driver: he just raised his hands as if to say, 'It's broken down; there is nothing I can do.' And the truck driver just nodded and drove past us.

Unbelievably, Tariq knew someone in the area and he told us he would be with us in ten minutes. I thought it had to be a miracle that he knew someone who was so close that they could get to us. The relief I felt was immense. I explained to the driver that help was on its way. He was absolutely dumbfounded.

Meanwhile, another taxi had pulled in and its driver attached a rope to our taxi and started to tow us. I immediately texted Tariq and said to tell his contact that he would see two taxis, one towing the other, on the same road.

Over the following fifteen minutes or so we were towed through this big mountain range with nothing else around us: no birds, no animals of any sort, no noise and hardly any traffic. It was a very weird area covered in sand.

Suddenly we came to what I thought was another checkpoint, but it turned out to be a kiosk of some sort. There were a number of men standing around, and they all started to stare into the car. The taxi driver came to the door and he told us to get out. '*Yalla, yalla*,' he said. May and I both grabbed what we had with us and jumped out. With that, the driver put us into another car and a young man in the front said to us, in perfect English, 'It's OK, you are safe now.' I couldn't believe it. He also said, 'Don't mention money to the taxi man. Say nothing. I will sort it.'

He then got out of the car and walked over to the two taxi drivers. He asked the driver who had stopped to help us if he would continue to tow the car behind us, as he knew of a garage that could fix it. I saw both the drivers nodding in agreement.

And so we started on the next leg of this journey to freedom. May and myself were in one car with the new driver, and the two taxi men followed behind. The new driver said to May, 'We are nearly there. I know you have had a long journey, but it will be fine.' I remember how he told May that she was a beautiful little girl and her smiling back at him.

We drove for about 15 minutes and then we pulled in at a garage. My new driver walked over to the first taxi driver and started to chat. The first taxi driver thanked the driver who had towed him, who got back into his taxi and drove off.

As my new driver and the taxi driver chatted away, I remember thinking that Mostafa would never find us if he drove by now, as we were sitting in the back of a car that had its windows blacked out and had a Damascus registration plate. We were safe. It felt slightly surreal, though. I thought, 'How the hell did I do this? I am in Syria, a country ravaged by war where people are being shot dead in their droves, daily.' It was hard to believe.

The taxi driver got into the front of the car, sitting next to our new driver, and we drove into Damascus. As we drove along, our new driver had a conversation in Arabic with the taxi driver, explaining to him that he would have to drive a certain way to avoid checkpoints.

Suddenly we arrived onto a huge street with garages everywhere and shops selling spare parts. With that, the taxi driver got out and I saw our driver handing him money. The taxi driver then opened our door and in Arabic said, 'May God bless you and your beautiful daughter.' I wanted to cry, and I thanked him from the bottom of my heart for what he had done for myself and May. He simply smiled and nodded his head. I owed that man our lives. I thought he was another angel in this terrifying country. He probably had his own family and yet he had put his life on the line for two strangers. Even when the taxi broke down he never cursed us or shouted; he just accepted what had happened and went along with events as they occurred.

As he walked away, our new driver told me that we would be meeting our new contact in five minutes. We pulled in to the side of the road, and soon a silver Transit van appeared.

Its driver walked over to us and said, 'Well, what an ordeal! You are safe now, so come with me.' He went over and asked the other man how much he had paid the taxi driver and then walked back to me and said it had cost 100 euros. I immediately took the money out and handed it to him.

The two men had a brief chat, and then the driver of the van got back in and started to drive us to his home. We drove and drove for about an hour up into the mountainside, and the man, who introduced himself as Sayed, said that the house he was taking me to was a 'safe house' and that we would be fine there until we got the Irish consulate's office to get us out of the country safely.

The relief I felt when we reached Sayed's apartment was immense. May was so excited. She kept hugging and kissing me. We thought we would only be here for a couple of days, maximum, before we made our way back to Dublin. We could not believe we had made it this far, either of us.

The area around the apartment block looked very run-down: dilapidated and unfinished. There was no entrance to the block as such, just an open hallway, and we immediately started to climb the five flights of stairs to Sayed's apartment. When we got to his door, his wife and three children came to greet us. As we walked in I felt so at home, because the apartment was lovely.

I was told to come in and freshen up, and I could smell food cooking. I went into a bedroom and asked May whether she thought I should take off the hijab in their home or leave it on. I hated wearing it because I wasn't used to having to cover up all the time. May didn't know what to say.

I asked Sayed what he thought was the right thing to do, as I had been taken in by his family and I didn't want to insult them. He told me to wear whatever I was comfortable with and that there was no need to cover up in his home. He told me that his home was our home while we were there. I had a shower and put on the European-style clothes I had been wearing under my long black dress. I remember feeling a little uneasy, being dressed like this and having my blonde hair exposed, but as soon as I went out, Sayed's wife, whose name was Rahil, held her arms out, welcomed me to her home and ushered me to sit down at the table to eat with her family.

I felt so privileged that night to be with them in their home. I owed a lot to them already for putting themselves out for me and being so hospitable. But, as much as I was appreciative of their help, I hoped that I wouldn't have to impose on them for too long.

That night May and myself had the first taste of comfort we'd had for weeks. We sat down to a lovely chicken soup and rice, and we all ate together. It was a million miles away from what we had become used to in Idlib, and I couldn't thank them enough.

I could see in May's little face that she was so relieved to be safe. But she looked absolutely exhausted. It was etched all over her tiny features. Her eyes were puffy and there were dark rings beneath them. She looked drained. I felt exactly as she looked, and I remember thinking that it was fine for someone of my age to feel and look that way but not for a little girl. And Mostafa, her own father, had done this to her.

As I sat there, I thought of all the physical pain I had felt in the taxi on the route to Damascus. It was mostly chest pain, caused, I would say, solely by fear: the fear of being caught. I thought about how great May had been through it all, holding my hand and squeezing it every now and then and telling me all the time that it would be OK. She was three foot nothing, but in my mind she stood ten feet tall, because she had been my rock throughout this whole nightmare. I lived for her and I knew she lived for me. It was an unspoken love between mother and child that can never be explained.

After the meal I sat out on the veranda with my head covered, a bowl of fruit beside me and a welcome cigarette in my hand. I felt all the stress leave me. I took my mobile phone from my bag and I called Mandy. I told her that we were fine and in a safe house. I told her to make sure my dad was OK and to reassure him that I was on my way home.

She was absolutely delighted. She felt a bit uneasy about where we were staying, as she didn't know these people any more than I did. As far as she knew they could have been anybody. But, had she been in their home and felt their genuine love and care for myself and May in our situation, she would have been reassured that we were in the best place we could be at that time.

Sayed had said that we would travel to the office of the honorary consulate the next morning to start planning our escape. Mandy had been in contact with them as we made our way to Damascus by car, and they had sent me a text along the way, telling me to contact them on my arrival. So I decided to ring straight away.

They sounded relieved to hear my voice, as I honestly think they believed that I would never make it to Damascus with the situation as it was in Syria. They told me that I would need to meet them immediately. The next morning would be too late. Sayed suggested a hotel he knew and said that he would take us along a certain route that would be less risky for me if we came upon checkpoints. It was a Monday evening, exactly two weeks to the day after I had arrived in Syria, and luckily the checkpoints were not manned so often early in the week. Sayed had hoped that we might just make it to the hotel without being stopped at all. Either way, I needed to wear a hijab.

I knew that I couldn't take May with me, and I dreaded telling her that I would have to leave her with a family she had only just met. She was terrified to even go to the toilet alone, and when she did go, I had to stand outside the door until she was finished. She was so fearful that I would disappear again. But this was one trip I had to make alone.

Sayed had three children: one was a teenager and the other two were aged ten and six. They had already gone to bed that evening, as they had school the next day, but Rahil reassured May that she would be safe with her and that I would be as quick as I could be. Reluctantly, she agreed to stay. I pulled on a cardigan that Rahil had lent me, which I wore with dark trousers and the hijab. I was well covered up just in case anything happened along the way.

As we travelled to the hotel we didn't come across one checkpoint. I was shocked. When we arrived, the representative from the consulate ordered us some coffees. He told me that I would have to be very careful now and they would have to check that Mostafa had not gone to the police to register me and May as missing. If this had happened it would be a huge problem, he said. When I asked if I could go home the next day, he said, 'Certainly not. There are a lot of things that need to be checked before you can go anywhere.'

I suppose I expected his response, but I was still upset. He apologised for not being able to get to Idlib to help us and told me that I was very courageous and very lucky. He actually said that they thought there was no way I would ever escape when they heard where I was. They had tried to contact the police in Nairab and Idlib to alert them to my situation, but he said it was impossible to get anyone on the phone so it seemed like there was no law enforcement there. He assured me that he would contact me as soon as he had more news and that the consulate would start making plans to help me. Sayed drove me back to the apartment and tried to convince me that everything would work out for the best, soon.

On our way back, he took me to a spot in the mountains where local people had stalls and sold their wares. The views were absolutely spectacular. I looked up at the sky, filled with what looked like a million stars, and I remember thinking how beautiful Damascus would be if only the situation was different. It was breathtaking up there, and looking down on the city it was hard to imagine the turmoil taking place in and around it.

May was ecstatic when we arrived back and squeezed me so tightly that I could hardly breathe. She asked me to promise her that I wouldn't leave her again. But I explained that I sometimes needed to go to away to try to get us back to Ireland and that it was just too unsafe to take her with me, and she nodded. She knew the situation on the streets only too well herself, despite her innocence and tender age.

That night we slept together, wrapped around each other, on two mattresses pushed together. To most people that would seem like a less than ideal situation, but for me it was heaven. I cried for about an hour with sheer relief, and then I thanked God for getting me to where I was that night and I asked him to get us home swiftly and safely. I knew that we probably had a long and stressful journey still ahead of us, but at least we were one step closer to home. Then I slept peacefully.

On the Tuesday morning I had a call from the Irish embassy in Cairo asking me to confirm that I was in Damascus. They asked if I felt that I was in a safe-enough house. The night before, the official I met had told me that he did not want to know where I was staying, as it might have put either him or us at risk, so I just told the embassy that I felt relaxed and happy where I was. I declined their offer to be moved elsewhere, as I genuinely believed that myself and May would only be there for another 24 to 48 hours and I felt fine with that. I just hoped that all the paperwork would be sorted quickly and we would be on our way. I prayed that Mostafa hadn't been bad enough to report us missing. I hoped that he would feel guilty about what he had done and feel some sympathy for us. Deep down I knew that wouldn't be the case, but it didn't stop me praying for it.

The days went by, one by one, and there was no news. I was waiting on tenterhooks, making sure that my mobile phone was always charged. Mandy was ringing me constantly or else I was ringing her, but nothing was happening. It was as if everything had just stopped.

Each day Sayed and Rahil went to work and the three kids went off to school, and myself and May stayed in the apartment watching English news channels. May had left all her Barbies, DVDs and books back in Idlib. She only had her Nintendo DS to occupy her. We were bored silly, but more than anything I was frightened in case everything was falling apart at the seams

and the embassy was afraid to tell me. I could see on the news
how the situation in Syria was getting worse by the hour, which
terrified me. We couldn't walk outside the door, not just because
of the fear that Mostafa might be waiting outside in a car so he
could pounce on us but also because things were really heating
up on the streets. Protests were happening more often and
more people than ever were being shot dead in broad daylight.
We were monitoring everything as it unfolded on TV and it
was very scary. I knew that consulate officials were talking
about pulling out of Syria altogether in fear of their lives and
that no journalists were being allowed to enter the country to
report on the situation. It was a waking nightmare.

Mostafa was unable to contact me by phone because I had
got rid of my old Cypriot SIM card on the night I arrived and
Sayed had bought me a replacement Syrian card, but it didn't
stop me worrying about Mostafa tracking me down. I knew he
had friends and contacts everywhere and anything was possible.

As the days went by, I started to get what they term
'obligatory' calls from officials in the consulate or the embassy
just telling me there was no news. Nothing more. Then one day,
one of the girls from the embassy told me that they were having
difficulty finding the entry visa I had used to get into Syria. If
there was no entry visa, I couldn't get an exit one. It was a
disaster. I told them that there should have been two entry
visas, as I had one issued on my initial entry and on the day I
fled Mostafa had had another one stamped to extend my visit.
But they still couldn't find anything for me or May. When it
came to the Friday I knew I was in trouble, as Fridays and
Saturdays are holy days in Syria and everything shuts down
then. It opens again on Sunday, but then everything is closed in
Ireland. Nothing would happen for the next few days, and,
although I was devastated, there was nothing I could do. It was
all out of my hands.

On Monday, Mandy and my aunty Kathy had a meeting with
the Department of Foreign Affairs in Dublin, so I waited and
waited all day for news. That evening, Mandy rang. I knew

immediately from her voice that something was seriously wrong. She said, 'Louise, I don't know how to tell you this, but it's bad news and this is the hardest phone call I have ever had to make.' My heart missed a beat. 'The Department said that they had received information from the Syrian government to say that you are wanted for kidnapping May.' I felt weak.

She went on to tell me that this was a very, very serious charge, and if I was caught I would be imprisoned for life or stoned to death under sharia law. I didn't know what to say. I had no words. Mandy said, 'You are in severe danger. Do not leave the apartment. This is very serious, Louise. Your lives are at risk.'

But, even though I understood the severity of what I was hearing, it just didn't seem right. I knew that something was wrong. I told Mandy not to worry. I rang the embassy and asked them to confirm what I had heard. The ambassador rang me back and verified what Mandy had said. She told me to keep my head down and stay indoors. She said she had no evidence in writing, though, and I begged her to find something because I just wasn't convinced.

The next day I spoke to another official at the embassy, and he said they were still waiting for written confirmation of the arrest warrant, but they insisted that the warrant was in place. I asked if they could send their diplomatic car for myself and May so it could take take us to them, but they said the car was in Egypt and it was too dangerous to drive to Syria, as the car would be searched at the border and the embassy had no powers in Syria.

They told me that the Cypriot embassy was in talks with the Interior Minister and the Minister of Foreign Affairs in Damascus about the international arrest warrant in place for Mostafa for kidnapping May. They were hoping that this would allow them to get an exit visa for myself and May. However, there were no guarantees, and I felt completely let down by everyone.

Then, out of the blue, I received what they call a 'comfort

box' from home. The Department of Foreign Affairs had asked Mandy if she wanted to send me any items, as they could be delivered through diplomatic post, so a package would get to me more quickly and with fewer problems. I had never been so happy to receive something. It was a link to home, as I saw it. As soon as I opened the box, May's favourite toy, Justin, the doll that she had had from the time she was a baby, tumbled out. I couldn't believe it. This toy was like a comfort blanket to May, and when Mostafa abducted her I was disgusted with him for not making sure she had Justin with her, knowing full well how attached to him she was. But now she was finally reunited with him. She was jumping up and down, hugging him and kissing him, and it was so encouraging for me to see her happy, even if only for a moment.

Mandy had also sent me new underwear and two books – one about a Columbian named Pablo who was the most wanted man in the world, which I read within days, as well as *The Girl Who Played with Fire* by Stieg Larsson – and she also sent me Mac and Lancôme make-up, which I was delighted with, as I had been feeling so unfeminine.

She sent books for May to read and copybooks for her to doodle on, along with a lovely Barbie doll in a swimming costume with little puppies on it. And I was delighted to see that she had sent me a lovely gold-coloured dress with a black top underneath, and thick black tights. I remember laughing when I saw the clothes, thinking how little Mandy knew about the dress code in Syria, but I was still delighted to have got everything she sent. She also sent new clothes for May, including a little white shirt, purple leggings, a little purple jumper and hair bobbles. These small things, which we would all otherwise have taken for granted in our everyday lives, were suddenly like a treasure trove to me. I was thrilled. It somehow helped me to cope with the days that followed.

By the following Tuesday, there was still no news. And the embassy still had nothing in writing that would confirm there was an arrest warrant in place for me. I was getting more and more exasperated. It was very warm in the apartment, as the weather was stifling outside, but because of the fear that Mostafa would find us I couldn't even sit on the balcony to have a cigarette. It was hell. But through it all Sayed and Rahil were a tower of strength, and they remained amazing hosts and never showed any sign of annoyance that we were still there, even though we had all thought that the situation would last for two or three days, not nearly two weeks.

Sayed could see how exhausted I was, and on Wednesday night he started to make calls to some contacts in high places he had. He asked them to check out the system for arrest warrants to see if my name was on anything. The next day Sayed rang me from work, a whole eleven days after I had arrived at his home, and he told me that he couldn't talk but that he was furious. He said he knew that I would understand why and he would explain all later. I knew what he was about to tell me. That evening he informed us all that there was no sign of an arrest warrant out for me in the name of Monaghan or Assad. He said his friends had checked with the Department of Immigration, giving both my passport details and May's to those in command, and there was absolutely nothing to say that the police were looking for us. I was livid.

On the following morning, which was Friday, a holy day, Sayed told me that the government offices were open for some reason, although they were short staffed, and he was going to head straight there. He said he would take myself and May with him, and we could stay in an apartment belonging to a friend of his until he had sorted things with the officials.

I called the Irish consulate first, and it turned out that Mostafa had been in Damascus and had arrived at the consulate, threatening the staff. He told them that he knew that they were protecting me, and he actually used very offensive language to one of the staff, cursing his mother. The staff were very worried over his behaviour, as he appeared to be very violent. I couldn't believe what I was hearing: that he had walked into the Irish consulate and no one had arrested him, despite there

being an international arrest warrant for kidnap for him issued
by Interpol. When I asked them about this, I was told that
they didn't actually have the arrest warrant in front of them
because they were still waiting for it to be sent to them and
were therefore powerless. It was a joke as far as I was concerned.
But the big worry now was that Mostafa was actually in
Damascus. Now, more than ever, I had to be careful. I felt
totally disillusioned, and it was probably the first day that I was
totally without hope.

Sayed had a meeting with the consulate officials at 7 a.m.
that Friday morning, where he told them face to face that he
had been informed, by his own contacts, that without a shadow
of a doubt there was no arrest warrant outstanding for myself
or May. They asked him to come back later that evening so that
they could try and confirm what he had told them in the
meantime.

That night we all headed out to the van: Sayed, Rahil, their
children and myself and May. We all carried down plastic garden
chairs and lined them up in the back of the van. In any other
situation it would have been funny. This was perfectly legal in
Syria, although it would have been considered highly unsafe
anywhere else in the world, and we all squeezed into the van.
May was in a corner and I told her not to move an inch. I was
terrified in case Sayed had to hit the brakes suddenly and we all
went through the windscreen.

I was covered up in the hijab, luckily, as we got stopped at a
checkpoint within minutes. They asked Sayed for his ID and
stared in at us all in the back of the van. I remember thinking
how calm and clever Sayed was that day. He even took out
some nuts he had in the front of the van and offered the soldier
a handful. It seemed to calm the guy down immediately and we
were allowed to go on our way. It was pitch dark, and Sayed
dropped us all off beside a park with a fountain in it and told us
to wait there until he got back.

I was anxious in case someone spotted me, but May was
having a great time, having finally been given the chance to get

a bit of fresh air. I remember looking at Rahil and thinking how unperturbed she was and how terrified I was. I told Rahil that I honestly felt that Mostafa was around, watching me. It was a stupid fear, I realise now, given that I was one person in a city of millions, but at the time it was real and uncontrollable. We must have been there a couple of hours and I was absolutely scared stiff.

Eventually Rahil rang Sayed and asked him if he would come back as quickly as possible. He was with us within a half an hour of the call. He looked absolutely livid when he arrived. When he eventually calmed down, he said that he had absolutely no faith in the Irish. He actually called them donkeys, in Arabic.

He said that he'd had arrangements to meet the official from the Irish consulate at 9 p.m., but he hadn't turned up. Sayed then went to someone else that he knew within the Syrian government, who, once again, confirmed that there was nothing on the systems about myself or May. Sayed then rang the official from the Irish consulate, who happened to be having dinner with the Syrian Interior Minister, and Sayed put his contact on the phone, who confirmed to the official that there was nothing on the system.

The official then apologised to Sayed. He asked if he could meet him there and then. Sayed was furious. He knew that the Irish government, on the previous Sunday, six days earlier, had sent five copies of a passport each for myself and May, emergency copies, to Irish officials in Jordan, Lebanon, Egypt, Turkey and Syria, but they had refused to give me the passports, as they said it would be too dangerous for me to have them on my person if I was stopped or anything happened to me.

I couldn't believe it. Sayed said that I would have to go with him to meet the Irish officials face to face. We drove down to a lovely, very affluent-looking area surrounded by trees. It was my first time going to the consulate office itself, and I felt some sort of relief when I spotted the Irish flag flying high. Yet I was also totally exasperated by how irresponsible they had been by not carrying out simple checks with regard to the so-called arrest warrants when Sayed, who was not a government official, had managed to get answers.

We got out of the van, and I told May to wait with Rahil. As we went to walk in to the consulate, the official came out to Sayed. He opened his arms and approached him to kiss him on both cheeks, a normal practice for Arab men. In the official's hands were our passports. In Arabic, he said, 'I am so sorry, my friend. You do everything now. Organise the exit visas; we trust you.'

The official said that there was nothing preventing me from leaving the country, but May had been put on a stop list. It was put into effect at 4.10 p.m. the previous Sunday. It meant that we could have escaped prior to that, as the passports had arrived that Sunday morning.

I remember thinking that we would have probably been able to escape even with May on a stop list, as her father got her in and out of three countries in total with a cancelled passport. But I knew that I needed to stay calm at this stage if we were to get out at all.

As the official chatted to Sayed, his phone rang. It was the Irish ambassador in Cairo. She spoke to the official and then asked for me to be put onto the phone. I asked her straight out what had happened. Why had I been told there was a warrant out for my arrest when there had never been one? She apologised profusely to me. As we spoke, there were six security men keeping watch beside the official's Audi and a high-powered jeep that displayed the Irish flag. She said that they had had a phone call from a number in Idlib stating that Louise Monaghan was wanted for abduction. She admitted that they never got this allegation confirmed in writing; instead they took it at face value and were very concerned about it, because the number appeared to be an official government number. She then said there was nothing could be done about that now, because the reality was that May was now on a stop list.

The ambassador argued the fact that the passports only arrived on the same day the stop list came into place. There was no point in me arguing back. In fairness to the ambassador, she said that this didn't happen every day and it was a very unusual situation for them to deal with. She also told me that she was coming in person to Damascus on Sunday and she was going to meet me face to face. This was Friday.

I rang Mandy as we drove back to the apartment in the van, and I felt vindicated in that I had tried to convince the Irish consulate all along that there was no arrest warrant for me, but no one was listening, and now I had been proved right. At least now I felt that they might try that bit harder to get us out quickly. I told Mandy that we had our passports now and I felt that things might happen quickly. I told her that myself and Sayed were going to the police station to see if we could now report my old passport missing and get me an exit stamp on new emergency documents.

However, when we did the police told us we would have to come back as they didn't have the relevant stamp. There was nothing I could do until we got the stamp.

Sunday came, the day we were to meet the ambassador, so that evening we headed to the old town, a historical part of Damascus that is a bit more cosmopolitan than the rest of the city. Sayed told me to bring the hijab with me just in case we were stopped, but explained that this part of town was normally, when times were not as volatile, an area where young people hung out and journalists had coffee and where the hip and trendy set of Damascus met up.

I was wearing a shortish skirt with dark tights and a dark top. I left the hijab off as we travelled in the van, because I felt a bit braver now that I actually had my Irish passport. Luckily we weren't actually stopped at all along the way.

I remember as we drove through the old town I was thinking how beautiful it was. There were people everywhere using little toothpicks to eat corn on the cob covered in paprika served in little Pyrex-type dishes, and the smell of Arabic coffee lingered everywhere.

We were looking for a hotel, a very luxurious one, where the ambassador was staying. Sayed held my hand as we walked around to deflect anyone from paying too much attention to me. He explained to me how people in this area many years ago would have lived in big old townhouses with lovely courtyards and exotic plants everywhere. The courtyards would have a fountain and the ground would be covered in cobblestones. Some of those homes were still around, despite the troubles, but they were few and far between.

It took us a while to find the hotel, but when we eventually got there we were approached by three very big men. However, the official from the embassy appeared and told them we were with him and to allow us inside.

We walked in through large automatic doors and were faced with three more big men, who I think were armed. The hotel security was extremely high, and I got the impression that it was a place where a lot of dignitaries or embassy staff stayed when in Damascus. It was definitely geared towards the more elite people who visited the city. It also turned out to be one of the old houses that Sayed had been telling me about on the way here, and it was stunning. It had a huge fountain in the middle of the ground floor and the decor was amazing.

We walked over and I was introduced to the ambassador for the Irish embassy in Egypt, whose name was Isolde. I was delighted to get to meet with her face to face, and as I sat down she handed me a present, which she said she had bought for me in the duty-free shop on her way to meet me.

We started to talk, and she commended me on how I had escaped from Idlib. She said that she would rather we spoke alone, without Sayed, explaining that it would be better for him, for his own safety, not to be aware of anything we spoke of.

I sat with the ambassador and another official, and Sayed sat with a second official not far from us. Isolde apologised for the errors that had occurred up until then and said that they were going to approach the Syrian Minister of Justice and the Interior Minister the following day with the international arrest warrant issued by Interpol for Mostafa. I gave them all the paperwork I had, which was all wrapped up in my bag. It included my divorce papers, the stop list and every other paper I had. The officials said that they would approach each department and ask what could be done to get me and May out of Syria with an exit visa. They said that they had to accept that May was on a stop list, but if this plan didn't work they would go to a judge later that afternoon and present the whole case to him.

I asked the official about our chances of being granted an exit visa, and he said that, although he knew the ministers and the judge in question, it was going to be 50/50. There was no way of telling how it would go until he got face to face with them armed with the file.

Isolde told me that things were getting very bad in Syria and that she felt that at any moment a civil war could erupt. She said that it looked like the Irish consulate would also be evacuated, as it just wasn't safe to stay there. Things were getting worse, not better. The Irish consulate was watching the British embassy and the American embassy, and once they knew what they intended to do, the Irish embassy would follow.

We finished our meeting and I honestly felt so optimistic. I kept thanking Sayed for looking after us until that day, and I remember telling him how I was going to start packing up some stuff as soon as I got back to his apartment because I felt we would be going home the next day. He was still very hesitant and kept telling me not to build my hopes up. 'Just wait, Louise, just wait until you hear,' he said. He had his doubts, but I wasn't being swayed. I was going home the next day and that was that. I had to stay positive.

I rang Mandy and told her how excited I was. I could tell that Mandy was hesitant. There had been let-downs all along the way, and she wasn't building her hopes up too high. But I went to bed that night so happy.

I woke the next day with butterflies in my stomach. I told May that hopefully we would be heading home very, very soon, and she was all excited too. But I waited all morning, then all afternoon, and there was no call from anyone. I was texting Mandy telling her that I was still waiting and we were all in bits.

At about 5.30 p.m., Isolde rang me and asked if I could come down to the office, as she needed me to sign a form giving the consulate power of attorney to act on my behalf. She said that they had explored every angle they had discussed the night before; however, as an honorary consulate they could not approach any official in Syria, so they had suggested that I give their solicitor a letter to allow him to act on my behalf to get the paperwork they needed. I was furious over this, because I couldn't understand why I could not have done it the night before when we met. I felt like it was just one hurdle after another.

Sayed was working, but he organised for a taxi to get me to the office. This driver was another angel, as he knew that I had no ID – I had a passport but no entry visa, so it was useless if we were stopped – and he took me on a route where he knew that there would be no checkpoints. We drove all around the mountain and passed by military bases where all you could see were signs saying 'No Cameras in This Area' and 'No Media in This Area'. In the distance I could see a man with a gun patrolling up and down, and I remember thinking, 'How the hell can anyone live like this?'

It took us about an hour and a half to get to the office. By the time I got there, Sayed had already arrived and he took me inside. I spoke to the solicitor, signed the forms and left. I was convinced that on Tuesday we would have the green light to leave the country.

I was worried sick yet again over what was to take place the next morning, and I slept badly. And at about 5.30pm on Tuesday I eventually got a call from Isolde asking me to come down to see her and to bring passport photos. I asked her what had happened, but all she would say was, 'It all failed. I need you here.' I didn't know what to think.

Rahil took me down to an old shop not too far away from the

apartment and we got the photos taken. I remember looking
around more closely that day at the poverty in that little region.
There was rubbish littering the place, the smell of sewage was
rotten and there were people begging everywhere. It was
heartbreaking to think that people were forced to live like this.
I had witnessed scenes like this all over Syria as I made my way
to Damascus. The government just didn't seem to care about
its citizens. While I was waiting outside the shop waiting for
my photo and smoking a cigarette, a little girl walked over to
me. She said nothing, but her little face and her pleading eyes
said it all as she gently pushed her hand out and into my face,
looking for anything I could give her. I felt so bad, because I
had no change to give her, and I was absolutely appalled that
this little child, not much older than May, was forced into
begging on the streets to get food. It was horrific.

When the photos were ready, we headed through the
mountains and back down to the honorary consulate. By now I
was so irate I wanted to scream the place down. I was just sick
of what I saw as bureaucracy at its worst.

I decided to take May into the office with me. It would be
the first time the staff had met her, and I wanted them to see
who I was risking my life for: a beautiful little child, an Irish
child with an Irish passport, innocent in all of this but who
deserved a chance in life. I wanted them to know that if they
couldn't or didn't help me, I would die trying for my child. I
wanted them to know that if it couldn't be done legally I was
willing to risk my own life as a non-national in this country to
get her to safety. I remember getting really upset when they
asked me if this was May, and I said, 'I need to get out of here.
This is about her life and my life, and we are losing valuable
time here.' I burst into tears and clutched May close to me as I
watched her sad little face stare up at me. I had always tried my
best to hide my emotions from my daughter, because she was
only a baby in my eyes, but this was a waking nightmare for me.

The consulate staff took me into an office and they told me
that they needed the extra passport shots for emergency travel

documents. I asked them why they hadn't organised this two weeks earlier – why hadn't I got out of this place two and a half weeks ago if these photos were all that was needed? I said, 'You told me I was wanted for abduction. You told my family the same thing. So why am I still here? As an Irish consulate, have you no power to help your own?' I couldn't hold back.

Sayed and Rahil were waiting outside. The ambassador said, 'OK, Louise. We need to get you to a safehouse. Every effort we have made has failed. You are not safe where you are now.'

The consulate staff told me to say goodbye to Sayed and Rahil and that they would take me to a safe place. I didn't know how to feel. I had got very close to this family, a family who, nearly three weeks before, I had never met. Now I was quickly thanking them for everything they had done for me and, without even going back to their home, I was leaving them, just like that. I was happy and yet I was sad, because although I was getting nearer to home, or so I thought, there was nothing to say I would definitely make it.

Sayed and Rahil were devastated. They begged me to go back to their home for just one more night to have a final farewell. But it was out of my hands now. I was at the mercy of the Irish officials, and I was willing to do anything they told me to at this stage if it got me out of there.

Rahil was so upset. For the last few weeks we had cleaned and cooked together, swapped recipes and done everything in the home together. Her English had improved and she had been delighted to have another woman to spend her time with. It was the quickest friendship I had ever made as I had been thrown into the situation, but she was someone I would never forget. We had formed a bond; she had consoled me, and she had opened up to me about her own personal situation and I had consoled her. She explained that honest and sincere Syrian people saw how foreigners, especially Westerners, were treated in her country and it made her ashamed to be Syrian. And, as a mother, she felt embarrassed at how I was being treated when I only wanted the best for my child. She and Sayed and many others along my journey had proved to me that most Syrians were lovely people. Even Rahil's parents were concerned about me and would ring Rahil each day to see if myself and May were all right. It was such a lovely gesture from people who were complete strangers to me, and I to them.

Despite Sayed and Rahil begging me to go back with them for one more night, to sit down and eat together, I explained to them that I had to leave there and then. They were upset, but they understood. Sayed said he would go back to the apartment and pack all of my belongings and drop them back at the consulate's office. He was so good.

We went down to their van and May had to say goodbye to the children she had become so attached to over the weeks. I remember how Rahil's eldest girl kept kissing May's head over and over again, crying as she did it, and saying, 'I am sorry. I am so sorry. It is all our fault,' even though that was so far from the truth. The Syrians I met always blamed themselves in some way for the working of their country's government, yet they were some of the nicest people you could meet. I remember the younger children calling May into the van and asking her to stay, and then hearing Sayed's words: 'No, children. You are not going to see May again.' Those words will echo in my ears for ever, and I still cry every time I think of them and all of the children's little innocent faces. The 12-year-old was howling with tears as we walked away, and all of the children were telling May that they loved her.

Rahil had tears streaming down her face, and she said to me, 'Promise me we will always be sisters.' And I did, because she will always have a special place in my heart. She couldn't bear to say goodbye to May; she simply patted her on the head with her back turned to her. It was heartbreaking for everyone.

Sayed called me to one side and said, 'Louise, you are not supposed to tell me where you are, but please ring me or text me when you get to safety and let me know that you are fine. Please.' I promised him I would, despite knowing how dangerous it was supposed to be. Up until that day they could have done anything they wanted to get me out of their home, but they hadn't, and that meant the world to me. I trusted them with my life.

I told Sayed that I loved him so much and I was indebted to him. And then they drove off.

I walked back inside and waited for what was to happen next. I didn't know where I was going or if I would ever get out of this godforsaken country, but I had to do whatever I was told from here on in if I was to have any chance of an escape.

As I sat there, I felt so lonely. Within a short time, a car pulled up and the ambassador and another official told me that we were going to a Catholic convent where we would be safe. The convent housed both an orphanage for children who had lost parents in the war and an old folks' home for people with no family members and no home. I was shocked that something like this could actually exist in such a Muslim country.

As we pulled up at the convent, I saw massive walls; they must have been about 40 feet high. There was a huge iron gate, which opened automatically as we pulled up. We drove up a long driveway to an enormous four-storey convent with big steps leading up to the door. As we got out of the car, a lovely little nun came out and embraced the official. She obviously knew him well and seemed delighted to see him.

As we walked in, it reminded me immediately of the convent I had attended as a child, Loreto College, as it had old blue linoleum on the floors, walls with holy relics hung on them, statues of Our Lady and St Andrew everywhere, and rosary beads hung all around.

The little nun showed us around a canteen where all the orphans, ranging in ages from around eight to their early 20s, all sat eating. She spoke softly in French and Arabic. I watched as these young, and not so young, girls, all 22 of them, who had just finished their dinner, sat quietly and recited the Hail Mary in French. May asked me what they were saying and I said, 'Do you remember the prayer that we were reciting all the way along in the taxi, May, the Hail Mary? Well, that is what these girls are saying, only in a different language.'

As they left the room, they all said, 'Bonjour,' and off they went to bed. We were showed around some rooms, which looked like prison cells, and I think my reaction must have said it all. I was reluctant to take one of them because I had no idea how long we would have to stay there. In fairness to the ambassador, she asked if they had any rooms with a TV, and the nuns said they did but that they were up on the old folks' floor. However, if I wanted to go up there they were the nicest rooms they had.

I was delighted. On the way we saw a lovely old lady who must have been in her 90s, but she jumped up off the bed on seeing us and embraced the official who was with us. They obviously knew each other well. On seeing May, the old lady grabbed her and started to hug her, calling her a 'baby'. She pulled three bars of chocolate from her bedside drawer and passed them over to an elated May. We later found out this lady spoke six or seven languages.

When we got to our room, I was really pleased. We had two big beds, an en suite bathroom with a proper shower, a fridge, a TV and now some chocolate. The nuns told us that we could either eat in the room or in the dormitory downstairs. The ambassador went over to the TV and tuned in two English-speaking stations for us. I knew that the ambassador was leaving Damascus the following day, Thursday, to meet the then President of Ireland, Mary McAleese, who was flying into Beirut, in Lebanon. But the ambassador said, 'Look, don't get your hopes up too much, but we are going to give this one more chance. We are going to the highest sharia judge in the country to ask him if he will override the stop list. We cannot promise you anything, but we will talk to you tomorrow when we have more news for you.'

I was happy that they were still trying, and I relaxed a bit and went down for something to eat in the canteen. The little nun sat with us as we had a cup of tea, two triangles each of Laughing Cow cheese, Arabic bread, which is like pitta bread, an omelette and a yogurt. And when we finished we had a little bar of chocolate each. It was meagre but absolutely delicious.

I went back to our room feeling so positive. I found a deck of cards, and we sat down on the bed and played Snap. May loved it and kept asking to play again and again. She was so much more relaxed.

We had a shower with the lovely shower gels that the ambassador had bought for me in the duty-free shop, and I felt so refreshed. Before I went to bed we headed down to the courtyard and I read a little, sitting on a bench as May frolicked around with the many cats that were running playfully around us.

When we went back to the room, which was on the third floor of the building, I remember looking out of the barred windows and seeing a chicken restaurant on the other side of the high wall. I couldn't believe what I was seeing: so near and yet so far. That night I would have done anything to have been able to walk out those gates and buy some southern fried chicken, but I knew that there was no way we could risk it, much as May longed for the taste of Western food. It was so disheartening knowing that it was within reach but that we couldn't get there.

I was totally chilled out that evening and convinced that once we'd had a good sleep we would be bright and breezy the next morning and ready for our trip home. I was sure that this would be our first and last night in this lovely but lonely little convent, and I fell asleep praying for a positive outcome the next morning.

CHAPTER SEVEN

———◆———

The Escape

I had a very fretful night's sleep. We were in very unusual surroundings, and all night long I could hear the cries of old people who were clearly not well. I could hear doors banging and people shuffling around. The convent wasn't a house or an apartment; it was more like being in a hospital, and I just felt uneasy all night.

The nun knocked on our door at about 6.30 a.m. with an unusual concoction of two bowls of yogurt with some sort of oil on the top and some olives. She brought tea for me and hot milk for May. I remember thinking that when May woke up she would be in shock at what was for breakfast. She had a big appetite for a little girl and loved her food, and I knew that she would be absolutely starving once she was up and dressed. Her eating pattern had been ruined over the last few weeks, and I could see the weight walking off her day by day.

Just minutes after the breakfast was delivered, there was another knock on the door. This time it was a young woman who I had been introduced to the night before. She spoke very good English and she had been told to come up to us that morning to see if we needed anything. She told me that she was Syrian, from the north of the country, and 25 years old. She had been in the convent since she was two years old, and her younger sister lived there with her. She went to college each day. I was fascinated as to how she and her sister, two Muslim girls, ended up in a convent, but I dared not ask. Her one hope, she told me, was that she would meet a man and settle down. 'I just want to get married and I hope that he will let me work,' were her very words. Even in the convent she had accepted that this would be her life as a Syrian woman: no matter which man she met, she was prepared to be subservient to him, just hoping that he would allow her the freedom to get a job. She was a lovely girl and I was delighted to see her, because I knew that May would have a heart attack when she woke and saw olives for breakfast. The girl would be a distraction for her.

Sayed had dropped our cases off at the embassy the night before, and the taxi driver actually handed them over the convent wall to us. However, there were some things missing, so I asked the girl if she would get us some toothbrushes and some toothpaste and whether there was any chance of some fruit for May.

While we waited for her to come back, we played a few games of Snap with the playing cards I had found the previous night. As the time ticked by, we watched *King of the Hill*, an American TV programme that I was shocked to see on the television in Syria. About an hour after she had left, the girl arrived back with a lovely little hamper containing two bananas, an orange and a lotus, and May ate every bit of fruit there was. I watched her enjoy every little mouthful, and I was delighted that we had been able to get something for her that she actually liked.

It was Wednesday morning, and work started very early in Syria. I was a nervous wreck, as I was aware that the embassy officials were to meet with the top judge in Damascus and beg for his help. They had told me that all of their hopes hinged on this meeting, so I knew that today would be the day that would shape the rest of my life, for better or for worse. The official had said that he would ring me as soon as he had any news for me, and I remember looking at the clock all morning, waiting in fear of what the outcome of that meeting would be.

Then, all of a sudden, the phone rang, and I scrambled to answer it. It was the call I had been waiting for. The official said that he and the ambassador had to go to Lebanon immediately, as the Irish president at the time, Mary McAleese, was arriving there the next morning and they needed to be there for any preparations. Then he broke the news.

'I'm afraid it's not good news, Louise. The judge said that although we have a very strong case, he could not allow May to leave Syria, as they would lose another Muslim.'

I thought I was going to collapse. 'Lose another Muslim.' The cheek of him! I was absolutely disgusted by his insensitivity. All the judge was interested in was his religion, not the future of an innocent child, and an Irish child at that. May still had no Syrian passport. She was Irish. I hated Syria, its religious beliefs, its political bureaucracy and everything that it stood for at that very moment.

I was absolutely devastated. I could not believe what I was hearing. I said, 'Please don't tell me that I have to stay here indefinitely.' But the official just said that I had to keep my head down and stay where I was for now, as it was the safest place for me. I said, 'Please don't leave me here. I know you have been very good to me, but I have to get out of here. How long will I have to stay here?' I was shocked when he said, 'Sunday.' Without meaning to raise my voice, in a state of shock, I shouted, 'Sunday? Sunday?'

'Yes,' he said. 'Just stay there, Louise. It will be Sunday before we get back to you, but you are safe there. I wouldn't be happy with you anywhere else. God bless you.' And he put the phone down.

I turned and looked at poor May's face, and she knew immediately that we were stuck there. All hope had gone from us both. I sat on the bed and tears welled up in my eyes. I couldn't disguise my feelings, not even in front of May, who I had tried to protect for so long, and had tried not to hurt by not allowing her to see me hurting. But here I was in a convent, behind high walls, with no friends and no way out, as far as I could see. I would much rather have been locked inside Sayed's apartment with people I knew than be stuck here for weeks, maybe even months. In the worst-case scenario, I could end up like the young girl who had been here for 23 years, for reasons I didn't know. At that very moment I felt completely abandoned. Completely hopeless. May was on a stop list, and I knew that the Irish officials were not even in the country now and it would be three more days at least before I would hear from them again. I had no energy, and I sat on the bed wanting the room to cave in on me.

I picked up the phone and rang Mandy. I told her the embassy's effort was a lost cause and that I was on the verge of giving up. I didn't know what to do next.

But we both knew about the only other option available to us, and we also knew that if we went down that route we would need the full support of the Irish officials in foreign affairs. Mandy had been exploring every avenue, and although the Turkish smuggling gang hadn't worked out, we had a second-best scenario up our sleeves. There was a group of Syrians ready to help us, for the right price, and all they needed was the green light. We knew we had no other choice. Mandy told me to sit tight and she would start to make the necessary calls.

Within five minutes, everything changed. The phone rang in the bedroom, and it was the little nun on the internal line. She asked me if I was OK and said that there was a call for me from the ambassador. I didn't know what to expect. I held on while she transferred the call. It was great to hear Isolde's voice and even better when I finally digested her words: 'Pack your bags now, Louise, you are going home today. You have five minutes. The car is collecting you and it's on the way.' She had been chatting to Mandy, and although Mandy and myself had to organise everything ourselves when it came to paying the Syrian men to get us out, the Irish embassy had agreed to help us once we got to Lebanon.

I didn't know how far Lebanon was or how we would get there, but a rendezvous had been arranged and we had to get out of the convent and to the meeting point immediately. I couldn't believe what I was hearing. I was in total shock. It was as if the conversation I'd had with the official just minutes ago had never actually happened. I said, 'Can I have a quick shower?'

'Absolutely not,' was Isolde's reply. 'Get to where you have to go quickly. The car is coming now.' She said Mandy had arranged everything and the officials were just there to ensure that, whatever happened, myself and May, as Irish citizens, were safe.

I picked up May as she played with a little toy dragon I had made her from Play-Doh and I said, 'Quick, May, we are going home. Pack your bag.'

'Going home to Ireland?' she asked.

'Yes, love, now hurry up, get everything together quick as you can.' And I never saw a child as organised. She was so quick at packing that she started pulling things out of my drawer and packing my case as well. She was running around putting clothes away and singing, 'Yay, yay, we are going home, we are going home.' She tumbled all the little cosmetic bottles from the bathroom onto the bed and then threw them into the bag, and I reached over for the mobile phone and dialled Mandy's number. I had put the phone down to her, having told her that I had lost all hope. I had said to her minutes earlier, 'I'm here to stay. I can't get home. The judge won't allow us leave and there is no hope now.' And yet minutes later I was back on the phone saying, 'I'm coming home.' All thanks to her.

Mandy was silent on the other end of the line, but I knew that she was crying. She said that she had been on to the Department of Foreign Affairs in Dublin as soon as I had put the phone down five minutes earlier, and they had got back to her and told her to make her way into the city centre to meet them. She said she had to sign a document in Dublin, and through tears she simply said, 'God bless you, Louise, and

Godspeed.' I told her that I would call her as soon as I could, and with that I heard a car beeping outside.

We ran down to the courtyard we had been in the night before, dragging our bags behind us. There was no one around, and I knew that there was no way I could open the gate, which must have been about 12 feet high, so I just flung the cases over it to the taxi driver parked outside and May climbed over. Just as I started to follow her, the girl who spoke English came out and started to laugh at me, struggling, at my age, to climb over a massive gate. She shouted at me to hold on, as she would press the button that would open it for me.

She came across to me, and we said our goodbyes and she wished me good luck. We were absolutely over the moon when we got in the car, and May held my hand, smiling all the way to the meeting point.

We hadn't a clue how we were getting home, but we expected that we were about to be taken to the airport for a flight back to Ireland via another country, as there were no direct flights from Syria, but at this stage we knew absolutely nothing. It was all up in the air, and no one seemed to be saying anything.

We arrived at the spot where we were to meet the men who we had to trust with our lives. We had no idea who they were or what they planned to do with us, and they had little or no English. But we had little or no hope. They were all we had left now. To my mind, being in the hands of these strange men wasn't any worse than the situation already was, in this war-ravaged country where I would face death if I was caught. I had no choice but to trust them.

I knew that the Irish officials were in fear of their lives in Syria and that the situation was getting worse by the day, and I knew that they were terrified for myself and May but that their hands were tied and they had no option but to step back. In fairness to them, they offered to talk to the Syrian guys for us if we had any problems and promised that if we made it to Lebanon they would be there to take care of us. They just couldn't help us in Syria.

I rang an official from the consulate's office and he said that they would meet us in Beirut. He wished us good luck and said that everyone was praying for us to make it there safely. My stomach was in a knot, but I put on a brave face for May, who I could see was terrified of the men.

As I finished my conversation with the official, a very abrupt man walked towards me and put out his hand, directing us, saying in Arabic, 'This way.' I felt very uneasy. Poor May was very worried; she stared up at me all wide-eyed.

We were ushered into a dark-coloured Audi, and the man, who spoke no English at all, started to talk to someone on his mobile phone as we drove along. He was obviously organising where he would pick up his colleague en route, as we later stopped along the way on a main road and collected another man.

I was conscious of the fact that I wasn't wearing a hijab that day. I was wearing a gold-coloured dress and tights and a pair of wedges, because when I got the call to say we were being taken back to Ireland I honestly thought we would be either going by plane or in a nice taxi. My attire was definitely not suitable for the route that lay ahead of us.

The man who got into the car spoke a little English, and he turned to us and asked where we were from. He asked for our passports and I handed them over. I had to put my trust in these men; I knew this, no matter how terrified I was of them.

We drove for about an hour and the men chatted amongst themselves. I could make out some of the conversation, and I realised that they were discussing changing the car for another vehicle, but I didn't understand why.

We drove for a while longer through a very derelict part of Damascus where the roads were just sand and the houses were falling down and dishevelled-looking. There was rubbish strewn everywhere, and rocks that looked like they might have come from a building site had been dumped every few feet along the way. All of a sudden we came to a housing estate that was accessed through big iron gates. There were houses and apartments that looked like they'd only been built in recent years. You didn't see many estates like this in Syria. I didn't know what was going on.

The man in the passenger seat turned to me and said that we would have to go into a house. He said it in Arabic, but I began to panic. I rang the official in the embassy on my mobile phone and told him that I knew it wasn't his problem but that I was a bit worried. I asked him to help us out by talking to the guy in the passenger seat, but after a very brief conversation between the two men, the phone was handed back to me and the official simply said, 'Louise, are you all right?' I told him that I hadn't a clue what was going on, but I realised that there was nothing they could do. He asked if I would ring him back in an hour to update him.

When we finished the conversation, I turned the phone off to save my battery, knowing that I would definitely need to make a call later in the day.

The man in the passenger seat got out of the car, approached two different houses and then got back into our car and we drove off again. He said a few words, which I couldn't make out, to the driver, and I thought that everything was OK and we were back en route, but within a few minutes we had stopped again. This time he said to me, 'We are going to change cars. You stay in a house.'

I felt sick. I didn't want to ring the official again because I didn't want to harass him. But then we started off again, without stopping at any house, and we drove into a garage. We pulled up alongside a 4x4 jeep, and the men directed us to get out of the Audi and into the jeep.

We did what we were told. I noticed that the windows were all blacked out in the jeep, so I thought this would be the vehicle that would take us all the way to safety. I relaxed somewhat. May was as quiet as a mouse. I knew that she was terrified, but she was being so strong. She was absolutely fantastic, and she just made sure that she cuddled into me and was holding my hand all the time.

As we got into the jeep, I noticed that all of the men in the garage were staring at me, because I had no head covering and looked totally out of place with my blonde hair and short dress. Most of them would have never seen a woman like me before. I was totally foreign to those men. But we didn't hang around for long, and within a couple of minutes we were on the road again.

We drove again for about a half an hour through tiny back lanes, which were hardly passable. The houses in this area were extremely run-down. The smell of sewage was very strong and the roads were filthy. Wherever we were, it was definitely the back of beyond. Young children were running around in dirty clothes and bare feet, and they looked as though they hadn't eaten a good healthy meal for some time. This was poverty at its worst.

In this area, we stopped at another house and picked up another man, who jumped in the back of the car with myself and May. He said nothing and we drove off again. Then, suddenly, we stopped at another house, and the man in the back of the jeep told myself and May to get out and go into the house. He told me that I was to wait there for a while. A woman came out of the door, and the man shouted at her in Arabic to mind myself and May for a while. She took us in, but we had no way of communicating with her because she had absolutely no English whatsoever.

I remember that she had a little garden with a few shrubs and trees growing in it, and she directed us around the back of the house and up the stairs into her sitting room. It was a typical Arabic house, with cushions on the floor all around the walls. She could see that we were very agitated and nervous, and she made chai for myself and May. I told May to play with a young baby who I think might have been the woman's daughter. I knew that it would occupy May while I tried to find out what was going on.

I asked the woman if she could tell me where exactly we were. I asked in Arabic if we were still in Damascus, and she said that we were just outside Damascus, but she was very careful not to tell me too much. I realised that she must have been in this situation before. This was obviously used as a safehouse on other occasions for people, foreigners more than likely, trying to flee.

Time dragged by and May was getting very bored and very hungry and was starting to worry, as was I. I looked at the clock and realised that we had been there for nearly four hours. That was not good as far as I was concerned. I wondered what the hell was going on. Were they holding us captive, trying to get more money for our release? Did they somehow know Mostafa and were trying to contact him to tell him where we were? My mind was racing.

May's grasp of Arabic was much better than mine, so I asked her to ask the lady if she would ring the men and ask them what was happening. Fair play to her, she understood May and she dialled a number. After a minute or so I heard her say, 'OK, OK, you will be here in a few minutes.'

I turned my mobile phone on and I rang the official again. When he answered he said, 'Louise, where are you? Are you there yet?'

I said, 'No. I don't know what is going on. I am in a house with a woman. We have been here for more than four hours now and the men are gone.'

He asked to speak to the woman, and when I put her on the phone I could see that she was very nervous and wary of what to say. She simply told him that we were in a house with her and we were OK. She wouldn't tell him anything else.

The official came back on the phone to me and he said, 'Louise, I am not happy with this situation. Do you know the man's name or what he looks like?'

I told him I didn't know anything about him. I could describe him, but my description could have fitted any number of Arabic men so it would be of no use. I asked the official what we should do next. Should we run? He asked me to keep my phone on and told me to stay calm. I knew he had no control over what happened in Syria and I tried to be as relaxed as possible. He told me that he couldn't be privy to what was happening, as it would put him and myself and May in danger, so he told me to call the ambassador myself and ask her advice.

I went through my contacts and dialled her number immediately. She answered almost instantly and frantically said, 'Louise, where are you? We are waiting for you.'

I said, 'Your Excellency, we are in a house and we don't know what is happening. We have been here for hours; I don't know if we are being held for ransom or what. Please help me.'

She said she would ring me back in five minutes, but she rang back almost immediately. She had made contact with the driver, and he had informed her that they'd had to take the jeep off to get new tyres, as the tyres they had would not get us over the mountains. I didn't have a clue which mountains they were talking about, but I just listened to what Isolde had to say. 'So you are going to be delayed for much longer than we thought, Louise. Please God, be safe and just stay focused.'

Another hour passed. I became very nervous. I kept telling May that we would be fine and that we had to have trust. She just nodded.

Suddenly the jeep pulled up outside and the man came in and said, '*Yalla, yalla.*' I thanked the woman for keeping us, as I'd realised that she'd had no choice in the matter; she was just being used by these men and had no control over the situation. She started to cry. I think she was worried about our safety from there on, to be honest, especially about May, as she was only small and so innocent in all of this.

We left the house and got into the jeep. The man asked May if I was able to walk for ten minutes. He must have noticed me limping as I came out to the jeep. May relayed the question to me, and I said, 'Of course. Ten minutes is fine.' And we started to drive off.

The man who was last in the back of the car with us had got in beside us again. We never came across one checkpoint, which I was surprised by, as they were absolutely everywhere, but I soon realised that these men knew the routes like the backs of their hands and they knew where not to drive; that was why they had been chosen for this operation.

After about a half an hour, we started going up a mountain. Dusk was falling by now and with the blacked-out windows it was very hard to see outside, but I could feel the drag on the engine and I knew that we were climbing – and climbing quite high. The roads were getting rockier and rockier and it was quite scary. But I never saw any other cars behind us or coming towards us. I knew we were in the middle of nowhere.

The man in the back had a bandana wrapped around his head, and I noticed that he had a gun on his hip. I tried not to worry about this and knew that it was being carried as much for our safety as for theirs. I took some comfort in this, but I just prayed that we would never have to see it and he would never have to use it.

The man tried to talk to May and I heard him tell her that she was a lovely little girl, but I could tell by her body language that she didn't like him and she was trying her best to ignore him. I hoped this wouldn't upset him and that he would understand that she was just a frightened little girl.

As we drove along, it was clear that the roads were getting narrower and narrower and we were driving on the edge of a precipice a lot of the time. You could feel the jeep struggling to get up the road, and many times I grabbed onto the seat, terrified that we would go over the side of the mountain. I remember praying over and over again in my head and asking my mam to get us through this ordeal safely and back to my dad and Mandy. I knew if she was with me she would do everything in her power to help us.

As we went along, the jeep suddenly started to slide, and I gripped May tightly to me. I looked out the window and could see us going around a big ridge. I spotted a big valley beneath us and smaller mountains and rocks everywhere. Then, all of a sudden, we came to a stop. I looked out and could see that there was no way we could go any further. The terrain was just too rough and narrow. The driver and his friend got out of the front seats and we were directed to get out of the back.

The man with the beard took my handbag, and the other man, his friend who had some English, simply said, 'OK. Bye bye. You go now.'

I looked around at everyone and said, 'What?' I couldn't believe what was happening. I clutched May's hand and I could see her little eyes filling up. It was getting darker and we were standing in the middle of a mountain range with sand and rocks everywhere. We didn't know where the hell we were. The men just kept directing us with their hands to walk. And so we did. What else could we do?

The first 100 metres or so of the walk were the most level, but there were stones and rocks everywhere and even here I could feel my feet going from under me. May never complained. She just kept saying, 'Come on, Mama. You can do it.' I couldn't believe the courage of my little girl through all of this. I knew that despite her tiny size and her tender years she was focused on getting out of Syria, getting home to see her granddad and aunty and her cousin, and I had to force myself to be as strong as this six-year-old child. She was truly amazing.

As I looked behind me I realised that one of the men was following us, and within a few minutes he had caught up. He made his way ahead of us, and we followed as close to him as we could, trying not to lose our balance as we tried to judge where we were walking. We climbed up a big hill with little stones and rocks everywhere, and we tried our best to hold our balance and not to twist our ankles on the uneven terrain. Then we came to flat ground, but as I looked around I could see that there was nothing but mountains for as far as the eye could see. I couldn't believe we were in this situation.

I kept thinking that at any minute we could be shot, because it was an obvious route for Syrians trying to escape. But escape to where I didn't really know, as no one had told me anything. I just had to trust in God and these men, who were clearly the only ones who could get us out of here alive.

I remember thinking as I struggled across that terrain that if I died there it would be better than the prospect of being stoned to death, which was one alternative, or being locked up in a Syrian jail for the rest of my life for a crime that the Syrian authorities believed I had committed, simply because it was their law and not European law. I remember thinking, 'Why the hell were they not forced into being part of the Hague Convention? Was their religion so powerful that they could refuse what most other countries would see as a basic human right: for a child to be with the parent that was legally entitled to have responsibility for him or her following a judgment in a court of law?' Courts don't give custody to a parent without having good reason, yet the Syrians were exempt from that. I just couldn't rationalise it. And I kept thinking, 'If I am caught now, not only with May but trying to escape the country with her, I am doomed.'

I looked up to see a beautiful orange sunset that at any other time in any other country would have been absolutely breathtaking. But on that day, it signalled to me that within a short time everything around us would be pitch black and we would really struggle to judge the territory.

There was not a sound to be heard. I didn't even hear any animals around us, shuffling by, which was odd in itself. There was just a deathly silence. The only sounds we heard were the shuffling of our own feet as we scrambled to find solid ground.

At one stage I was startled to see two men up in the distance ahead of us. I called to our guide to tell him in Arabic that there were men ahead, but he just said, 'Shh. It's OK. They are with me.' The relief I felt at that moment was indescribable. I knew that if we were spotted crossing the mountain by guerrillas or the army we were dead. I had no doubt about that.

We continued on and on, and about half an hour or so into the journey a man approached us from up ahead. He was one of our guide's men, and he had his face totally covered with a bandana and his neck covered with a scarf. He was holding a large gun in one hand, like an AK-47, and a bottle of water in the other hand. He offered both myself and May some water, but I said no, and even though I thought that May must have been famished and very thirsty, she too refused his offer. We were just too scared to take any chances, even by accepting a drink from someone we did not know, because we still didn't know where the men were taking us or what they could do to us. We knew these men were bandits and that even the Irish embassy knew nothing about them.

As it got pitch black, the men started to use what looked like cigarette lighters with small LEDs on the end of them, and they would communicate with each other as we walked along the side of the mountains. Every now and then they would alternate, and the man ahead would come back and walk with myself and May and allow the second man to go ahead as a lookout. We soon realised that the lights were being used to signal that everything was OK to continue forward. I realised that up to now we had been very lucky, because it was obviously a route others used as well, and at any time we could meet other people, maybe even security forces patrolling the area, and if that happened we were done for.

I hated it when the man with the beard had to leave us, because there was something that I trusted about him. Any time I fell, which was quite often, he would come back and give me his hand to help me back up and on the road again. On a number of occasions when the drop got really steep, this man would walk in front of me and allow me to put my arms on his shoulders so he could lead me down.

The second man wasn't half as nice. He looked evil. I think May was terrified of him, but she never showed her fear at any stage of the journey. In fact, she was just worried for me and kept taking my hand and telling the men that her mammy couldn't see in the dark, bless her. She was such a tower of strength for me that night.

I remember at one stage we were trying to get down this steep mountain covered in rough briar and stinging plants, and my and May's arms and legs were torn to pieces as we tried to negotiate our way down. We thought that it would never end and we could see no destination in sight, just a sheer blackness. When the moon shone down we could only see miles upon miles of mountains. There was no beacon of light from a town or a little village to keep our hopes up. But we had no choice but to keep going no matter what.

Minutes felt like hours, and hours felt like days. We continued climbing and dropping and going from side to side on the bigger mountains.

We were coming down the side of a mountain when all of a sudden the men started to signal to each other with the lighters, and I knew that something was wrong. The guide whispered, 'Get down, get down,' in Arabic. But it was so hard to get down, because we were at an angle and there was nothing to grab onto on the side of the mountain.

May lay down beside me as best she could. She started to whisper something to the man, but he said, 'Shh. Stay quiet.' I knew there and then that we were in danger.

I craned my head, trying not to be noticed but at the same time attempting to see what was causing all this worry. In the distance I could sort of make out headlights from three or four vehicles driving along below us and I could hear the slight hum of their engines. We stayed deadly silent. I knew they were obviously Syrian army vehicles, and we froze to the spot, all of us. We stayed lying against the mountain for about three minutes, although it felt like an hour, and not for one second did I think of running. I remember thinking that these men were my lifesavers. I had to put all of my trust into these two people who I knew nothing about and had never met before, but if I didn't do what they told us to do we were doomed. I told May to listen to everything they said and obey them. She agreed, and although she was clearly frightened of them she never disobeyed them once. She did exactly what they said.

After a few minutes, the man said, '*Yalla, yalla*,' and we started off again. I remember that we hit one very difficult spot on a mountain as we climbed again, and I looked up and thought, 'I can't do this.' I was distraught. I tried to find rocks to grip onto with my wedged shoes but kept losing my footing. I thought, 'I will never get up to the top, not a chance. I need a rope to pull me up.' But, despite my concerns, I knew that I had to keep going. I had no choice. There wasn't just me in this situation; I had my child to think of as well.

I grasped the top of the mountain, and the man who had already reached the top with May stretched down and gave me his hand to grab onto. He literally dragged me up onto that mountaintop and I desperately clung to him.

I could see May was OK and I begged her to wait for me, but she said, 'It's OK, Mama, I am fine.' And she said to the guide, 'Please help my mama, she has very bad legs.' I could see her brushing her clothes down, bless her, trying to get rid of the muck. As I got up I could see May already starting to make her way back down the other side of the mountain. She was unstoppable.

All of a sudden we got to a terrain with a very big rock in the middle. It was clear that the men knew exactly where they were going and it was obvious that this rock was always their stopping point. They offered us some water, but we still said no, despite our thirst. Then the man who spoke a bit of English, the one with the beard, said to me, 'Money. I need money.' I wasn't arguing. I would have sold my soul to the devil to get down off that mountain range safely with my little girl.

I knew how to appease Syrian men. The main thing was not to be disrespectful to them and not to lie. If I lied I would only be making things worse for myself. I knew that I had to respect them, because being lied to is seen as a personal insult, and I knew only too well from my experiences with Mostafa never to do this. I had to respect them no matter what the situation was. I took out my wallet and I showed them that all I had left was 150 euros. The bearded man said, 'Dollar, dollar?' I told him that I had no dollars, just euros. Then he said, 'Phone, phone.' And I told him that I had to keep my phone. It was my phone and I needed it. And he just said, 'OK, *yalla*.' I was so relieved, because losing my phone would have been the worst thing that could have happened to me. I had all the phone numbers I needed in there, and even though we had no coverage in the mountains, I knew that I would need it when we arrived wherever it was we were going.

I got a bit worried over whether the money I had given them was enough. As we sat there, I prayed to God that they wouldn't rape me in front of May. I hoped that if it was in their plan, they would do it out of sight of my daughter. I didn't want her to witness such a thing. It was a real fear of mine, because I had been conscious of these men staring at me all along the journey. I was not covered up like their own women; I was wearing a short skirt and had my hair exposed. This was not normal in Syria. I tried putting the thought completely to the back of my mind, but I then started to fear that they might actually rape May. And that, for me, really would have been the very worst thing that could have happened. I had already planned to offer myself if I even thought for one second that this was on their minds. I just hoped and prayed that they were decent men and that they had children of their own so that this thought would not arise at all. But I had to be prepared for everything. I wasn't in control here.

Every fear I could possibly have had went through my mind. I also worried about the men simply abandoning us in the mountains. I didn't know how they operated, and I hoped that we wouldn't see another cavalcade of vehicles in case they panicked and decided that it was just too much of a risk to carry on. I remember thinking that if that happened we would just keep going, myself and May, because we had no other choice. But I prayed it wouldn't come to that.

After about 15 minutes the lighters started to go again, but it turned out that these signals were just letting our guide know that everything was OK to keep going. We started to go back down the mountain again and the ground was, once again, extremely rocky. It was pitch black and the moon barely shone any light around us, making it very difficult to judge what we were walking on.

I fell a number of times, struggling to hold on to a rock or a piece of loose ground, and then all of a sudden my foot dropped into a hole and slipped to the side and I lost my balance. I couldn't scream, because it was too risky to make any noise, but the pain was unbearable. I was sure that I had broken my ankle or, even worse, my leg.

May grabbed my hand, and the man came back and asked me if I was OK. I told him that I thought I might have broken a bone, as my leg and foot had swollen up immediately. I could feel my shoe getting really tight. But I told him I had to go on, and although the pain was unbelievable, I continued to walk, trying not to put too much weight on that side of my body. In fairness to the guide, he was more helpful than ever on this leg of the journey and he allowed me to put all of my weight on him during the steep declines. I could see May was worried about me, but I told her that I was fine and to keep going.

After about 20 more minutes of a really steep decline, we spotted little lights twinkling in the distance. I hadn't a clue where we were and whether these lights were a good thing or a bad thing, but it showed that we were near civilisation at least. The guide turned to me and pointed down and showed us that one village was in Lebanon and one in Syria. I was so relieved, because I suddenly realised that they were taking us to Lebanon. They were actually taking us where they had promised.

I had read on the Internet when I was with Mandy how Lebanon was a much safer option for escape. I knew that there were Irish troops or Irish UN workers in Lebanon, if I was just able to find them. I knew our journey was by no means over, but we were nearer to freedom than ever now.

The route down the mountain was extremely steep. I could see May just in front of me, going down the rocky incline on her back, and so I did the same. We both went down very slowly, as it was really uncomfortable, and although I had pain in my back and in the foot I had injured, I remember thinking it odd that despite all the challenges along the way on the mountain range, I never once had pain from my hips, which had caused me agony for years. It was very strange, but I was grateful for the lack of it. We had pain from everything else anyway.

As we struggled to get down that mountain, walking and sliding, I remember saying to May, 'I am so proud of you, darling. You are just unbelievable and I love you so much. You are the best child that ever lived.'

She just kept saying, 'I am OK, Mammy. I am OK.' As we continued down through the rocks I heard her making the odd noise, oohing and aahing as she was cut by the briars or lost her balance, but nothing deterred her. Like me, she was on a mission and she wasn't stopping until she got to the end.

We suddenly reached a pool of water, and I was totally exhausted. I had to keep telling myself to keep going; we had gone this far and I couldn't give up now.

The man who had been up ahead for a long time made his way back to us, and he started to help May, who was struggling to make her way down. It was extremely unstable ground and we were both slipping and sliding everywhere. When I saw him coming back, having been leading the way, I knew that we must be near whatever spot we were aiming to reach.

All of a sudden May disappeared, and I heard her laughing and going, 'Wheeeeee!' She was obviously sliding down the mountain. The man turned to me and said in Arabic, 'Can you do this?' I didn't know what 'this' was, but I assumed it was going to be worse than anything we had gone through to date. I just said, 'Yes. Yes.'

As I looked down, I saw how steep it really was. I started to slide, and the man was in front of me. As I slid, he would stop me with his boot if I went too far; it acted like a brake for me. This went on for about ten minutes, when suddenly I saw a 4x4 vehicle with its headlights flashing in the distance and little May standing there covered with mud up to her chest. I can't describe the relief I felt when I saw her. I just smiled. As I got to the other side of another, smaller pool, I tried to get up, but my feet felt like they had been covered in drying cement. They felt so heavy.

I saw a man helping May to get up and then he came over to me to help me up. I looked up to see an open-top Suzuki jeep and a tall, very slim man speaking very briefly with the bearded guide. Nothing was said to us; they simply put May in the back of the jeep and myself in the front. Then the man with the beard, who I think had some feelings for us, came across to me. He grabbed my hand, took me out of the jeep and took me around to the back of the vehicle, and I swear to God I thought at that point that he was going to rape me. I cannot explain the relief I felt when he simply pointed to the Lebanese registration plates. I was so happy I just gasped for fresh air and I started to cry. I was so grateful to him, and I took his hand to kiss it, but he grabbed his hand back and very seriously said, 'No.' I knew that he meant he did not want me to disrespect myself by doing something like that, even though kissing his hand would not mean that to me. I was just so grateful to him for all that he and the other men had done for us.

We went back to the jeep, and the bearded man spoke to the driver. Then, turning back to me, he asked me for my phone. I took a deep breath, because I needed my phone now more than ever, but I handed it over. I had no choice; I had placed my trust in these men through the night and knew they had put their own lives at risk for me and May. He then opened the phone, took out the SIM card and broke it in two. I sat there with my mouth open, absolutely shocked at what he had done, as I now had no numbers to contact anyone. I remember going into a sudden blind panic, thinking that not only could I not contact the ambassador but she could not contact me.

It was only later that I realised that they needed to do this to protect themselves, just in case I had any of their numbers in my phone or in case there was a way of tracking my calls once I got to safety, because I had made calls in one of their safehouses and that would pinpoint where they lived. I wasn't thinking like that at the time, though. I was just distraught.

We began to drive off, still in a very mountainous area with narrow roads and rocks everywhere. May simply said, 'Mama,' and as I looked around she signalled with her eyes for me to look on the floor. I was shocked to see the floor littered with guns: what looked like more AK-47s and an array of handguns. I told her to pretend they weren't there and not to touch them. I looked at the driver, who clearly understood what we had been talking about and smiled.

As I sat in the jeep, I could feel every muscle in my body ache: they were strained from my neck down to my toes. I was in absolute agony, and I knew that May must have felt the same and that she must have been absolutely starving and thirsty. We had only made one toilet break on a mountain trek of four hours or longer, and that had been behind briars with no toilet paper while feeling totally vulnerable and embarrassed. I knew that May must also be dying to get to a place where we could use a toilet, wash our hands and faces and freshen up. I prayed that wouldn't be too far away now. The driver turned to me and offered me a cigarette. I was so delighted to have that stick of tobacco. I gladly took it and lit it and felt immediate relief.

We drove up to two checkpoints, and it was obvious that the driver knew everyone and had probably paid the guards to give him the green light to drive on, because we were just waved through both of them. I was so much calmer at this stage, having realised that we were as safe as we could ever be now.

As we drove along through a little village in the dark, I puffed away on my cigarette. All of a sudden I saw a car coming towards us, too close for comfort, and as it passed it whipped the side mirror from the jeep. What happened next was surreal.

The other car screeched on his brakes, and our driver skidded off to the side of the road, jumped out of the jeep and started to curse profoundly in Arabic. The other driver screamed back at him, and next thing our driver pulled out his gun and started to wave it in the air, still screaming at the other guy.

I told May not to look back. I didn't know what was going to happen next and was terrified that he might just fire the thing. All of a sudden, an old man ran out of a nearby house and tried to calm things down. The two drivers were furious, shouting and roaring despite the presence of the old man, and our man was still flinging his handgun around into the air. But fair play to the elderly gentleman, because he somehow managed to calm them both down, and within a few minutes they were exchanging details on pieces of paper. I was so relieved.

And as if nothing had happened, our driver just got back into the jeep and started to drive off again, and I remember thinking what a chance he had taken, pulling a gun out over a broken wing mirror even though he was smuggling two illegal immigrants in his vehicle. It was like something from a movie.

We carried on for about another half an hour and eventually we arrived at an apartment. When we walked in it was obvious that there was no electricity, but there was evidence that at some stage there had been children living there, as there were pictures of Santa on the walls and teddies dressed as Santa scattered all around. There was even a big Santa in the corner that the family obviously plugged in when there was electricity. It seemed very odd that among Muslim communities in some parts of Syria Santa figures were hugely popular, yet Mostafa hated anything to do with Christmas. I wished he had welcomed that time of year for May's sake, but it was too late to even try to change that now.

We were told to sit down and wait for a few minutes. The driver asked me for my mobile phone, and I told him that it didn't work, as the man who had brought us to him had taken out the SIM card and destroyed it. He seemed OK with that, but he then asked me for the number of my contact in the embassy. I told him that I didn't have it; it was on the SIM card. He got very agitated then, as he needed to contact the ambassador. I asked him to give me his phone, as I knew my sister's number off by heart, thank God, and I told him that she could contact the Department of Foreign Affairs, who would then make contact with the ambassador.

As he was fumbling for his phone, I looked down at my foot and my leg, and they were both swollen up like balloons. I told May to go into the kitchen and get me some cold water so that I could try and bring the swelling down.

While she did that, I took the man's phone and rang Mandy. She answered and in a panic said, 'Louise, where are you?'

I said, 'I am in Lebanon, Mandy.' She started screaming, celebrating, but I roared back at the poor girl, 'Stop it, stop it. Help me. Help me. I am in Lebanon and my bloody leg, never mind my ankle, is probably broken and I have no bloody numbers in my phone to contact the ambassador, so shut up shouting and help me. I am with a bloody headcase here and in an apartment with no bloody electricity so stop screaming and get me help.'

Looking back, I must have seemed like a lunatic myself, but I was totally stressed out and I knew that this would be my one chance to tell Mandy exactly what the situation was like and hope to God she could get us help. I was terrified in case this man's phone would suddenly be cut off for lack of credit or something, and I knew I had no time to lose.

Poor Mandy, she stopped straight away, knowing I was in a panic, and she said, 'OK, Louise, I'll get on to someone now. Hold on. Hold on.'

Ten minutes later, the man's phone rang and arrangements were made to meet. Mandy had given the official the number that had come up on her phone. They planned to meet at 8 p.m. It was 10 p.m. then, and I suddenly realised that we must have taken about three and half to four hours to go through the mountains. I have to say it felt as though we had been walking for a lot longer than that, but I was just grateful we had got here in one piece.

The official spoke to me, and he told me not to panic; we were nearly there. Poor May was starving, and she kept saying, 'Mama, I am hungry. I need food.' I felt awful, because I had nothing to give her. I explained that we would be safe soon, and I would get her food as soon as we got to our next destination.

We got back into the jeep, and this time I put May in the front and I sat in the back seat with the guns beneath my feet. It was only then that I realised there must have been seven or eight guns, bits of broken shotguns and .22 rifles, and round upon round of ammunition. It wouldn't have taken a genius to realise that these guys were probably also gun smugglers, and I thanked God that we had got this far safely.

I remember looking out of the window as we drove along and thinking how different Lebanon was to Syria, how much cleaner the country was and how people appeared to have substantially more in Lebanon than they did in Syria. The scenery was even nicer, and there were more plants and trees than in Syria. It was a completely different country, yet they were land-linked and Lebanon had its own problems when it came to war and poverty. It just seemed to be more civilised somehow.

We drove for about an hour and a half, driving through more checkpoints, and not one of them even looked at myself or May; they just looked in at the driver and waved us on. This guide didn't talk to us much at all, he just concentrated on the road ahead, yet I was feeling more relaxed with every mile we drove.

All of a sudden I saw a very big city ahead of us, a huge city with tall buildings that seemed very commercialised. As I looked to my right I thought I was seeing things; it was absolutely like how I imagined seeing a mirage in a desert: I saw a big McDonald's perched there as if calling on us, drawing us into its doorway with a magnetic force, absolutely starving as we were. I think I was subconsciously licking my lips at the thought of what was there to be eaten inside, just yards away from us, and right on cue I heard a scream from May in the front: 'McDonald's! Mama, McDonald's!' May thought that all of her birthdays had come at once. I'd never seen her so excited about food. But we hadn't eaten for hours and hours, and both of us were overcome by hunger.

I could also see that right in front of us was the very last checkpoint we needed to go through to get to safety, and sitting there like something from a dream was the Irish diplomatic car. It was such a relief to see the Irish flag again. Finally, I knew that we were safe.

Up ahead was the ambassador, Isolde, and in her hands were pizza boxes, and I remember thinking how thoughtful she was. But she looked concerned and absolutely distraught, and I knew that she was obviously worried sick over us. As an Irish official in a foreign country, she must have felt some sort of responsibility for our safety. She will never know how relieved I was to see her too, and how grateful I was for everything she had done for us.

As we pulled up, one of the officials ran to the car and dragged May from the front seat. He then came to the back seat and grabbed me, but it was difficult for me to get out, as my legs had started to go stiff and I had pain everywhere. As we walked away from the car, he said, 'What happened?' I realised that myself and May were both filthy, and he must have been wondering how the hell we had got in that state, as the Irish officials were probably unaware of the routes these men had had to take to get us to safety.

I hobbled into the diplomatic car, with pain coursing through my injured leg, but the seats were so comfortable and clean that I remember looking up to the skies and quietly thanking God for getting us through that journey alive and well.

Isolde handed May the pizza boxes, and she was absolutely hilarious to watch as she ripped them apart to get to the pizza. And as she stuffed a big slice into her mouth, the official handed me a phone. On the other end was a man who asked me to confirm that I was in Lebanon, which I did. Then he asked me something in broken English and Arabic that I couldn't understand, so I handed the phone back to the official to let him interpret for me.

What the man had been asking was if any of the Syrian men had taken anything from me on the journey. To be honest, I didn't want to tell him, because I was so grateful to those strangers for getting us safely to Lebanon, but I knew I had no choice in case it happened in the future to other people who might have no money to hand over. So I said, 'Yes. One of the men took 150 euros off me in the mountain.' The official wanted to know who it was, and, although I felt really bad, I explained that it was the man with the beard. Yet that man had saved my life. I knew I was doing the right thing by telling the official, but I also knew that I would have given the bearded man a thousand euros if I'd had it in my purse that day. I could never repay those men for what they did for us.

However, the Irish official explained that this had to be said to help others, and I had to accept that. When the call ended, the official and the ambassador asked me what had happened to my leg and my foot. I explained to them that we had been walking through the mountains for hours in the dark on very uneven ground, and I remember their faces: they were just staring in disbelief at the dangerous route we'd had to take to get to Lebanon. But to me it was all now a distant memory, and freedom and my family were waiting for me back in Dublin.

The officials and the ambassador were so upset. They were visibly shaken, and I think they were very relieved that we had got there safely. The ambassador and I had a long conversation, and I will never forget how encouraging she was to me, telling me how proud my family would be of what we had done and how courageous we were to have faced that journey. She was genuinely delighted to see us and to know that we were safe and out of harm's way.

As I sat there in the car, covered in filth and muck and ripped asunder from sharp briars and broken rocks, I kept thinking of the words Mostafa repeated to me day in and day out as he held me captive in Syria: 'May will never leave Syria. Put that into your mind. May will never, ever leave Syria; put that into your head.' It was a mantra he tried to brainwash me with ten times a day if not more as I sat alone in his home behind barred windows and a locked door. I looked out the window as we drove along, still in disbelief that we had made it. I took deep breaths and held my baby's hand tightly, kissing her on the head and telling her that I loved her so much. This horrible ordeal was nearly over. I had my little girl back in my arms. I just felt so proud that I had got my daughter to safety, so proud and so relieved that we were finally here.

As we drove through another checkpoint, waved on because we had the Irish flag flying proudly from the bonnet of our car, I said another Hail Mary and thanked Our Lady and my mammy for all of their help and assistance over the last few days, and especially the last few hours.

We drove through a beautiful area with wooden houses laden down with hanging baskets, like something I had seen many times on skiing holidays in Switzerland and Austria, and I remember thinking, 'How beautiful is Lebanon?' It was a beautiful country with so many amazing towns to see and so much scenery to take in. I knew it had its fair share of problems, too, but it was stunning.

We were taken to a safehouse to clean up and relax for a while. A beautiful lady opened the door, a Lebanese woman with matt black hair tied back in a bun, wide, sparkling eyes and an amazing smile. This woman, who was in her 60s but still oozed natural beauty, welcomed us in. She made no comment on our appearance, which I was surprised about, considering I had scratches all over my body and mud up to my neck. She just welcomed us with open arms.

I was informed that this woman knew nothing of my circumstances and I was to tell her nothing. She was simply a person they felt they could trust and that they had sought help from before and, luckily, she had a particular fondness for the Irish. To be honest, I didn't care in the least if she knew my business because she seemed genuinely lovely. A very warm-hearted person.

As I entered her home I went to take my shoes off, and she said, 'What are you doing, love? There are no Muslims here. We are Christians.' I think it was then that I knew we were truly safe.

CHAPTER EIGHT

———◆———

Going Home

The Lebanese lady's house was absolutely beautiful. She had white leather chairs and really modern furniture, and I was delighted when I looked at her pictures on the walls to see photos of her nieces wearing the most elaborate white Holy Communion dresses. It just made me think of home even more.

That evening, this lady who had so kindly agreed to help us without knowing anything about us, cooked for us and made us feel so welcome, and when we could no longer sit up straight from tiredness, she led us into our beautiful bedroom, adorned with plush bedding and big cushions. She heated the water so that we could bathe and showed us the TV, which had hundreds of stations, mostly in English. It was fantastic. I hugged May tightly, and I said, 'Can you believe we are here, May, and that we are on our way home?' I could see the happiness in her little face.

I was shocked to think that we were actually in Lebanon after doing what so many people had told me I could never do: escape from Syria.

Poor May said she was too tired to have a shower and she lay on the bed, but I couldn't wait to jump in under warm water to wash all the dirt from my body.

The lovely lady handed us fluffy peach-coloured towels and led me into the bathroom where, thank God, there wasn't a hose in sight. She had a proper toilet and toilet roll! I was absolutely delighted. I remember thinking there and then how much we take for granted in our civilised world and how when we have lost it we are so much more grateful. I had a lovely shower that night with proper shower gel, shampoo and conditioner, but as I went to get in, little May knocked on the door and said, 'Mama, I think I need a shower.' Her face was hilarious as she had finally realised, after her tiredness wore off a bit, just how dirty she actually was. We both stood into the shower together, laughing and joking and feeling so thankful for the lovely hospitality and warm, welcoming home we had just walked into.

I woke the next morning to the most surreal sound. I heard birds singing. It was something that I had never heard in Syria, and which I only realised that very morning. Birds are said to sing when they are happy, so I knew that, unlike when I was in Syria, I was in a happy place.

As I turned over in bed, I thought I was imagining things. The smell of breakfast frying away in the kitchen came drifting in and I genuinely thought that I was dreaming. The thought of sitting down to a cooked breakfast was just amazing; it was something I'd thought I might never do again. I knew that May would be delighted when I told her that we were about to eat a fry-up.

I looked around the bedroom and noticed two white louvred doors, and as I opened them up I had to rub my eyes to make sure that I wasn't imagining things. Outside the window was a sparkling blue sea, and I could see little boats bobbing around on the horizon. And surrounding the house were the most beautiful pine trees, everywhere. I walked out onto a veranda and saw a stunning view of lots of little wooden houses adorned with flower boxes. May followed me out onto the veranda and when she saw the sea, the one thing we loved most about Limassol, she said, 'Mama, it's Cyprus.' I laughed at her

innocence and explained where we were, but she was just so
happy to see that we were in what looked like a very safe area.
And we felt safe. I remember at that point taking a deep breath
and just relishing the moment.

We hurried inside and got dressed and then we headed
outside to the sitting room. I noticed the owner of the house
was smoking and I was delighted, as I was longing for a cigarette.
She said to me, 'Why don't you go out to the veranda and sit
down and relax with a cigarette and your breakfast will be out
in a few minutes.'

As we sat there trying to take in the moment, this beautiful
moment, she started bringing out the breakfast, which was an
absolute feast. There was a big cafetière of coffee, a platter of
ham all rolled up neatly, thick slices of cheese, beautiful fresh
muffins and croissants and loads of greasy, fatty bacon and eggs.
When May saw the food, she said, 'Oh, Mama.' And before I
could do anything she started to dig in.

The officials arrived in the middle of breakfast, and when I
told them exactly what had happened to us and the route we
had taken they were absolutely shocked. They'd had no idea of
the escape route we were to take and they actually told me that
I was lucky to have made it. In fact, one of the officials said
that they had had a very big fear that we would never be seen
again, as some of these smugglers have their own agendas and
at times they rob the people they are trafficking or kidnap
them for big ransoms.

We knew ourselves how blessed we were. We didn't need
anyone to tell us that.

We sat for a while, and then one of the officials called me
into the sitting room. I didn't know what he was going to say. I
hoped for the best but had learned to fear the worst. This time
I was prepared for the latter. He simply turned to me and said,
'Right. Don't get too excited.' And with that he produced two
airline tickets. 'These are your tickets home. But we are not
safe just yet.'

He said that he had gone to the various Lebanese officials,

and unfortunately most people didn't want to get involved because of how we'd got into the country and the fact that May was deemed to be a Syrian child and was on a stop list. But the official said that he'd gone through another channel and pleaded my case. Eventually, he saw a man who held a high position in Immigration but was notorious for being very intolerant and hostile. However, the official gave him the paperwork. It took the man nearly a half an hour to read through it. The official said that he waited with bated breath as this man never spoke a word, he just kept reading. Thankfully the officials had all of my documents translated into Arabic and that was the only reason the man had even bothered to read on. As he finished, he told the official that I had got into the country illegally and he wasn't happy with that but that he understood the dilemma. He asked for an hour to make a decision.

As we sat in the sitting room we were still waiting for his answer, good or bad. The official was clearly worried, but he said that he was so desperate for us to get home, after all that we had been through, that he actually walked into a travel agent's and bought our airline tickets. The tickets were for the Lufthansa airline and would take me from Beirut to Frankfurt and finally on to Dublin. I was ecstatic.

No sooner did I have the tickets in my hands when the official's phone rang. I looked down to see his hands visibly shaking as he answered it. His face gave nothing away, but he kept saying the word 'sorry' in Arabic to whomever he was talking to and I immediately feared the worst.

But suddenly he said, 'Right, I will be there in the morning for the papers.' I knew there and then that we were OK. And as the official put down his phone he started to cry, and we all cried with him: tears of joy and absolute and utter relief. We were all ecstatic.

He turned to us and said, 'You deserve everything. We did the easy part; you got yourself here. The ambassador has told me that I am here on a mission, and if I do nothing else today I have to take May Mandy Monaghan to McDonald's.'

May's eyes lit up, even though she had barely finished her breakfast. She had been deprived of food for so long that she was wolfing down every little morsel that she could get her hands on. It was as if she might never see food again. But the poor woman in the house was already preparing lunch! So we said that we would go to McDonald's later in the afternoon, as there was no way that we could shun the woman's hospitality.

We ate lunch two hours after breakfast in a huge dining room, and we actually all had a glass of red wine in beautiful crystal wine glasses. It was slightly surreal. The lunch was a feast, and after all the stress I had been under I could feel myself getting woozy after just one glass. But it was a lovely feeling.

After lunch we drove into Beirut, driving through the most amazing scenery into the beautiful city. It was very cosmopolitan with bright lights and amazing architecture. I was shocked that there were all sorts of fast food outlets, just as we had back home, and eventually we came to a McDonald's. May ordered a Happy Meal with chicken nuggets. She had a big smile on her face and she tore the box open. We sat watching her for 45 minutes as she ate her nuggets, nibbling every tiny corner as if she was terrified that she would never get to taste them again. I could see that she was enjoying every moment. It made us all smile, and, to be honest, it made us all cry. It was something that made the officials realise just how deprived this little girl had been during our ordeal and how it had affected her. For her, food was now a luxury, and I knew that it would take some time for her to realise that she didn't have to worry any more about getting fed. It would never be a worry again.

She had lost so much weight from the time she had left me in September, and I could tell that in a way she had been slightly institutionalised in Syria. She had been deprived of the basics that she was so accustomed to in Cyprus, stupid little things like toilet paper, shampoo, soap and even food, and it would take some time to readjust to having all those things once more and to realise that from here on in they would always be there.

That night we relaxed in bed, watching TV, thinking about the trip home and feeling absolutely ecstatic. We were hopeful that all of the paperwork would be filled out the following morning so that we wouldn't miss the booked flights. I spoke to Mandy for ages on the mobile phone, and I could hear the excitement in her voice as she waited anxiously for us to complete the final journey back to safety. I knew that although she was excited about seeing us, she was still a bit nervous that something would go wrong, as it had done many times before. She would only relax once she saw us walk through the arrivals gate at Dublin airport.

The next morning the official picked us up as planned, and we said our goodbyes to the lovely lady who had so kindly put herself out to ensure our safety and comfort.

We headed to the immigration office, and myself and May were told to wait in the car with the air conditioning on high, as it was a very hot day. We watched as the official nervously approached the immigration building. His biggest fear was that someone would have had a change of heart overnight, and if that was the case we were in serious trouble. There would be no hope left.

We waited and waited, and it felt like an eternity. I felt so sick that I had to get out of the car to have a cigarette. May was worried about me, as she knew that I was very stressed. I just asked her to say a prayer that everything would be OK. We had been told already that if this plan failed we would have to go to a Catholic convent, and the reality was that it would be indefinitely. It was a scenario that I dreaded, but it was something I had to be prepared for. I hadn't told Mandy this, as I didn't want my family to worry any more than they already were. Most importantly, I didn't want my dad to worry.

The time was ticking away and I noticed that the full car park we had entered earlier was quickly clearing out, a sign that we had been there quite a long time. I had no watch on my wrist, but I knew that this wasn't the quick visit I had expected it would be. I remember looking up at the rooftops for snipers and then realising that that wasn't necessary here in Lebanon. I started to think that something had gone wrong, when I saw a figure in the distance approaching us from behind a soldier's station where two men were standing fully dressed in army clothing. I couldn't make out whether it was our man or not until I saw him wave his hands in the air: hands that were holding our two passports. I was ecstatic. He started to run towards us, and I broke down crying. I jumped into the passenger seat, and as he jumped into the driver's seat he reached over and gave me a big hug and a kiss. I could see that he was genuinely happy for us.

He started to laugh and he said, 'You are not going to believe this. They have given you an exit visa allowing you two weeks to stay here for a holiday.' He turned to May and, laughing, he said, 'May, do you want to stay here for a holiday?' And she shouted, 'No!' And we all started to laugh. After all we had been through, it was quite funny that the Lebanese people were allowing us a holiday when, bless them, all we wanted to do was to get home to the safe bosom of our family. But we were so grateful to whoever it was who signed those forms to get us home. We knew we owed them a lot. We were actually fined for entering Lebanon illegally, and the penalty we paid was around $1,500: a small price to pay for our freedom.

We started to drive to the airport, and the official made a call on his mobile's speakerphone to let the embassy officials know that we were en route home. The girl in the office, who by now I knew well, was screaming with joy when she heard the news. He told her to ring Dublin and tell everyone that we were on our way. I was beaming. I took his phone and I apologised to the girl on the other end of the phone, who I had shouted at many times in the previous weeks as I'd become frustrated by what I saw was a lack of effort on the embassy's behalf to save myself and May. Today I was thanking the girl for all the efforts she and everyone else had made to eventually get us home. She was so understanding, and she wished me every best wish for the future.

After she hung up I rang Mandy, and to this day I get upset as I recall saying the words, 'Mandy, we're coming home.' They were words that I'd never thought I would get to say while knowing, without a shadow of a doubt, that they were true. Mandy paused for a minute, and I knew that she too was crying. It was so emotional for us both. After all that we had been through, both together and separately, we were finally all going to be reunited. Alive.

I can admit now that I never thought I would see that day.

As we pulled up at the airport, I could see the plane that was to take us home, and I cried again. My emotions went through the roof. It was very difficult to comprehend the enormity of the situation.

I was shocked by how big and modern the airport was. It had every amenity there was, just like any big European airport. I think everything seemed very surreal, as I had been used to associating Beirut with war because of programmes on TV, yet here I was in this beautiful city and its ultra-modern airport. It all seemed very odd, but so welcome.

And as we went our separate ways, I thanked the official, a man who had been one of many lifesavers along our arduous and sometimes horrifying journey. I told him that he would always be in our hearts and our prayers, and I meant every word of it.

As we queued up to go through security I thought how amazing it was to be boarding a plane home with people who didn't know me at all, who didn't know what myself and May had gone through to get here. I looked to my right and saw a sight that I never would have imagined possible in a country that housed so many Muslim people. Standing there in bikinis were two stunning young women draped over a Ferrari, advertising a raffle for the car. It was very funny.

We sat in a coffee shop with one hundred dollars that our lovely official had handed me to use to get something to eat in the terminal, and I looked up and saw that a coffee would cost a whopping ten dollars and a milkshake twelve dollars. I couldn't believe how expensive it was. But there we were in a very expensive coffee shop watching amazingly stunning women dressed in the most beautiful clothing passing by. It was a scene I will never forget. It was great to just sit in a coffee shop and order whatever we wanted. I hadn't had the opportunity to do that in so long, and I realised that even that is something we all take for granted every day, not knowing what some people are going through just a few thousand miles away.

When it came time to go through to board our plane I remember handing the man at immigration our passports and him looking at us very oddly and saying, 'Emergency passports? You have a two-week visa and you got them forty-five minutes ago.'

I said, 'Yes.'

'And you don't want to stay? Can I ask you why not?'

And I laughed and said to him, 'It's a very long story and I don't think you would want to hear it.'

He smiled uneasily at me and said, 'Go ahead then.'

And in we went, stocking up on Cadbury's milk chocolate before we boarded the plane to Frankfurt.

We were so relaxed sitting there as the plane taxied down the runway. The flight took two and a half hours, but we were so excited that we didn't feel the time go by.

When we landed in Germany, we raced to catch our connecting flight to Dublin. By this stage we were so excited, knowing that in fewer than two hours we would be seeing all of our family again. It made me realise just how important your family is in times of trouble, and mine had been relentless in helping us.

As we disembarked from the plane in Dublin, an announcement was made for Louise Monaghan to make herself known to airport staff. I did, and I saw a wheelchair sitting there waiting for me, just in case I needed it. The staff had been made aware of my health situation, and they didn't know how bad I would be when I arrived, after all that I had been through. But I thanked them and said that I could walk. I had walked for so long to get there that another few steps, my last few steps to freedom, would be my easiest.

I was on home soil at last.

I was met by a lovely Irish official from the Department of Foreign Affairs whom Mandy had been dealing with throughout our ordeal, and he told me that they were taking me out through another exit, as the family were waiting to see me. I was delirious.

We walked through passport control in Dublin with a government official, and I remember a Gardai saying, 'I'm sorry but I have to check your passports; it's a formality.'

I replied, 'I am so happy for you to check our passports after all that I have been through. You have no idea.' I thought that I would never have been in this situation in the first place if the same procedures had been adhered to elsewhere. It was a relief to see it happening in my own country.

When I walked into the arrivals hall, I remember that the first voice I heard was that of Yvonne Kinsella, a journalist and TV producer who had been helping my family get my story out there from day one. Although I had never met Yvonne, I recognised her voice immediately from having spoken to her on the phone, and I ran over to give her a big hug and to thank her for everything. Yvonne went on to become a good friend to us all, and she has helped me to put my story in book form.

As I walked away from her to go into a private room to be finally reunited with my family, I saw two reporters, one from the *Irish Daily Mirror* and one from the *Irish Sun*, and two photographers waiting to chat to me. I knew that they had helped highlight my plight all along while still respecting our family's desire for privacy, and I thanked them for coming. But I wanted to see my family first, and as I walked through the door to the private room I was greeted by my very tearful sister; my poor dad, who looked heartbroken; my nephew, Josh; my brother-in-law-to-be, Sean; my aunty Kathy; and my cousin Elaine, and I'd never been so happy to see them.

We all burst out crying, and everyone was hugging and kissing myself and May. I had a surge of happiness that was beyond words. My heart was thumping in my chest and my mouth was dry, but I knew that I had to try to keep it together. Mandy and I just stared at each other in disbelief!

My dad came over to me, and as he hugged me I could feel his whole body shaking and his tears on my shoulder. As my aunty Kathy came over I just wanted to hug her and not let her go, as she had been a rock through this ordeal, helping us at every turn.

My cousin Elaine was just standing in the corner crying, and I remember thinking back to other family tragedies and how Elaine would always be standing in the corner crying, and in a way it was funny, because this, thank God, had not become a tragedy, although it so easily could have.

Poor Josh was in tears, and I remember having to look up when I gave him a hug, as I hadn't seen him for more than a year and he had grown so tall.

I looked around that tiny room and I was consumed with love and pride. I was so proud that I had managed to get May home safely, back to a family who clearly loved her immeasurably. I remember thinking that even if I died now, as I still did not know for sure whether or not I actually had cancer, I knew that May was safe. That at least I had accomplished.

It was only later that night that I brought up the subject with Mandy, and she showed me the paperwork confirming that I had the all-clear. That was the icing on the cake for me, as now I knew that I had many years ahead of me to love and care for my child.

I was only in the airport for about half an hour, and then I was whisked off to a welcome home party in our nearby GAA hall, a sports hall for Gaelic football. As I walked through the doors with May I was greeted by cheers and claps from all of my family, my aunties, uncles and cousins, as well as neighbours

and friends. The photographers from the newspapers had
followed us to take some family snaps.

May was thrilled with our welcome home party and she
looked so happy that night. It was so hard to believe that we
were finally safe and in the arms of the people who loved us
most.

CHAPTER NINE

———◆———

Moving On

When we finally got home that night, both myself and May got into our lovely new pyjamas that Mandy had bought for us and we cuddled up in bed. I remember asking May if she was all right, and her answer said it all: 'Yes, Mama, I think I'm dreaming.'

No words can ever express how elated I am to be safe and alive and reunited with my little girl.

There were so many days when I thought that I would never see my family again, and the fear of being stoned to death under sharia law haunted my every hour.

I now watch the news each day, looking at people being shot to death or killed in mortar attacks in many of the cities that I drove through on my way to safety and in the city in which I was held captive with May, and I pray for all the innocent children and parents so brutally murdered in the turmoil, which has escalated to even greater heights than when we were there. And as I pray for those still stuck there, in that living hell, I thank God that we managed to get out when we did. It is hard to believe that the violence could have got so bad so quickly, but I know that if I hadn't run that day when the chance presented itself May and myself would either be dead or holed up for the rest of our lives in a country desolated by war.

I love my family and our home in Dublin, and I tried to settle there immediately after my return from Syria, but May was missing her friends and I was missing the sun, sea and sand. It took a lot of soul-searching before I finally decided to go back to Cyprus and try to rebuild our lives. It wasn't an easy decision by any means, but I now know it was the right one.

I contacted friends back in Cyprus, and I explained to my dad and Mandy that I really felt that Mostafa would have won if I didn't return to what was by now my home. Thankfully, they understood. I finally took the big step of going back in early 2012 and, in many ways, I faced my fears. Thank God it has all worked out.

As soon as we returned, May went back to school, and within a short while she started attending counselling for post-traumatic stress. We had been told in Ireland that it would have taken months before she could have had similar therapy there and that was very disheartening to me, because I knew she needed it badly. In fact, we both did. But now I am probably happier than I have ever been, and May is slowly but surely going back to being the happy little girl that she was before that horrible day when her father dragged her away from her idyllic life. Thankfully, we are getting back on track. And, more importantly, I feel safe. When I was making my decision I worried about that, but I am very happy here and so is May, and I have amazing friends who are there for us day and night. Without them, things would be very different.

Passport control in Cyprus clearly failed myself and May, and this is still of huge concern to me and it is something that I want to try to change, if I can, to stop something like May's kidnap ever happening again. As it stands, there is free movement when travelling between southern and Northern Cyprus. There are no border controls, as Cyprus does not recognise Northern Cyprus as being under Turkish control. This is a massive security risk for parents of children either living in or on holiday in Cyprus if there are disputes over custodial rights. It is an issue that needs to be addressed as a matter of urgency. My focus now will be on helping others in similar circumstances in whatever way I can. I hope now, having gone through this horrific journey, that I will be able to help many other families caught up in what has to be described as the most terrifying and frustrating experience that any parent can endure in a lifetime.

I have learned a lot along the way about what you should and shouldn't do in the immediate aftermath of a child's abduction, and I know the ins and outs of the system when it comes to dealing with embassies and the various departments of foreign affairs. I have spent the months since I returned home trawling the World Wide Web looking at ways in which other parents of abducted children can be helped. I genuinely feel that I have been given the gift of my child, and I should do everything in my power to help anyone I can with the knowledge of the system that I now have.

I hope, once civil unrest has died down in Syria, to be able to push as much as I can to encourage it and countries like it to sign up to the Hague Convention, although I accept that this is a huge challenge given that in most, if not all, Islamic countries the father holds most of the rights when it comes to his child and anything he does is deemed fit and right in the eyes of the law.

The words of the sharia judge in Syria who refused to give me an exit visa will echo in my mind until the day I die. His excuse, that he would refuse May an exit visa because the country would lose another Muslim, still makes me feel physically sick. I believe that it is up to heads of state the world over to push for a World Court of Human Rights to ensure that people everywhere in the world have to accept and adhere to rulings that encourage equal human rights for men and women, no matter what your religious beliefs. Each case should be assessed on its own merit, and should not take into account whether you are a Muslim or a Catholic or a Protestant or Jew.

Despite religion, women should be equal to men, and the protection and welfare of the child should be the main consideration in issues of parental abduction the world over.

The abduction's effects on May will only really come to the fore as she grows up, and no one knows what those will be. I see her today as she tries to move on, one step at a time. She is still extremely close to me and hates for us to be parted, even if I am simply going shopping and leaving her in the safety of home with family or close friends. I know it will take time for May to feel safe, and I hope counselling will help her and that in time she once again becomes the confident little girl she was before. I have no doubt in my mind that she will, as she will have the support of a very loving and caring family and a close circle of friends to guide her along every step of the way.

As for her father: because of the situation in Syria I am unsure of where Mostafa is right now. I was told in the weeks after our escape that he had been arrested and was in prison in Syria. If he is deported to Cyprus, as planned, to face charges of parental abduction, it may well be a monumental case, as we have been told that it will be the first time this has ever happened to a Muslim father. Ours might become a landmark case and will hopefully be used by lawyers seeking to help other parents in a similar situation. However, I have no way of knowing what is actually happening, as the staff at the Irish consulate had to flee Damascus when things got really bad. I have been told the situation is now out of their hands: this is yet another complication that can arise when a parent abducts a child and takes them to a country in the grip of war.

I just have to hope and pray that he is out of our lives for ever.

I wish to God Mostafa had never taken our daughter out of Cyprus, because he is May's father and I feel every child should have both parents in their lives if possible, but that control was taken out of my hands on the day he illegally took May. I hated him for taking her, but I hated him even more for taking her to a war-torn country and putting her life in danger.

People ask me all the time, 'What did you see in him?' Well, it wasn't just what *I* saw in Mostafa; it's what every woman who met him saw in him. He was absolutely charming when he was in a good mood. He was an amazingly good-looking guy with a very commanding presence. He had a strong jaw line, rugged features, big brown eyes, beautiful shiny black hair, white teeth and broad shoulders, and he was always dressed immaculately. He spoke very softly, and he came across as a very well-mannered, charismatic man who would stop any woman in her tracks. When we were out together I was shocked by how women would react to him, even when I was sitting at his side. They loved him. He definitely had a gift when it came to the ladies, and he would charm them all night long, given the opportunity.

I remember after we married, we flew home to Dublin via Manchester so that he could meet all of my family and friends, and in Manchester airport I became aware of his command of a room: women were staring at him and nudging each other, sheepishly pointing over at him, clearly saying to each other how attractive he was. Because I was used to Cyprus, where there were plenty of other men who had similar looks, I didn't pay any attention to the difference in appearance between Mostafa and men from the UK, but it was more obvious when we were actually there. At one point May lost her comfort blanket in the airport, and as I was frantically looking around for it I suddenly looked up to see a group of women clearly flirting with him – and he was loving it. In fact, on the plane even the air hostesses were making eyes at him. It was as if he was a famous male model or actor that day. The attention he was receiving was unreal.

In Dublin, friends of mine actually told Mostafa to his face that he was the most handsome guy they had ever seen. He simply had what it took to win over the ladies. One night on that visit we went to a major nightclub in Dublin called the Wright Venue and, despite the fact that I was standing right beside him, one girl came over to him and asked if she paid him ten euros whether he would kiss her friend, because it was her birthday. Obviously he didn't, because I would have killed him, but this was the kind of thing that I had come to expect when we went out, be it in Cyprus or Ireland, although definitely more so in Ireland, and it was something I simply grew to live with.

I look back and laugh at it now, but, when my ordeal was over and we had got home safely, a neighbour actually approached me and said, 'Oh, thank God you are home after such a horrible time. But isn't it a shame, because he was such a gorgeous-looking fella.' That says it all about Mostafa: he knew how to charm, and charm he did.

I suppose his charm, when the relationship was going through its hard times, was always what won me back into his arms. I was just smitten back then and always hoped that Mostafa would change and that he could once again be the nice guy I had met in a bar one night when we were both infatuated with each other. Of course, it never works out that way.

Do I feel any sorrow or pity for Mostafa Assad? I ask myself this every day. In some ways I do, because I know that, although he rarely showed it, he must love his child, as she is his own flesh and blood. He had visitation rights and I never stopped him from seeing her and taking her out for the day and spending time with her. May never liked going, but I always explained to her that she had to, because he was her daddy and he loved her. However, Mostafa had no such consideration for my rights. I was not allowed to take May out of Cyprus even if I'd had a passport for her, as Mostafa had put her on a stop list, preventing me from taking her outside the country without his written consent. I would have had to have his permission to take her on holiday to Dublin, so he had no fear that I would do anything underhanded. But Mostafa had no such qualms himself, and his attempt to ensure that May lost all her Western habits and that he had complete control over her life caused all our heartache. For that I will never forgive him.

Of course, I wish things had been very different. I put up with his abuse, both physical and mental, for all those years and was still willing to allow him into my home to see our child, yet he clearly had no respect for me.

Today, I am a very different person. I am much stronger than I ever thought I could be. I never want to be perceived as hating Islamic culture; in fact, on my horrendous journey I met so many genuinely decent and loving people who did everything in their power to help us, even putting their own lives at risk, that I have the utmost respect for them.

However, I have to admit that I worry about mixed marriages between Muslims and non-Muslims, and I would urge anyone contemplating starting a family in a relationship like this to look at and discuss all their plans for the future, especially when it comes to raising a family. I know of many other Western women who have been in abusive relationships with extremist Muslim men and who, like me, endured it and continue to do so, but then again, I also know of many married couples of the same religion who go through similar troubles. It is not at all straightforward. But I do believe that there can be very big differences of opinion in intercultural marriages, and it is something that everyone should be aware of before committing to starting a family in that situation.

My ex-husband's selfish actions undoubtedly turned our world upside down in 2011. He truly shattered our lives and has left us cautious of the future, but he will never be able to break the bond of trust that myself and May share, now more than ever. I look back on all that we have been through, all that we have survived, and I know that he might have shattered our lives but he will never shatter our love.

Louise Monaghan studied travel and tourism at college and formerly worked as a senior travel consultant. She is is now trying to rebuild her life in Cyprus surrounded and protected by a large group of friends.